Whole Earth Thinking and Planetary Coexistence

Like never before in history, humans are becoming increasingly interconnected with one another and with the other inhabitants and habitats of Earth. There are numerous signs of planetary interrelations, from social media and international trade to genetic engineering and global climate change. The scientific study of interrelations between organisms and environments, Ecology, is uniquely capable of addressing the complex challenges that characterize our era of planetary coexistence.

Whole Earth Thinking and Planetary Coexistence focuses on newly emerging approaches to ecology that cross the disciplinary boundaries of sciences and humanities with the aim of responding to the challenges facing the current era of planetary interconnectedness. It introduces concepts that draw out a creative contrast between religious and secular approaches to the integration of sciences and humanities, with religious approaches represented by the "geologian" Thomas Berry and the whole Earth thinking of Stephanie Kaza and Gary Snyder, and the more secular approaches represented by the "geophilosophy" of poststructuralist theorists Gilles Deleuze and Félix Guattari.

This book will introduce concepts engaging with the ecological challenges of planetary coexistence to students and professionals in the fields of environmental studies, philosophy, and religious studies.

Sam Mickey is an adjunct professor in the Theology and Religious Studies Department at the University of San Francisco, USA.

The *Routledge Environmental Humanities* series is an original and inspiring venture recognising that today's world agricultural and water crises, ocean pollution and resource depletion, global warming from greenhouse gases, urban sprawl, overpopulation, food insecurity and environmental justice are all *crises of culture.*

The reality of understanding and finding adaptive solutions to our present and future environmental challenges has shifted the epicenter of environmental studies away from an exclusively scientific and technological framework to one that depends on the human-focused disciplines and ideas of the humanities and allied social sciences.

We thus welcome book proposals from all humanities and social sciences disciplines for an inclusive and interdisciplinary series. We favour manuscripts aimed at an international readership and written in a lively and accessible style. The readership comprises scholars and students from the humanities and social sciences and thoughtful readers concerned about the human dimensions of environmental change.

Rethinking Invasion Ecologies from the Environmental Humanities
Jodi Frawley and Iain McCalman

The Broken Promise of Agricultural Progress
An environmental history
Cameron Muir

The Biosphere and the Bioregion
Essential writings of Peter Berg
Cheryll Glotfelty and Eve Quesnel

Sustainable Consumption and the Good Life
Interdisciplinary perspectives
Edited by Karen Lykke Syse and Martin Lee Mueller

The Anthropocene and the Global Environmental Crisis
Rethinking Modernity in a new Epoch
Edited by Clive Hamilton, Christophe Bonneuil and François Gemenne

Nature, Environment and Poetry
Ecocriticism and the poetics of Seamus Heaney and Ted Hughes
Susanna Lidström

Whole Earth Thinking and Planetary Coexistence
Ecological wisdom at the intersection of religion, ecology, and philosophy
Sam Mickey

Endangerment, Biodiversity and Culture
Edited by Fernando Vidal and Nélia Dias

"Sam Mickey has produced an insightful study of the intersection of religion, ecology, and philosophy. Drawing on such seminal thinkers as Thomas Berry, Gilles Deleuze, and Félix Guattari, the author weaves an engaging narrative of a way toward Whole Earth thinking."

Mary Evelyn Tucker and John Grim, Forum on Religion and
Ecology at Yale University, USA

"Philosophically precise, ethically capacious, and accessibly written, *Whole Earth Thinking and Planetary Coexistence* is a wonderful addition to discourses on religion, philosophy, and ecology. Sam Mickey's careful and generous depictions of geophilosophy (informed by Deleuze and Guattari) and earth community (informed by Thomas Berry and others) serve as helpful guides to some of the vexing environmental issues facing different parts of the planet in the present day. His treatments of various religious and philosophical traditions demonstrate the vitality of multiple ways of human knowing and relating in an era of ecological change. Both erudite and accessible, this text is a wonderful guide for students and will also serve as a useful resource for interdisciplinary scholars of environmental philosophy and religion and ecology."

Christiana Z. Peppard, Fordham University, USA

Whole Earth Thinking and Planetary Coexistence

Ecological wisdom at the intersection of religion, ecology, and philosophy

Sam Mickey

Routledge
Taylor & Francis Group
LONDON AND NEW YORK

from Routledge

First published 2016
by Routledge

2 Park Square, Milton Park, Abingdon, Oxon OX14 4RN
711 Third Avenue, New York, NY 10017, USA

*Routledge is an imprint of the Taylor & Francis Group,
an informa business*

First issued in paperback 2017

British Library Cataloguing-in-Publication Data
A catalogue record for this book is available from the British Library

Library of Congress Cataloging-in-Publication Data
Mickey, Sam, 1981–
    Whole earth thinking and planetary coexistence : ecological wisdom at
    the intersection of religion, ecology, and philosophy / Sam Mickey.
        pages cm
    Includes bibliographical references and index.
    1. Ecology—Philosophy.   2. Ecology—Religious aspects.
    3. Environmental responsibility.   4. Environmental responsibility—
    Religious aspects.   I. Title.
    QH540.5.M54 2015
    577—dc23   2015000496

ISBN: 978-1-138-88854-8 (hbk)
ISBN: 978-1-138-74355-7 (pbk)

Typeset in Times New Roman
by Keystroke, Station Road, Codsall, Wolverhampton

Contents

1 Introduction   1

2 Ecology: a household word   17

3 A geologian meets geophilosophers   32

4 Integrating environments, societies, and subjects   50

5 Roots of ecological wisdom   65

6 Reinventing the human   83

7 Emerging Earth community   97

8 Cosmic connections   109

9 Narrative imagination, dangerous dreams   120

10 Energy   132

11 Conclusion   144

   Index   151

1 Introduction

Like never before in history, humans are becoming increasingly interconnected
with one another and with the other inhabitants and habitats of Earth. Signs of
planetary interconnectedness are everywhere. For instance, think of the ways
that Twitter, Facebook, and other social media contribute to connections between
people, or think of the ways that trade and transportation link people and resources
together from hundreds and thousands of miles away. Think of cloning, genetic
engineering, hydroelectric dams, and global climate change. Those phenomena
indicate that humans are entangling themselves in the Earth's life, land, air,
and water.

Increasing interconnectedness can be beneficial, but it can also involve a tremendous amount of destruction and violence. Cars and airplanes provide a good
example. On the one hand, they provide people with more and easier access to
the world. On the other hand, the production and operation of cars and airplanes
causes pollution, which is destructive to the integrity of the climate and harmful
to the health of humans and other species. This does not mean that cars and
airplanes are bad or that the people who make them or use them are bad. It
means that increasing connectedness is complicated. Although connections can
be beneficial, peaceful, and creative, they can also be detrimental, violent, and
destructive. Currently, the predominant patterns of increasing interconnectedness
are excessively violent and destructive. They are unraveling the health and integrity of the Earth community, obtaining good things for only a few humans while
impoverishing many other humans, degrading ecosystems, and endangering the
future of all life on Earth. In short, the current era is a time of crisis. Deriving from
the Greek *krinein* ("to separate"), a crisis is like a fork in the road. One path leads
toward more destruction, more pollution, more poverty, more extinction, and
more inequality, and the other path leads toward a recuperation of life forms, ecosystems, and cultures that are currently undergoing exploitation and destruction.
A crisis is risky and threatening, but it also opens up possibilities for change. This
ambivalence of crisis is expressed in Chinese, where the ideogram designating
crisis is a combination of the symbols for danger and opportunity (Hathaway and
Boff, 2009: 8).

From social media and global trade to genetic engineering and global climate
change, it is apparent that existing on Earth in the twenty-first century means

coexisting with countless other beings in a time of planetary crisis. To be is to be situated in a multifarious crisis composed of numerous problems ranging from species extinction, water scarcity, pollution, and nuclear waste to poverty, discrimination, war, and human rights violations. To exist on Earth today is to face the challenges of planetary coexistence. The challenges are urgent. Action needs to be taken promptly, but how? Many of today's planetary problems are unprecedented. Humans have never had to figure out what to do with things like plastic, Styrofoam, a globalized economy, or the planet's climate. How, then, can one act with resolve and vision? Challenges of this scale require planetary ways of thinking. This book presents "whole Earth thinking" as a way of understanding and responding to the challenges of planetary coexistence.

There are many fields of study that contribute to an understanding of planetary coexistence, but one field stands out in particular: ecology. Since its beginnings in the nineteenth century, ecology has usually been defined as the study of the interrelations between organisms and environments. However, that is not the whole story. Ecological theories and practices are diverse and contested (see Chapter 2). There are many contrasting perspectives on what an ecosystem is and how to study it. Furthermore, those perspectives are changing as they account for interrelations in a more planetary context, wherein the impacts of human civilization have grown so large that they now pervade the water, air, land, and life around the planet. In response to our interconnected planetary context, wherein the natural and biological are becoming inseparable from the artificial and technological, ecology is becoming more inclusive and comprehensive, accounting for local as well as global interrelationships and for Earth's physical and biological systems as well as the social systems, cultural values, traditions, technologies, and ideas populating the planet. In that sense, ecology is more than a science, more than an academic discipline. It is a cross-disciplinary engagement in whole Earth thinking, where knowledge from many sources (including sciences and humanities) comes together to facilitate ecological wisdom (see Chapter 5). To practice ecological wisdom is to practice integrative ways of being and knowing that cultivate care for the interdependent flourishing of the whole Earth community.

The whole Earth

From the Copernican revolution to Gaia theory, from colonialism to environmentalism, the past five centuries have seen the human species become increasingly planetary. It is ironic that, just as we are learning how closely humans are woven together with one another and with the rest of the planet, we are learning that we are unraveling the fabric of life on Earth. At the same time that we are learning about our evolutionary and ecological context, we realize that we are destroying that context. Although humans are more aware than ever before that they live on a planet in a time of ecological crisis, we still do not know what to think about that. We still do not know how to think through planetary problems. We are only just beginning to learn how to think of ways to contribute to the mutual flourishing of humans and the rest of the Earth community. For instance, even though we have more scientific information about climate change than ever before, the problem is getting worse. Carbon emissions are still increasing globally, contributing to the increasing destabilization of the planet's climate. Many individuals, communities, and organizations are doing great work facilitating personal and political responses to climate change. That is necessary work, and people should keep doing it, but obviously it is not sufficient. As members of a planetary civilization, we still need to figure out how to coordinate a global response to the challenges of planetary problems like climate change. It is important to think like an individual, to think like a local community, or to think like an environmental organization, but more is needed in order to think through planetary issues. Baird Callicott (2013) makes this point in his recent work on the planetary implications of the land ethic of the American forester and conservationist Aldo Leopold. While Leopold is well known for his land ethic, which advocates "thinking like a mountain" (i.e., thinking at the scale of ecological community), Callicott shows that Leopold's work also advocates "thinking like a planet," which extends the land ethic to an Earth ethic (pp. 11, 30).

By introducing whole Earth thinking, this book provides some guidelines for undertaking a path toward ecological wisdom. Taking that path means crossing many disciplinary boundaries. Ecology is not just one academic discipline among others. Ecology is more than a physical or biological science separate from social sciences like economics, psychology, and sociology. Furthermore, ecology is not merely a scientific mode of inquiry separate from the philosophical and religious perspectives studied in the humanities. Ecology has always involved ways of thinking that move across the boundaries that separate academic disciplines from one another and separate ideas from practices. As ecology undergoes a mutation to adapt to its planetary context, it is turning its transdisciplinary investigations toward the study of the whole Earth. To engage in whole Earth thinking, one must question the meaning of Earth, examining one's assumptions and inherited opinions. In short, Earth cannot be taken for granted.

Earth is not just a stage upon which humans play out the dramas of existence. Earth is not a giant background for human cultures. Earth is itself an actor, an active participant in history. This means more than saying that *parts* of Earth are active participants in human history, such as the volcano, Mt. Vesuvius, whose eruption destroyed the ancient Roman city of Pompeii, or the tsunami that triggered the nuclear disaster in Fukushima, Japan in 2011. Not only do volcanos, oceans, mountains, rivers, and other parts of Earth play significant roles in cultural events. The *whole* Earth is an actor. Earth has been contributing to cultural developments with increasing frequency in recent centuries, beginning around the time of Nicolaus Copernicus (1473–1543), who revolutionized the science of astronomy in the sixteenth century by developing a theory that Earth revolves around the sun. Copernicus went against the grain of his time, asserting something that was contrary to the traditional understanding passed down from ancient astronomy: Earth is not a motionless center around which the rest of the universe turns. Earth is not a stable location surrounded by wandering heavenly bodies.

Earth is itself a wandering heavenly body – a planet (from Greek *planasthai*, "to wander"). Although the ancient Greek thinker Aristarchus developed a similar heliocentric theory centuries earlier, it was only after Copernicus that there began a widespread recognition that humans are living on a moving body, a planet (Gassendi, 2002). It is a shocking realization. Taken out of their place in the center of the universe, humans were left with no stable place at all. The ground is shifting underneath our feet. Our place is spinning and flying around the sun in an evolving universe (see Chapter 8).

The Copernican revolution gradually changed people's understanding of the world. Having understood their location to be a stable center in the universe, humans became decentered and disoriented as they learned about this astronomical revolution. With the decentering of earthly existence, the social systems and cultural traditions built upon the old model of the universe were forced to adapt to this new planetary discovery. The scientific evidence thus caused controversy throughout society, not only among scientists but also among political and religious authorities. The Copernican revolution opened up new questions about the place of humans in the universe and new questions about how we know who and where we are. Who are we? Where are we? Who gets to decide who and where we are? How do we know what to do? Living on a moving body, how should we act? Thus began the entrance of the whole Earth into human awareness.

Around the same time that Copernicus was starting a scientific revolution, explorers like Ferdinand Magellan and Christopher Columbus were starting to navigate uncharted territories and thereby contribute to the mapping of the whole Earth. Such mapping was one of many projects involved in the European colonial period, when missionaries, merchants, and political rulers made contact with other peoples and places, spreading Western culture around the planet through means that often involved violence, slavery, oppression, and coercion. In the tumultuous events of colonialism, there was a proliferation of world maps and globes. The whole Earth was coming into view. Even if most of the people looking at those maps and globes were interested mainly in finding riches, converting nonbelievers, or attaining power over conquered lands, the whole Earth was becoming an increasingly prevalent part of people's lives, entering their thoughts, feelings, and perceptions.

Maps, globes, and scientific representations of Earth increased in detail and accuracy over the centuries, but it was only in the twentieth century that a vision of the whole Earth became widely available to the general public. Beginning with photographs taken in the 1940s, space exploration made possible numerous pictures of Earth taken from outside of the planet's atmosphere, of which one of the most famous is the 1968 photograph of Earth taken from the moon, "Earthrise." Of course, even a picture of the whole Earth does not show every single part of Earth. As one side is revealed to us, the other becomes hidden, and even if all sides could be represented simultaneously, Earth's mantle and core would still remain invisible, hidden beneath the clouds, water, and land. Nonetheless, "Earthrise" and similar photographs and pictorial representations provided a visual sense of the whole Earth to everyone who could experience it, and growing capabilities of mass media have made it increasingly easy for people to have that experience.

Many people find inspiration in the pictures of our planetary home. Those pictures convey a sense of the unity of the Earth community. Among the people who have first-hand experience of seeing Earth from space, such a sense of unity is often referred to as the "overview effect" (White, 2014). The overview effect indicates that the experience of seeing the relative smallness of Earth suspended in space can occasion a feeling that humans are far closer to one another and to the rest of the planet than is often realized. There are many important differences that divide the planet's denizens along lines such as species, age, gender, ethnicity, religion, race, class, and ability. Yet, as pictures of the whole Earth indicate, all of those differences take place in one planetary context. No matter how different we are, whether human or nonhuman, we are earthlings. We share a common dwelling, a singular home. There is only one Earth.

At around the same time that pictures of Earth began circulating widely, many people started to promote ideas and lifestyles oriented toward a concern for our shared planetary existence. For instance, in the 1960s, Stewart Brand began publishing the *Whole Earth Catalog*, which functions as a guidebook to give people access to tools, skills, and knowledge for living on an interconnected planet. As Brand (2009: 22) describes it, "The *Whole Earth Catalog* encouraged individual power," facilitating a do-it-yourself approach to human–Earth relations. Brand's work may be described not only as environmentalist but also as countercultural, emerging alongside many other 1960s countercultural movements, including feminism, civil rights, anti-war, and anti-nuclear movements. Brand's emphasis on interconnectedness runs counter to the fragmentation and selfishness that pervade mainstream culture. However, the phenomenon of the whole Earth was not something celebrated only by the 1960s counterculture. Planetary coexistence became the focus of international celebration with the inaugural Earth Day in 1970, which continues to be celebrated worldwide every year on April 22. The 1970s also saw the development of a science of the whole Earth: Gaia theory. By bringing together multiple scientific perspectives on the interlocking systems that compose the whole Earth, Gaia theory is capable of describing the complex relationships between planetary systems. A crucial task of whole Earth thinking is to account for interdependent and self-organizing dynamics of Earth's systems, including its living systems (biosphere) and its systems of water (hydrosphere), rock (lithosphere), air (atmosphere), and even human consciousness (noosphere) (see Chapter 7).

In recent decades, amidst the emerging scientific and cultural awareness of our terrestrial home, there has been a growing recognition of an ecological crisis. Whether mainstream or countercultural, many people began realizing that the dominant form of human civilization was severely damaging its own land base, fouling its own nest. In other words, it became obvious to many people that humans were killing themselves (suicide) by killing other organisms (biocide) and destroying the ecosystems (ecocide) on which human existence depends. The preservation, conservation, and environmental movements of the twentieth century raised awareness of numerous ecological problems, such as pollution, toxic waste, deforestation, water scarcity, soil erosion, and extinction. As the century progressed, the crisis became increasingly planetary, overflowing the boundaries of local and regional problems.

The planetary scale of the ecological crisis is reflected in the unprecedented challenges posed by phenomena like global climate change and the mass extinction of species. Those large-scale problems are symptoms of a transition out of the current geological epoch (the Holocene, which began approximately 12,000 years ago) into the Anthropocene – a term that an increasing number of researchers and scholars use to designate the currently emerging geological epoch, in which human actions impact planetary systems. The Anthropocene is named with the Greek word *anthropos* ("human"), but that does not mean that it is a time when humans are in charge. The Anthropocene is named after humans because it is a time when humans have massive, Earth-changing impacts, altering the chemistry of the atmosphere (climate change), changing DNA (genetic modification), and depositing non-biodegradable plastic, Styrofoam, and radioactive materials around the planet. A particular local community may have the knowledge needed to resolve a local environmental problem like an invasive species or a polluted waterway, but the planetary problems of the Anthropocene call for new ways of thinking. As Mark Whitehead (2014: 1) says in his analysis of the Anthropocene's geography, "the Anthropocene appears to require a change in the ways in which we study environmental transformation." It requires "a peculiar mix of analytic skills" from multiple disciplines to provide "a reliable toolkit for studying the geological force that is humankind" (p. 3). In short, it requires whole Earth thinking.

Planetary thinking involves more than following the slogan, "Think Globally, Act Locally." It means rethinking the very relationship between the global and the local, the macro and the micro, the planetary and the personal. It even means rethinking what it means to think and act. From a planetary perspective, does thinking happen inside of one's head, or does thinking emerge in relationship with the surrounding world? Do nonhumans participate in anything like thinking? Are actions limited to individual or local actions, or can action happen in massively distributed networks and groups that cross local, regional, and national boundaries? This book explores those and many other questions that are emerging as humans are becoming increasingly planetary. There is more than one way to address those questions. Indeed, there is more than one way to practice whole Earth thinking.

Religion, ecology, and philosophy

The phrase "whole Earth thinking" comes from Stephanie Kaza (2008), an ecologically oriented scholar and practitioner of Buddhism. She uses that phrase to describe a way of thinking she shares with another ecologically oriented Buddhist scholar-practitioner, Gary Snyder. She uses eating as an example. While some environmentalists or animal rights advocates argue that vegetarianism is more ethically appropriate than a diet that includes meat, Snyder situates the practice of eating within a more comprehensive context, what Kaza calls "Snyder's big view of the universe" (p. 11). Taking a big view, one sees that all eating involves harm to some kind of life. There is no diet that allows one to attain a purely innocent position where no harm comes to life. "Snyder urges us to face the fact that causing harm is necessary for us to live. There is no harm-free lunch. We all participate in the big story of eating and being eaten" (p. 9). The challenge of not harming life is not a challenge one can solve once and for all. It requires that you keep participating in the big story, continually paying attention to the whole context of your actions. The point, then, is not simply to be vegetarian or vegan. The point is to pay attention and stay committed to the task of reducing unnecessary harm to life. Be mindful of the context in which you are eating. If you try to eat vegetarian food, consider the context of the food. Is the source of the food local, or was it shipped over long distances? Is it organic, or was it produced using artificial chemicals for fertilizer, herbicides, and pesticides? How much do you want, and how much do you need? Whole Earth thinking keeps those questions open, letting them focus your attention on the many interconnected aspects of the world around you.

Snyder's big story draws on many sources, including poetry, Buddhism, indigenous traditions, and radical environmental movements like bioregionalism and deep ecology. Closely associated with the Beat movement in literature, Snyder is most well known as a poet and essayist. Like other members of the Beat Generation, such as Allen Ginsberg and Jack Kerouac, Snyder's work affirms creativity, freedom, and spiritual experience, and it is highly critical of many features of the cultural norms prominent in the United States after World War II, including growing trends toward industrialization, militarism, consumerism, and selfishness. Unlike the other Beat writers, Snyder is unique for his extensive inclusion of wilderness, nature, and ecology into his writings.

Snyder connects all of those themes in his big view of the universe, connecting social issues to spirituality, connecting spirituality to everyday practices (like eating), and connecting everyday practices to the wildness of the natural world. Much of this is expressed in what is perhaps his most famous work, *The Practice of the Wild* (1990). In that work, he summarizes his big view of the universe by describing the wholeness of things. For Snyder, your own body and local environment make up a whole: one place. Your place is whole, yet it is also just a part, which is situated in a larger whole. Your place is part of a whole region. That region is whole, and it is a part of a larger whole, a continent, and every continent is part of a more encompassing whole, the planet, and this nested hierarchy continues through solar systems and galaxies all the way to the whole universe. The universe is a network of parts containing parts, and every part is whole. To realize the unique situation of your place within this universe is to recognize the spirit of your place. "To know the spirit of a place is to realize that you are a part of a part and that the whole is made of parts, each of which is whole. You start with the part you are whole in" (Snyder, 1990: 41). Knowing the spirit of a place means knowing its wholeness, and knowing the wholeness of anything means knowing its position in the wholeness of everything.

Snyder's emphasis on place is indicative of his involvement in bioregionalism, a radical environmentalist movement that advocated for place-based ways of being in the world. Bioregionalists encourage people to practice "reinhabitation," to reconnect to one's place and ecological community (i.e., bioregion) (p. 191). Bioregionalists know the places where their food and water come from. They know that food does not just come from a store or restaurant, and water does not just come from a bottle or tap. They know which direction north is, and they are familiar with the species living with them in their place. Bioregionalists focus intently on the local. However, this does not mean that they oppose the global. Place-based knowledge does not disconnect the local from the rest of Earth. Quite the opposite: knowing the spirit of a place means understanding its position within the dynamics of the whole Earth.

If bioregionalism is against the global, it is only insofar as the global is not sufficiently planetary. The global often refers to telecommunications, finance, trade, and multiculturalism, with little attention paid to the actual planetary context within which those phenomena are taking place. Peter Berg (2015: 42), one of the first and most well-known proponents of bioregionalism, puts the distinction between global and planetary this way. "Globalists" hold that "human beings are important to the degree that they should actually control the entire biosphere," and in stark contrast, "Planetarians" are "people who view themselves from within the biosphere rather than from the top of it." Global civilization spreads consumer culture everywhere, turning everything and everyone into resources, making everything look the same. Avoiding such homogenization, planetary civilization cultivates biological and cultural diversity, attending to all planetary beings on their own terms, each according to its own place.

Along with bioregionalism, Snyder's big view of the universe is also indicative of his involvement in another radical environmentalist movement: deep ecology. Proponents of deep ecology aim to include philosophical and religious perspectives into ecology, complementing the scientific, economic, and political perspectives with which ecological phenomena are often viewed. The metaphor of depth suggests that philosophies and religions are "deep" ways of engaging ecology, whereas science, economics, and politics are "shallow." That metaphor sounds disparaging to science, economics, and politics, as if they are not only different from philosophy and religion but are somehow less thoughtful or less wise. The point, however, is not to disparage the so-called "shallow" perspectives but to include other ways of thinking into ecological inquiry. Snyder is an ally of the deep ecology movement insofar as he complements ecological and evolutionary sciences with perspectives from religions. In particular, Snyder draws on Buddhism and Native American traditions. Like sciences of ecology and evolution, those religions contain many ways of attending to the interconnectedness of beings, although they do so with different ideas, symbols, and practices.

Whole Earth thinking involves more than talking about connections between local and planetary scales. It also involves the task of bringing together multiple perspectives on those connections. When Kaza defines whole Earth thinking by pointing to Snyder, she is indicating something about *what* whole Earth thinking attempts to know and *how* it attempts to know it. What? Whole Earth thinking stretches toward knowledge of our planetary context. How? It brings into dialogue multiple kinds of knowledge, including knowledge based in sciences, knowledge based in intimate experiences of place, and knowledge based in the religious traditions of the world. Whole Earth thinking facilitates the integration of many sources of ecological wisdom (see Chapter 5). Furthermore, whole Earth thinking is not restricted to deep ecology in its understanding of religious perspectives on the natural world. More than just deep ecology, it draws upon a vast array of theories, ideas, methods, and practices that engage religious perspectives on ecology. Whole Earth thinking draws upon the entire field of religion and ecology.

Religion and ecology emerged as an academic discipline in the 1990s. Its development was spurred by the Forum on Religion and Ecology, co-founded by Mary Evelyn Tucker and John Grim. Currently stationed at Yale University, the Forum is a diverse network of people from around the world who are interested in ecology, including teachers, researchers, activists, advocates, scholars, and adherents of various religions. An example of the work of the Forum may be found in the book series on Religions of the World and Ecology published through the Center for the Study of World Religions at Harvard and based on conference proceedings that took place between 1996 and 1998. The series includes multiple perspectives on the ecological implications of Christianity, Judaism, Islam, Hinduism, Buddhism, Jainism, Confucianism, Daoism, Shinto, and indigenous traditions. One conference focused entirely on interdisciplinary dialogue between religious, scientific, and ethical perspectives on animals (Waldau and Patton, 2006). With the success of that series of conferences and books, the Forum contributed to the development of a new academic discipline, a field of study called religion and ecology. Along with the conferences and the book series, the Forum website was developed "to assist in fostering research, education, and outreach in the area of religion and ecology" (Tucker, 2007: 410). The website for the Forum presents a summary of its project:

> The Forum on Religion and Ecology is the largest international multireligious project of its kind. With its conferences, publications, and website it is engaged in exploring religious worldviews, texts, and ethics in order to broaden understanding of the complex nature of current environmental concerns.
>
> The Forum recognizes that religions need to be in dialogue with other disciplines (e.g., science, ethics, economics, education, public policy, gender) in seeking comprehensive solutions to both global and local environmental problems.
>
> (http://fore.research.yale.edu)

There are many influences that guided Tucker and Grim in their contributions to the field of religion and ecology, including some of their teachers. One such particularly important teacher is the cultural historian Thomas Berry (1914–2009).

As Grim and Tucker (2014: 6) recall, Berry passed on to them "an abiding interest in the cosmologies embedded in the world religions, that is, the ways in which these orienting narratives bind peoples, biodiversity, and place together." Berry's passion for religious cosmologies accompanied his understanding of the immense challenges facing the current era of planetary crisis. In short, Berry may be considered a practitioner of whole Earth thinking. "The present urgency is to begin thinking within the context of the whole planet, the integral Earth community with all its human and other-than-human components" (Berry, 1999: 105). To this end, Berry proposes an "integral Earth study" (p. 90). Like Snyder's big view of the universe, Berry situates planetary thinking with a comprehensive cosmological context in which all parts find wholeness, which Berry, together with the cosmologist Brian Swimme, calls "the universe story" (Swimme and Berry, 1992). Berry's work with Swimme illustrates the importance of scientific cosmology (see Chapter 8) and the imaginative practice of storytelling (see Chapter 9) for whole Earth thinking.

Kaza mentions Berry and the universe story in her presentation of practices for whole Earth thinking. She mentions a practice developed by Sister Miriam Therese MacGillis, a Dominican nun who founded Genesis Farm as a place to put Berry's ideas into practice. One such practice is a "cosmic walk," where a spiral path is set up with markers along the way to designate different events in the evolutionary story of the universe, "beginning with the first flaring forth of the Big Bang" and proceeding through the evolution of life on Earth and the emergence of human beings (Kaza, 2008: 48). Kaza goes on to describe her experience of the cosmic walk: "I could feel in my mind and body a sense of immensity, that these gifts of time – our sun, the planets and stars, our home earth – were the results of systems within systems operating across many timescales." Whole Earth thinking is a practice of attending to those systems within systems. It is a practice of attending to our planetary coexistence and our place within immensities.

Drawing upon figures like Snyder and Berry, Kaza's whole Earth thinking may be situated within the field of religion and ecology. Of course, Kaza, Snyder, Berry, and others associated with religion and ecology are not the only people developing something like whole Earth thinking. The field of religion and ecology represents one kind of approach to understanding the challenges of planetary coexistence. Drawing a creative contrast with the approach emerging from religion and ecology, there is another approach that I present in this book, one that uses philosophical inquiry to respond to the questions opened up by the planetary crisis. Unlike fields of religious studies and sciences, philosophy is known for being unruly and difficult. It has been this way since its beginnings in ancient Greece around two and a half millennia ago. Socrates is exemplary in this regard. He was put to death because his philosophizing was considered a threat to the youth and the traditions of Athens. In Plato's dialogue about the trial in which Socrates – Plato's teacher – was sentenced to death, he has Socrates make an analogy between his relationship with Athens and the relationship that a stinging fly has with a lazy horse. Socrates says he lives in that city "as though upon a great and well-born horse who is rather sluggish because of his great size and needs to be awakened by some gadfly" (Plato, 1998: 82). The sting of the gadfly (philosopher) hurts, but it helps to get the horse (society) moving.

The philosophical approach represented in this book is known for its intense sting. The representatives of this way of thinking are known for ruthlessly criticizing tradition and questioning the status quo. They are known for attempting to develop new ways of thinking that challenge people to become more deeply engaged in their existence and to affirm the messy ambiguities, complexities, and chaos of life. Coming primarily from French philosophers in the second half of the twentieth century, this approach is often known in English-speaking circles as "poststructuralism," mainly because it came after a movement called structuralism – a slightly earlier theoretical movement that aimed to analyze all human cultural phenomena in terms of the overarching contexts or structures in which they appear. For a structuralist, the task of understanding a Tibetan sentence requires an understanding of its relationship to the whole grammatical structure of the Tibetan language. To understand the meaning of a Christian holiday like Christmas as it is celebrated in London, you have to study the whole system of practices and relationships that make up meaning for British culture and the Christian religion.

Structuralism seems useful for understanding how things relate to the larger systems and contexts in which they exist, including the planetary systems within which humans, organisms, and ecosystems exist. However, thinkers coming in the wake of structuralism, such as Michel Foucault, Jacques Derrida, and Gilles Deleuze, suggest that things are more complicated than that, more dynamic and open-ended. It is not always easy or even possible to neatly define an overarching context. To define a culture once and for all is to ignore the fact that the boundaries between what does and does not belong to a culture change over time, and even when they are not changing, those boundaries are more blurry than clear, more flexible than rigid, more porous than closed, and more uncertain than obvious. Furthermore, things cannot be completely explained by their contexts. Even if you understand British culture with profound insight, you cannot completely explain Christmas in London. Even if you understand the whole planet, you cannot fully explain an owl living in northern California. It is too unique, too singular, too different. It resists being reduced to an overarching context. There is an inexhaustible mystery to things and their contexts, an unknowable dimension that no theory can grasp.

Foucault, Derrida, Deleuze, and other poststructuralists were doing more than just criticizing structuralism. They were engaging many different theories and issues. Along those lines, poststructuralists sometimes find themselves situated within a broader category, "postmodernism," mainly because they are part of a new historical period that seems different than the "modernism" of the previous five centuries, which differs from the preceding medieval and ancient periods of human history. However, those labels for historical periods are very vague and do not say much about the specific content of the work that any artist, scientist, or philosopher might have done in any particular period. For example, even though Deleuze is considered postmodern, he explicitly aligns his work with modern and even ancient thinkers. Moreover, Deleuze and the actual representatives of this approach do not use the labels of poststructuralism or postmodernism for themselves, and in general they resist any easy application of "ism" labels. Many other labels are variously associated with this group of philosophers, including materialism, critical theory, deconstruction, atheism, feminism, and existentialism.

While poststructuralism, postmodernism, and other labels may sometimes be useful, it must be borne in mind that these thinkers are not easy to categorize. Their resistance to simple categorization is one of the factors that make them relevant to the task of navigating challenges that are difficult to categorize – the uncertain, complex, and unprecedented challenges of planetary coexistence. Indeed, two of the thinkers that represent this philosophical approach – Deleuze and Félix Guattari – worked together to develop an explicitly planetary philosophy, a philosophy of Earth. Among other so-called poststructuralists and postmoderns, Deleuze and Guattari are the most explicitly oriented toward Earth and ecology. "Philosophy," as they put it, "is geophilosophy" (Deleuze and Guattari, 1994: 95). The aim of geophilosophy is to make up powerful new ideas, to create concepts that can change lives and facilitate planetary renewal, "*to summon forth a new earth, a new people*" (p. 99).

Geophilosophy situates human existence within the vibrant dynamics of Earth and the evolving story of the universe, which they call "the song of the universe," in other words, "the great Refrain" (p. 189). Unlike deep ecology, for which philosophy is "deep" compared to the shallowness of science, geophilosophy has a much more hospitable approach to the profound knowledge that scientists articulate. Geophilosophy situates itself on the same level with science and art. Its relationship to religion, though, is more ambiguous. If whole Earth thinking adopts an inclusive attitude toward religions, then geophilosophy may seem like a poor companion to whole Earth thinking, as Deleuze and Guattari frequently criticize religion. However, just as the field of religion and ecology criticizes ecological illiteracy in religious traditions while also retrieving and reconstructing more ecologically sensitive aspects of those traditions, Deleuze and Guattari reconstruct what they consider to be the liberating aspects of religions while also adopting a critical and sometimes hostile approach to any oppressive aspects of religions.

Geophilosophy does not stay within the boundaries of academic disciplines. Traversing many fields of study and connecting multiple ways of thinking, feeling, and acting, geophilosophy produces concepts that facilitate creative, life-affirming modes of planetary coexistence. The philosophical approach of Deleuze and Guattari is representative of a larger trend in French theory to address ecological questions in ways that cross disciplinary boundaries with the aim of articulating complex forms of terrestrial coexistence, wherein culture can never be separated from nature, humans can never be separated from nonhumans, and global civilization cannot be separated from the planet (Whiteside, 2002). The way Guattari (2000) puts it is that an ecological philosophy must address connections between "three ecologies," accounting for the ways that problems of natural and living systems (environmental) are not separate from political and socioeconomic problems (social) or problems of human consciousness (mental) (see Chapter 4).

Pairing religion and ecology with this radical approach to philosophy creates a contrast that enriches both approaches in their respective efforts to integrate multiple ways of knowing and facilitate complex and creative forms of planetary coexistence. That pairing is quite complementary, but it also involves points of criticism and antagonism (see Chapter 3). Both approaches to whole Earth thinking emphasize the importance of engaging in dialogue with other perspectives, so it seems likely that they would be in dialogue with one another. However, despite their shared interest in including multiple perspectives to cultivate planetary renewal, people interested in the kind of French philosophy represented by Deleuze and Guattari are rarely engaged in the field of religion and ecology, and vice versa. In the rare case that those approaches are put into dialogue, as in Whitney Bauman's (2014) thoughtful and creative work, it tends to be presented at a level that is only accessible to advanced scholars. This book presents that dialogue in more accessible terms.

By maintaining a contrast between geophilosophy and the field of religion and ecology, those approaches stay in ongoing dialogue, with neither approach taking a dominant position. This not only indicates that there are different ways to undertake the task of whole Earth thinking. It also indicates that different approaches are enhanced through practices of dialogue, which is to say, practices of building "(un)likely alliances," which are exactly the kind of alliances toward which the geophilosophy of Deleuze and Guattari is oriented (Herzogenrath, 2008). In creative interactions with one another, geophilosophy and the field of religion and ecology open up more possibilities for making change, more possibilities for building alliances across differences, and facilitating vibrant, mutually enhancing modes of planetary coexistence.

Summary

Elaborating on contributions from the field of religion and ecology, represented by people like Berry, Kaza, and Snyder, and from the philosophical approach represented by Deleuze and Guattari, this book provides an introduction to whole Earth thinking, including an overview of multiple approaches to ecological wisdom and a presentation of concepts useful for crossing disciplinary boundaries and engaging the entangled coexistence of the environments, societies, and subjects of Earth. Each of the chapters may be read either independently or in sequence. The point is, what can you do with them? How can these ideas empower your participation in planetary coexistence? How can you tell your story, orient yourself toward wisdom, and find your place in the universe?

This introductory chapter discusses ways of thinking that integrate religion, ecology, and philosophy in order to address the challenges of planetary coexistence. Subsequent chapters focus on particular aspects of those ways of thinking. The focus of Chapter 2 is on the varieties of ecological inquiry, including a history of the idea of ecology beginning with ancient conceptions of the natural world and moving through modern scientific approaches to ecology and the current use of ecology and the "eco-" prefix in a wide variety of contexts. Chapter 3 presents a closer look at the contrast between geophilosophy, represented by Deleuze and Guattari, and the field of religion and ecology, represented by Berry, who calls himself an Earth scholar or "geologian." Chapter 4 discusses the intertwined environmental, social, and subjective dimensions of ecological phenomena, which correspond to what Guattari calls the "three ecologies" and what Berry calls the "cosmogenetic principle." Wisdom is the focus of Chapter 5, with attention to Berry's enumeration of multiple sources of wisdom, the love of wisdom (*philo-sophia*) inherent in the geophilosophy of Deleuze and Guattari, and the ecological wisdom or "ecosophy" that Guattari articulates in his analysis of the three ecologies.

The next three chapters rethink the meaning of humanity, Earth, and the universe in the context of whole Earth thinking. Following Berry's call for a reinvention of the human species, Chapter 6 builds upon environmentalist critiques of the human-centered (anthropocentric) values of modern humans, but not in order to articulate a non-anthropocentric position, which risks ignoring human problems of injustice, exploitation, and inequality. Instead of choosing between anthropocentric and non-anthropocentric values, sources of ecological wisdom point toward an anthropocosmic position, wherein humans and nonhumans are understood as mutually constitutive and not mutually exclusive opposites. Whereas the previous chapter discusses the role of humans in whole Earth thinking, Chapter 7 elaborates on the specific characteristics of the whole Earth, including its relationship to environmental, social, and subjective ecologies. This chapter discusses the condition of Earth during the Anthropocene by elaborating on what the theorist of complexity, Edgar Morin, describes as the evolution of the Planetary Era. Bringing together scientific, philosophical, and religious perspectives on cosmology, Chapter 8 presents an overview of the cosmic context for whole Earth thinking, what Kaza calls Snyder's big view of the universe, which is similar to the song of the universe for Deleuze and Guattari and the universe story for Swimme and Berry. In the wildly creative cosmos of whole Earth thinking, the universe is not a collection of objects but is permeated by creativity, subjectivity (self-organization), and intimate relationship.

Whole Earth thinking is not just about rational intelligence. It also includes emotions, perceptions, dreams, stories, and imagination. One way to include those kinds of experience into whole Earth thinking is through narrative imagination and the visionary power of dreams. Chapter 9 introduces concepts of narrative imagination and dream that draw on many sources, including the universe story of Swimme and Berry, the concept of refrain in Deleuze and Guattari, and the traditional ecological knowledge of indigenous peoples. To cultivate creative and mutually enhancing expressions of planetary coexistence, whole Earth thinking requires more than ideas. It requires stories and dreams capable of embodying and realizing those ideas. It also requires energy, which is the focus of Chapter 10.

Chapter 10 draws from Berry, Deleuze-Guattari, and Kaza to develop a concept of energy that integrates philosophy, science, and religion. That concept is relevant to the energetic challenges of global climate change, which is an energy crisis in many senses. It is a crisis caused by the excessive use of a particular kind of energy source (fossil fuels), and it demands the use of alternative energies. It is also an energy crisis because of the lack of personal and political energy to turn individual practices and social systems away from fossil-fuel-based lifestyles and toward sustainable alternatives. An integrative concept of energy indicates ways of energizing personal and political concern for mutually enhancing human–Earth relations. Finally, the concluding chapter gives a brief summary of some of the key concepts introduced throughout the book (e.g., wisdom, narrative, energy, and integrative conceptions of humans, Earth, and the cosmos), concluding with a call for the further development of multiple approaches to the integration of ecological perspectives in the sciences and humanities. Part of the development of such approaches is for them to enter into dialogue with one another, building alliances across differences. Out of such dialogue, the contrasts between different approaches can produce more opportunities for planetary collaboration, opportunities for the development of increasingly more inclusive and comprehensive responses to the complex challenges facing the emerging Earth community.

References

Bauman, Whitney, A. 2014. *Religion and Ecology: Developing a Planetary Ethic*. New York: Columbia University Press.

Berg, Peter. 2015. "Globalists Versus Planetarians: An Interview of Peter Berg by Michael Helm." In *The Biosphere and the Bioregion: Essential Writings of Peter Berg*, ed. Cheryll Glotfelty and Eve Quesnel, 41–51. New York: Routledge.

Berry, Thomas. 1999. *The Great Work: Our Way into the Future*. New York: Bell Tower.

Brand, Stewart. 2009. *Whole Earth Discipline: An Ecopragmatist Manifesto*. New York: Viking.

Callicott, J. Baird. 2013. *Thinking Like a Planet: The Land Ethic and the Earth Ethic*. New York: Oxford University Press.

Deleuze, Gilles and Félix Guattari. 1994. *What is Philosophy?* Trans. Hugh Tomlinson and Graham Burchell. New York: Columbia University Press.

Forum on Religion and Ecology. "About the Forum." http://fore.research.yale.edu (accessed November 6, 2014).

Gassendi, Pierre. 2002. *The Life of Copernicus (1473–1543)*. Fairfax, VA: Xulon Press.

Grim, John and Mary Evelyn Tucker. 2014. *Ecology and Religion*. Washington, D.C.: Island Press.

Guattari, Félix. 2000. *The Three Ecologies*. Trans. Ian Pindar and Paul Sutton. London: Athlone Press.

Hathaway, Mark and Leonardo Boff. 2009. *The Tao of Liberation: Exploring the Ecology of Transformation*. Maryknoll: Orbis Books.

Herzogenrath, Bernd (ed.). 2008. *An [Un]likely Alliance: Thinking Environment[s] with Deleuze|Guattari*. Newcastle upon Tyne: Cambridge Scholars.

Kaza, Stephanie. 2008. *Mindfully Green: A Personal and Spiritual Guide to Whole Earth Thinking*. Boston, MA: Shambhala Publications.

Plato. 1998. *Apology of Socrates*. In *Four Texts on Socrates: Plato and Aristophanes*, revised edn, ed. and trans. Thomas West and Grace Starry West, 63–97. Ithaca, NY: Cornell University Press.

Snyder, Gary. 1990. *The Practice of the Wild*. Berkeley, CA: Counterpoint.

Swimme, Brian and Thomas Berry. 1992. *The Universe Story: From the Primordial Flaring Forth to the Ecozoic Era – A Celebration of the Unfolding of the Cosmos*. San Francisco, CA: HarperCollins.

Tucker, Mary Evelyn. 2007. "Religion and Ecology: Survey of the Field." In *The Oxford Handbook of Religion and Ecology*, ed. Roger S. Gottlieb, 398–418. New York: Oxford University Press.

Waldau, Paul and Kimberly Patton (eds). 2006. *A Communion of Subjects: Animals in Religion, Science, and Ethics*. New York: Columbia University Press.

White, Frank. 2014. *The Overview Effect: Space Exploration and Human Evolution*, 3rd edn. Reston, VA: American Institution of Aeronautics and Astronautics.

Whitehead, Mark. 2014. *Environmental Transformations: A Geography of the Anthropocene*. New York: Routledge.

Whiteside, Kerry H. 2002. *Divided Natures: French Contributions to Political Ecology*. Cambridge, MA: MIT Press.

2 Ecology: a household word

Ecology is a household word. Deriving from the Greek *oikos* ("dwelling"; "home") and *logos* ("word"; "discourse"), ecology may be understood as a way of speaking about home. It is a way of speaking about the household of nature. Along with its Greek roots, ecology is a household word in another sense as well. It is a word that has spilled out of its academic context into the vernacular; that is, the language used in everyday life, the language used around the house. Ecology regularly shows up in numerous places throughout mass media and popular culture, sometimes appearing only in the prefix "eco-," which is attached to an increasing number of words and used extensively in marketing, design, and research. Although the word is extremely common, it is not clear precisely what it means.

In its common usage, there are two meanings of the word "ecological." First, something is ecological if it is good for the environment; in short, ecofriendly. In this sense, an organic farm would be considered more ecological than a farm that uses artificial chemicals in pesticides, herbicides, and fertilizers. A farm with free range animals is considered more ecological than a factory farm – more formally known as a "concentrated animal feeding operation" (CAFO). A disposable plastic water bottle is far less ecological than a refillable bottle that is made without the use of any plastics. Hunting for subsistence would be considered more ecological than trophy hunting. That popular usage of the term "ecological" is not entirely wrong. Many ecological researchers are often involved in some kind of advocacy or activism, and even those who are not publicly engaged in environmental issues are nonetheless often oriented toward actions that are beneficial for the health of ecosystems. Throughout the twentieth century, ecological theories and methods were used in numerous efforts to support ecosystem health, including in the preservation of wilderness areas, the conservation of resources, and the restoration of damaged ecosystems. However, ecology is not always ecological in the sense of ecofriendly. Ecologists and other environmental scientists are not always studying or advocating for healthy or friendly ecological relationships. This leads to the second of the two meanings frequently given to ecology.

Second, the word "ecology" refers to a scientific discipline. More specifically, it is a scientific discipline that began as a subfield of biology in 1866, when the

German biologist and naturalist Ernst Haeckel first coined the word *oecologie*, defining this field of study as a scientific mode of inquiry which furthers the development of Charles Darwin's theory of the evolution of life. Drawing explicitly upon Darwin, who had published his groundbreaking work *On the Origin of Species* in 1859, Haeckel defines ecology as the study of organism–environment relationships, saying that "ecology is the study of all those complex interrelations referred to by Darwin as the conditions of the struggle for existence" (Merchant, 2007: 178). Although Haeckel coined the word, ecology owes its existence to Darwin's theory of evolution. In short, as the environmental historian Donald Worster (1994: 114) puts it, Darwin is the "single most important figure in the history of ecology over the past two or three centuries."

Appreciating how Darwin's theory accounts for the ways that a species changes over time in relationship to pressures from the natural environment, Haeckel proposed ecology as science that would not just focus on the species or on environmental conditions but on the relationship between the two. Haeckel's approach may be described as mechanistic, which means that he accounts for ecological relationships in terms of the results of mechanical processes, such that organism–environment interactions resemble the interlocking parts of a machine, like the gears in an analog clock or the parts of a car. He excludes from his approach any supposedly unscientific phenomena such as agency, subjectivity, or soul. This does not mean that there is no theology or psychology in Haeckel's view. Haeckel (2004) was interested in connecting religion and science, particularly by reducing religion to scientific explanations. His interpretations of God and consciousness are described in terms of his monistic view, a view in which everything can be reduced to one substance. Haeckel believed that God, consciousness, and all of nature can be explained rationally insofar as they can be reduced to the mechanistic operations of one underlying material substance.

Subsequent developments in ecology maintained a mechanistic outlook. In this sense, ecology is not about being ecofriendly; it is about studying all aspects of the struggle for existence. Ecologists do not just study beneficial relationships between organisms and environments. They study all aspects of the struggle for existence, a struggle that involves predation, parasitism, death, decomposition, and other seemingly unfriendly phenomena, including toxicity, pollution, and industrial waste. Scientific ecologies do not limit their study to healthy or friendly ecological relationships, nor do they always advocate for healthy ecosystems. Some scientists attain ecological knowledge for the sake of exploiting resources or manipulating nature for human ends. In other cases, scientists consider their work to be exclusively oriented toward facts with no concern for ethical values, although it may not be so easy to neatly separate facts from values. In short, ecology studies the friendly and unfriendly aspects of the struggle for existence, and, along with ecofriendly attitudes, ecological inquiry can take on supposedly value-neutral as well as exploitative attitudes.

The second sense of ecology (a scientific inquiry) may seem more correct than the first sense of ecology (ecofriendly). However, the meaning of ecology exceeds both definitions. Ecology is not just ecological in the sense of studying or promoting friendly relationships between organisms and environments, and ecology is not just ecological in the sense of a scientific mode of inquiry that excludes non-mechanistic phenomena such as value, subjectivity, and soul. Ecology means much more than ecofriendly ecology and scientific ecology. Ecology is also philosophical. It is also religious. Ecology may be found anywhere there are words (*logoi*) about the places, life, water, air, and land that constitute one's home (*oikos*). For instance, humans must have had some knowledge of relationships between organisms and environments when they began practicing agriculture during the Neolithic Revolution approximately 12,000 years ago. Considering the oldest of human activities, from the control of fire and the invention of cooking to the cultivation of plants and the domestication of animals, one finds that those activities required humans to cultivate a sense of relationships (e.g., in the case of cooking, relationships between wood, moisture, friction, combustion, food, and hunger).

In this much more comprehensive context, ecology includes multiple ways of knowing the relationships that comprise the struggle for existence in the natural world. However, there is a terminology problem. If all ways of knowing relationships are considered to be "ecology," it is easy to lose sight of the unique contributions of the scientific approaches developed by Haeckel and his successors. After all, it is for such scientific inquiry that the word "ecology" was explicitly coined, and many of the concepts developed in scientific ecologies have become part of common discourses (e.g., ecosystems, niches, and food chains). Theories and methods developed by scientists in the late nineteenth and twentieth centuries have shown themselves to be effective in describing ecological phenomena. Without such theories and methods, scientists would not have the ability to understand problems like soil erosion, global climate change, and species extinction. Accordingly, it is important to use terminology that does not eclipse the unique contributions of the scientific approaches to ecology that emerged after Haeckel's response to Darwin's work.

One way of preserving the uniqueness of scientific ecology is to distinguish it from earlier forms of ecological knowledge by referring to the predecessors of Haeckel as "proto-ecologists," which means that they are people "who had ecological insights before a formal science of ecology was formulated" (McIntosh, 1985: 15). Accordingly, the concept of nature articulated by the ancient Greek philosopher Aristotle would be considered proto-ecological, whereas Arthur Tansley's twentieth-century concept of the ecosystem would be considered ecological. The term "proto-ecologist" helps to distinguish between ecological knowledge before and after Haeckel, but it does not distinguish between kinds of ecological knowledge. Along those lines, one can distinguish "scientific ecology" from "religious ecologies" (Grim and Tucker, 2014: 38). Scientific approaches to ecology may be found in people like Haeckel and Tansley, who base their work in empirical observations, models, and metrics. Religious ecologies use different methods than scientific approaches. Religious ecologies are embedded in the narratives, symbols, and rituals of religious traditions. Whereas ancient religious ecologies would be considered proto-ecological, contemporary religious ecologies are not exactly proto-ecological. In contrast to proto-ecology, contemporary religious ecologies often engage explicitly in the ideas and practices of the scientific ecology developed after Haeckel, specifically in response to the challenges posed by the environmental crisis and by increasing planetary interconnectedness. In short, "religions are now entering their ecological phase and finding their planetary expression" (Tucker, 2003: 9). Many artists, philosophers, politicians, entrepreneurs, teachers, and parents are also entering their ecological phase. Earth art, environmental ethics, political ecology, green business, environmental education, sustainable design, and ecological consciousness make the meaning of ecology even harder to pin down.

The meaning of ecology is incredibly multifaceted, taking different shapes throughout history, from proto-ecological expressions of humanity thousands of years ago to contemporary scientific ecologies, religious ecologies, and many other expressions of the entrance of humans into an ecological phase of existence. The various approaches to ecology do not always agree with one another. The theories, methods, and aims of their work can differ greatly. Regarding their aims, some understandings of ecology encourage care and concern for natural environments, but other understandings may be oriented more toward a value-neutral assessment of the facts or toward anthropocentric aims for which nonhumans have value only for the sake of humans. Regarding their theories and methods, some ecologies include more than others. From the beginning of scientific accounts of nature, the meaning of ecology has been caught between specialized approaches, which focus on one or a few facets of ecology while ignoring or opposing other ways of knowing, and integrative approaches, which include as many facets as possible in order to facilitate creative collaboration between multiple ways of knowing. Specialized approaches are not without merits, but their narrow focuses are insufficient for addressing the planetary scale of contemporary ecological problems.

In the current era of planetary interconnectedness, integrative approaches are needed for building alliances across differences and crossing boundaries between multiple ways of knowing. To provide some context for understanding the tensions between different approaches to ecology (religious and scientific; anthropocentric and non-anthropocentric; specialized and integrative), this chapter gives an overview of the history of ecology, from its earliest proto-ecological expressions embedded in religious traditions to its articulation as a science and its emergence as a household word.

Religious ecologies

Through the history of the human species, people have been practicing something like ecology, attempting in many different ways to figure out how things relate to one another. There is proto-ecological knowledge embedded in practices of gathering, hunting, starting a fire, and cooking. Subsistence activities are among the oldest forms of ecological inquiry. Those forms of ecology became more intricate with the beginnings of agriculture and animal husbandry during the Neolithic Revolution, which began approximately 12,000 years ago. The Neolithic Revolution marks a time when humans developed more complex ecological conceptions, such as conceptions of seasons, growing cycles, and sexual reproduction. Subsistence and agricultural knowledge may be understood as forms of traditional ecological knowledge (TEK). It still exists today in the knowledge embedded in the "sacred ecology" of indigenous traditions (Berkes, 2012). Such knowledge is not expressed using mathematical equations, computer models, or any kind of writing. Situated in oral, small-scale, place-based societies, that knowledge is embodied in the words and deeds of the members of a tradition. It is expressed in the stories and practices with which that tradition orients itself to its place in the world.

Because indigenous knowledge is embodied and place-based, indigenous ecologies are often well adapted to their local ecosystems. TEK provides effective means for managing local resources sustainably, and, more than that, insofar as an indigenous ecology is a sacred ecology, the natural world is understood not simply as a collection of resources to be managed but as an interrelated community of beings that have value in themselves (intrinsic value), not merely value for human use (instrumental value). Humans do not conquer or possess nonhumans. Rather, humans understand themselves as situated in multispecies kinship groups, such that humans and nonhumans are relatives. When people speak of "totem" animals, this is what they are talking about. Indigenous traditions are not anthropocentric. They are "kincentric," as indicated by the derivation of the term "totem" from *ototeman,* which means "that's a relative of mine" in Anishinaabe, a language spoken by many Native American (United States) and First Nations peoples (Canada) (Pierotti, 2011: 31). Similarly, the Lakota Sioux – a Native American people with lands in North and South Dakota – use the phrase *mitakuye oyasin* ("all my relations") in many of their prayers (Demallie and Parks, 1989). Kin are not just resources. Accordingly, this sense of kinship supports practices that do more than manage local resources sustainably. It supports practices that cultivate mutually beneficial relationships between the humans and nonhumans inhabiting a place together. In short, it supports practices that are beneficial to all my relations.

This is not to say that indigenous approaches to ecological problems are always the best. The models and methods used in contemporary scientific ecologies provide detailed information and projections that indigenous traditions and other religious ecologies are not always capable of producing. This is not to say that scientific ecology is better than religious ecology. It is more capable of analyzing different phenomena and different scales, from the microbiological level of cells to the geological level of planetary systems. With its focus on the local, TEK does not have the same perspective on the planetary scale of ecological problems. Furthermore, even at the local scale, indigenous traditions are not perfect. Indeed, no tradition is. There is no tradition that has not been complicit in some kind of environmental destruction. Some people, in attempting to honor indigenous ecologies, treat indigenous peoples as if they are pure, innocent, and perfectly harmonious with the natural world. In other words, sometimes indigenous peoples are treated like "ecological noble savages" (Buege, 1996). This attitude perpetuates nostalgic stereotypes that fail to do justice to the complexities of indigenous ways of life. There is no ecological noble savage. One example of an environmentally destructive practice that occurs in some indigenous communities is swidden agriculture, more commonly known as slash-and-burn agriculture (Grim and Tucker, 2014: 24). Although it can be sustainable in small-scale contexts, this kind of agriculture can also be quite destructive when practiced continually or implemented on large scales.

Proto-ecologies extend beyond traditional ecological knowledge. More proto-ecologies began emerging after the Neolithic Period ended approximately 5000 years ago, marking the end of the Stone Age ("-lithic" derives from the Greek word for "stone," *lithos*). The agriculture that was developed during the Neolithic Period supported the growth of cities and the expansion of territories, making possible the emergence of ancient empires like Egypt, Persia, China, and Rome. Along with empires, this period of history also saw the development of a new technology: writing. Human history now entered the phase known as recorded history. Along with the invention of writing and the building of large cities and empires, new cultural expressions began to form during this period, including new religious ways of life (e.g., Judaism, Hinduism, Buddhism, Confucianism, and Daoism) as well as new ways of thinking: philosophy and science.

With new religious traditions came new approaches to ecological knowledge. Like indigenous traditions, the religions that arose during this period use symbols, myths, and rituals to provide their members with a sense of their place in the world. Unlike indigenous traditions, these religions are not entirely oral but also incorporate writing into their modes of expression, and they are not always small scale but also extend to larger social systems. Writing is more abstract than oral communication, which is embodied in a speaker who is situated in a particular place. Writing can exist without any speaker, and it can be read in many different places. Writing and large social systems are two indications that, in these new religious traditions, place-based knowledge was supplemented with universal principles and laws that could be applied and extended in many different places. In some cases, this entailed a loss or suppression of place-based knowledge, such that religions would focus less on the relationships between humans and their local environments and more on relationships that humans have with one another or with some divine or spiritual powers.

A lack of attention to human–Earth relations may be seen in the otherworldly (transcendent) aspirations that are expressed in many religious traditions, such as a Christian focus on an afterlife in heaven or a Buddhist focus on attaining enlightenment and escaping from this world of suffering and death. Those are otherworldly approaches to soteriology, which is to say that they are ways of understanding salvation in a way that focuses on a transcendent world beyond this world, beyond the immanent world of sense, bodies, and matter. Furthermore, if the focus on salvation excludes nonhumans from any share in enlightenment and heaven, then those soteriologies are not only otherworldly but also anthropocentric. Anthropocentrism and otherworldliness are not uncommon features of religious traditions. However, that is not the whole story. No religion is simply anthropocentric or otherworldly. No religion is completely lacking in concern for the natural world apart from its value for humans. There are aspects of Christianity, Buddhism, and all religions that cultivate concern for the beings of the natural world, a concern that does not separate humans from the rest of the world. Such a concern could be described as anthropocosmic (see Chapter 6). For example, in Christianity, this may be seen in the idea of stewardship, which means that humans are assigned the task of taking care of the natural world – God's creation – in the same way that stewards or caretakers take care of land for the owner (Jenkins, 2008). Humans are not thereby centered exclusively upon themselves. Rather, they experience themselves in relation to God and God's creation. In Buddhism, a concern for the natural world may be found in the Bodhisattva, who vows to be reborn into this world to continue working to end suffering and facilitate the liberation of all beings, human and nonhuman. An ecologically oriented bodhisattva or "ecosattva" could be considered to be "someone who cares deeply about all beings and the health of the planet and is willing to take action after action to help all beings thrive" (Kaza, 2008: 13).

As Grim and Tucker (2014: 13) put it, every religious tradition has "problems and promise." Every religion has aspects that can be limiting and oppressive alongside aspects that are liberating and healing. Religious ecologies can be authoritarian as well as democratic. They can be violent as well as non-violent, otherworldly and this-worldly, and anthropocentric and non-anthropocentric. The task of the field of religion and ecology is to retrieve, re-evaluate, and re-construct the ecological dimensions of religions in order to better understand their problematic and promising potentials, both throughout history and in response to contemporary issues (p. 86). This does not just entail studying the ideas, texts, and doctrines of different religions. It also entails studying the practices, rituals, organizations, and other material conditions of religious ways of life.

Theories cannot be separated from practices, ideas from actions, or worldviews from lived experiences. Yet, it is also important to remember that the practice is never completely identical to the theory. Sometimes one's actions are completely contrary to one's own religious beliefs and ideals. This means, for instance, that there is a difference between Islamic environmentalism and Muslim environment-alism (Foltz, 2007: 208). The former involves the environmental implications of the Islamic worldview and its main principles, specifically as they are expressed in the Quran. In contrast, Muslim environmentalism is found in the environmental behaviors of the practitioners of Islam (i.e., Muslims) and may draw in many ways from diverse sources not limited to Islam or even to religion but also secular poli-tics, mass media, and personal experience. Similarly, in Catholicism, there is a gap between the ideals expressed by the Pope and the beliefs and practices of the other members of the tradition. For instance, the famous work by St. Francis of Assisi, "Canticle of Brother Sun," uses familial language (e.g., "brother" and "sister") that expresses a profound kinship with all of creation, including the sun, moon, water, and fire (Hart, 2007: 69). That kind of language is unique to St. Francis and is not explicitly articulated in Catholic doctrines.

More examples of the ideas and practices comprising religious ecologies are discussed throughout this book. For now, the important point is to recognize that religion and ecology are intimately related. Religions are not just about people and not just about God or some principle of absolute reality. Along with human–human relations and human–divine relations, religions also provide ways of understanding and responding to the dynamics of human–Earth relations. Any definition of ecology that does not include religious ecologies would be incomplete. It would fail to recognize the proto-ecological predecessors that paved the way for ecology, and it would fail to account for the way in which symbols, myths, narratives, rituals, and images contribute to human understandings of organisms and environments. Such a failure would not just be a mistake in a theory. A failure to address religious ecologies has serious practical implications. To exclude traditional ecological knowledge is to exclude knowledge that in some cases has allowed humans to live sustainably on a land base for hundreds of years. To exclude religious ecologies is to exclude perspectives by which many people orient themselves to the world. With the vast majority of contemporary humans claiming adherence to some religious tradition, current efforts to address ecological problems must engage with religious perspectives if those efforts are going to be comprehensible in multicultural contexts.

To meet the ethical and political challenges of facilitating responses to ecological problems like freshwater scarcity, toxic waste, factory farms, and climate change, an engagement with religious ecologies is required. Grim and Tucker (2014: 11) summarize this point, observing that religions "can be active participants in finding solutions along with scientists, economists, and policymakers. Religions are thus necessary but not sufficient in themselves for achieving a sustainable future." Religious ecologies are a necessary component of any comprehensive and effective approach to contemporary ecological problems, but religious ways of life are not substitutes or replacements for the ecological knowledge produced in contemporary scientific ecology, which itself developed out of a proto-ecological context – the sciences of the ancient Greeks.

Scientific ecologies

The relationship between religions and sciences is complex and contested (Clayton, 2006). To risk oversimplifying their rich contrast, one can distinguish between their focus on what is revealed in tradition (religion) and what is discovered through reason (science). While religions express themselves in narratives, images, and symbols handed down through tradition, sciences rely less on tradition and more on reason, specifically what can be rationally deduced from observations and measurements. The distinction between narrative and reason is another way of stating the difference between two ways of speaking: myth (*muthos*: "story," "narrative") and logic (*logos*: "word," "reason," "rational account"). When sciences like physics, biology, and geometry first emerged in ancient Greece, certain lovers of wisdom – philosophers (*philia*, "love"; *sophia*, "wisdom") – distinguished the logic of their scientific inquiry from the mythical meanings presented in their local religion. The difference between the two ways of speaking can be quite stark. For instance, in the fifth century BCE, the local religion in Athens held that the sun is a god, but the philosopher Anaxagoras contested that idea, claiming instead that the sun is a large burning rock or metal (Graziosi, 2014: 70). Anaxagoras was exiled from Athens for his lack of reverence, officially charged with *asebeia* ("impiety"). This example is meant to demonstrate how different religion can be from science. This does not mean that religions and sciences are always incompatible. Sometimes mythical and logical perspectives can be much more hospitable to one another. Plato is exemplary in this regard. His works are dialogues, which present his teacher Socrates speaking with a variety of other people about numerous topics like justice, beauty, truth, goodness, politics, and the origin of the universe. Those dialogues express logical arguments, yet Socrates and his dialogue partners are frequently telling stories and discussing myths, thereby keeping philosophy in close contact with religious discourse.

Like religious ecologies, philosophical and scientific perspectives on the natural world include diverse discourses and practices. Amidst that diversity, one may discern two distinct ways of thinking about organisms and environments. In his account of the history of ecology from the ancient world through the twentieth century, the environmental historian Donald Worster (1994: 2, 29) describes these two ways of thinking: first, the "arcadian" approach, which is oriented toward "peaceful coexistence" between humans and the rest of the Earth community; and second, an "anti-arcadian tradition," which maintains an "imperial" view of nature that is oriented less toward coexistence and more toward arrangements that situate humans on top of a hierarchy of beings, where animals, plants, and inorganic matter are subordinate to human values.

The tension between arcadian and imperial ecologies may be found in the beginnings of science in ancient Greece, with thinkers like Pythagoras, Aristotle, and Euclid. For example, one can sense arcadian as well as imperial perspectives in the proto-ecological view of plants expressed by Aristotle (384–322 BCE). For Aristotle (2001: 412a20), every living being has a soul, with "soul" (*psyche*) defined as the form that causes life in the material body. There are many different kinds of living bodies, and they can be distinguished by the presence of one or more of the following capacities of the soul: intellect, perception, movement with regard to place (i.e., locomotion), and nutrition (414a30). A plant has a share in the nutritive capacity of the soul, which manages the work of growth and nutrition. Animals also share in this nutritive part of the soul. However, unlike plants, animals also possess the perceptive capacity of the soul and the capacity for locomotion. Furthermore, some animals have the capacity to reason and think things through (415a). The way in which an animal's senses are directed and attuned to the sensible world is a kind of ratio or rationality (426b5). However, Aristotle indicates that this does not mean that animal thinking is identical with the kind of thinking proper to humans, for a human being is also capable of imagination and intellect, which make it possible to discern what is true from what is false (427b–429a). The continuity and difference between human and animal intelligence is still debated today, particularly within the field of cognitive ethology (Allen and Bekoff, 1997).

On the one hand, Aristotle's botany represents an arcadian ecology insofar as he affirms the soul or interior agency of plants, in contrast to the scientific perspectives developed during the modern period, according to which plants are studied primarily as calculable and measurable objects. If humans and plants have souls, then presumably plants do not have value only for humans but also have value for themselves. The good of a plant is not just what a human thinks it is. The good of a plant depends upon the soul of the plant itself. On the other hand, Aristotle's hierarchy of the different capacities of the soul privileges human intellect over the cognition, perception, and locomotion of animals, and those animal capacities are privileged over the nutritive capacities of plants. Why is human intellect privileged? More than the other capacities of soul, intellect allows humans to become virtuous and happy. In other words, "the higher faculties of soul are higher purely because they are thought to belong solely to human beings. This value-ordering is fundamentally anthropocentric, with humanity becoming the yardstick for value" (Hall, 2011: 25). That value-ordering denies any intrinsic value in plants, leaving them with only instrumental value as objects to be exploited and consumed according to human ends.

There is thus a tension between Aristotle's arcadian attribution of soul to plants and his more imperial view, which suggests that humans are the primary center of value, reducing plants to their instrumental value as objects to be used by animals and humans (for food, fuel, fiber, shelter, etc.). The arcadian side of Aristotle's philosophy of nature is carried forward by his pupil Theophrastus, who does away with Aristotle's imperial hierarchy. Theophrastus investigates plants on their own terms instead of measuring plants according to what they lack with respect to animals and humans (pp. 28–35). The arcadian view expressed by Theophrastus was subsequently relegated to the background in favor of Aristotle's more imperial view. The history of Western approaches to botany, from Aristotle through Carl Linnaeus in the eighteenth century, may be seen as propagating mostly an imperial view of nature (p. 36).

Although the imperial view of nature has dominated the history of science, the arcadian view has never been entirely absent. For example, around the same time that Linnaeus was developing the imperial system of taxonomy used in contemporary sciences, where Latin names are used for designating the genus and species of an organism (e.g., humans are *Homo sapiens*; wolves and dogs are subspecies of *Canis lupus*), the Romantic movement of German *Naturphilosophie* (philosophy of nature) was developing a more arcadian view. Two prominent Romantic thinkers, Johann Wolfgang von Goethe and Friedrich Wilhelm Joseph von Schelling, proposed evolutionary theories for which the material world and its ideal or psychic structures (archetypes) were not separate realities, but were manifestations of a unified and creative process, "*dynamische Evolution*" (dynamic evolution), a term developed by Schelling and adopted by Goethe (Richards, 2002: 10). For Romantics like Goethe and Schelling, natural phenomena are understood in terms of an organic process of development that cannot be captured by mechanistic explanations (p. 9). Plants and animals are not just objects. They have their own agency, their own subjectivity or psychic reality, such that they have value in themselves and not only for humans.

When Haeckel coined the term *oecologie* in 1866, he inherited the proto-ecological tension between interdependent coexistence (arcadian) and hierarchy (imperial). On the one hand, Haeckel's ecology promotes peaceful coexistence between humans and the natural world, particularly through his attempt to articulate a holistic or monistic understanding of evolution. On the other hand, Haeckel's monistic materialism (as discussed above) relies primarily on mechanistic explanations that fail to do justice to any subjectivity or intrinsic value in the natural world. Haeckel's arcadian side may be seen in his appreciation of the evolutionary perspective of Goethe, for whom organisms have internal dynamics that propel their evolution, and Haeckel's imperial side may be seen in his acceptance of Darwin's evolutionary theory, which states that there is no internal principle driving evolution but only the mechanistic function of natural selection (Grim and Tucker, 2014: 65). After Haeckel, the mechanistic side of ecology gained predominance.

Some ecologists extended Haeckel's approach to include social sciences in articulations of ecological phenomena, specifically economics. The possibility of this extension is implicit in his definition of ecology as the study of the "economy of all nature" and in the shared prefix of the words *eco*logy and *eco*nomy (Merchant, 2007: 178). Along those lines, the twentieth century saw the emergence of a *"New Ecology"* – an approach that brought biological and physical sciences together with economics to provide "an energy-economic model of the environment," in which ecologists like Charles Elton and Arthur Tansley used thermodynamics and economic models of production, consumption, and efficiency to describe the flow of energy through an ecological "community" (Elton) or "ecosystem" (Tansley) (Worster, 1994: 311). Having little use for arcadian theories like those of Theophrastus or Goethe, this approach attains accurate measurements of the ways in which energy moves through plants, animals, soil, water, and sunlight. One weakness of the New Ecology is that it still presumed that the natural world is basically a stable system tending toward harmony. That prevented ecologists from studying energy in a way that more effectively accounts for the role of uncertainty, unpredictability, disturbance, and disorder in ecosystems. The problem was resolved in the 1970s and 1980s with the inclusion of chaos theory into ecology, providing ecologists with metrics and models for analyzing the discord and unpredictable dynamics that accompany any harmonious balance which ecosystems exhibit (Botkin, 1990). Ecosystems are not stable. There is no such thing as a static system called "nature." The energy flows of ecosystems are less like stable systems and more like dynamic, finely textured patches, which are constantly shifting and changing in complex ways that cannot always be modeled or predicted.

Despite the success of the New Ecology with its shift toward an understanding of the chaotic characteristics of ecosystems, it is an imperial approach that does not facilitate peaceful coexistence between humans and the rest of the Earth community. It fails to recognize the interior agency or subjectivity of nonhumans. It reduces organisms and ecosystems to mechanistic causes, specifically through the calculation of energy flows. Attempting to rectify the situation, Eugene Odum (2000: 198) opposed that reductionism and proposed a different "new ecology," one that would function as an "integrative discipline," thus recovering a holistic approach over mechanistic and materialistic approaches. Odum's new ecology is a way of bringing together multiple scientific disciplines in a holistic framework that includes economic values as well as environmental values. "In summary, going beyond reductionism to holism is now mandated if science and society are to mesh for mutual benefit" (p. 203). However, Odum's ecology still contains aspects of the reductionism it proclaims to avoid.

Although Odum's approach aims for a mutual benefit of science and society, it does not include the arcadian perspective that aims for the mutual benefit not only of science and society but also of nonhumans. His inclusion of environmental values is more about values for humans than the values of organisms and environments on their own terms. To the extent that he does include the values of nonhumans on their own terms, it is only the values that show up in calculations of energy flows. He does not include values related to the agency, subjectivity, soul, or other interior or intrinsic dynamics of nonhumans. In the end, Odum's model is simply a more multidisciplinary version of the energy-economic model of ecology that dominated the twentieth century. Even his attempt to cross disciplinary boundaries is not very comprehensive, as he does not include any disciplines in the humanities (e.g., philosophy, literature, and religious studies).

Environmental humanities and everyday ecologies

The humanities can facilitate a deeper understanding of the ways in which subjectivity and culture shape and are shaped by the relations humans have with the natural world. The humanities can also nurture a critical understanding of the ways in which intelligence and agency could be present not only in humans, but also in the nonhuman members of the Earth community.

The humanities are increasingly finding their way into ecology theories and practices, as indicated by the twenty-first-century emergence of environmental humanities or ecological humanities (Rose and Robin, 2004). An important predecessor of ecological humanities is the American forester and conservationist Aldo Leopold (1887–1948). While the energy-economic model of ecology was dominant, Leopold articulated a way of thinking which anticipates the integration of the humanities with the ecological perspectives that come from the natural and social sciences. There are two ways in which Leopold's work anticipates such integrative approaches to ecology. First, Leopold accounts for interiority as well as exteriority, such that, "in addition to natural and social science perspectives, people need to bring to bear ethical, cultural, and aesthetic perspectives on land use (environmental) issues" (Zimmerman, 2009: 77). This is reflected in a transformative experience that Leopold had. After shooting a wolf, Leopold (1989: 130) approached the wolf, and as it lay dying, he saw what he describes as a "fierce green fire" in its eyes. Previously in his life, Leopold had never considered the possibility that a wolf and the mountain it inhabits have their own value apart from the measurements and calculations of human use. After experiencing the fierce green fire, Leopold began articulating his land ethic, which aims to overcome the rift between two distinct approaches to the values of the organisms and ecosystems comprising the land. There is an "A" approach, for which the value of land is given in terms of human use and economic value, and a "B" approach, for which the value of land is intrinsic to the land itself, including the integrity and stability of the land as well as its profound beauty (p. 221).

The second way in which Leopold anticipated integral ecology is that Leopold understands evolution as a unified and dynamic process which needs to be accounted for not only in biology but also in human moral development (Zimmerman, 2009: 78). Historically, ethics has extended to encompass villages and tribes, then cities, nations, and eventually all of humanity (e.g., universal human rights). According to Leopold's land ethic, the next phase in human moral evolution is the extension of ethics to the land.

> The "key-log" which must be moved to release the evolutionary process for an ethic is simply this: quit thinking about decent land-use as solely an economic problem. Examine each question in terms of what is ethically and esthetically right, as well as what is economically expedient. A thing is right when it tends to preserve the integrity, stability, and beauty of the biotic community. It is wrong when it tends otherwise.
>
> (Leopold, 1989: 224)

The land ethic calls for a moral transformation that reinvents the human species. More specifically, it transforms the role of humans "from conqueror of the land-community to plain members and citizen of it" (p. 204). Leopold's call for moral transformation and his attention to the subjective dimension of ecological phenomena were and remain highly influential. Leopold's work supported the growth of the environmental movement in the 1960s and the emergence of many ecologically oriented fields of the humanities in the 1970s, including environmental ethics, deep ecology, and environmental literary criticism (also called ecocriticism or ecopoetics).

Alongside the development of fields of ecological humanities, ecological perspectives have spilled out of academic research and into popular culture and mass media, becoming a household word. Advertisers market products that are supposed to be "natural" or "eco-friendly." Celebrities promote environmental causes. Films portray massive environmental destruction and post-apocalyptic landscapes. Scientific ecologies are now situated in a great abundance and diversity of ecologies. Some approaches are interested in peaceful planetary co-existence, while others are more interested in using resources to benefit humans. Some approaches cross boundaries to include other perspectives, while others overspecialize in one perspective to the exclusion of any other perspectives. Some ecological perspectives are explicit, while some are implicit, folded into the details of everyday interactions. Imagine the situation described by the ecological thinker Timothy Morton (2013: 99):

> You are walking out of the supermarket. As you approach your car, a stranger calls out, "Hey! Funny weather today!" With a due sense of caution – is she a global warming denier or not? – you reply yes. There is a slight hesitation. Is it because she is thinking of saying something about global warming? In any case, the hesitation induced you to think of it. . . . You can no longer have a routine conversation about the weather with a stranger. The presence of global warming looms into the conversation like shadow, introducing strange gaps.

Spilling outside of theories and methods in the humanities and sciences, ecology looms into everyday conversations and experiences.

As humans and all life on Earth face critical challenges, it is imperative to coordinate the multiplicity of ecologies to facilitate comprehensive and effective responses that benefit the interdependent flourishing of the whole Earth community. Religious ecologies are necessary for such responses, but they are not sufficient. Likewise, the metrics and models of scientific ecologies are essential, but alone they are incapable of addressing the moral and spiritual dimensions of human–Earth relations. Activists, advocates, policymakers, researchers, and families need more inclusive, creative, adaptable concepts to address the planetary scale of contemporary ecological problems like climate change, mass extinction, and freshwater scarcity. The problems facing the whole Earth community require ecological perspectives that integrate multiple ways of knowing to address planetary coexistence. Before moving on to a discussion of specific strategies for facilitating such integration (see Chapter 4), Chapter 3 presents a creative contrast between two integrative approaches to ecology in a time of planetary crisis, one represented by the geologian Thomas Berry and the other by the geophilosophers Gilles Deleuze and Félix Guattari.

References

Allen, Colin and Marc Bekoff. 1997. *Species of Mind: The Philosophy and Biology of Cognitive Ethology*. Cambridge, MA: MIT Press

Aristotle. 2001. *On the Soul*. Trans. Joe Sachs. Santa Fe, CA: Green Lion Press.

Berkes, Fikret. 2012. *Sacred Ecology*, 3rd edn. New York: Routledge.

Botkin, Daniel. 1990. *Discordant Harmonies: A New Ecology for the Twenty-first Century*. New York: Oxford University Press.

Buege, Douglas J. 1996. "The Ecological Noble Savage Revisited." *Environmental Ethics* 18(1): 71–88.

Clayton, Philip (ed.). 2006. *The Oxford Handbook of Religion and Science*. New York: Oxford University Press.

Demallie, Raymond J. and Douglas Parks (eds). 1989. *Sioux Indian Religion: Tradition and Innovation*. Norman: University of Oklahoma Press.

Foltz, Richard. 2007. "Islam." In *The Oxford Handbook of Religion and Ecology*, ed. Roger Gottlieb, 207–219. New York: Oxford University Press.

Graziosi, Barbara. 2014. *The Gods of Olympus: A History*. New York: Metropolitan Books.

Grim, John and Mary Evelyn Tucker. 2014. *Ecology and Religion*. Washington, D.C.: Island Press.

Haeckel, Ernst. 2004. *Monism as Connecting Religion and Science*. Whitefish: Kessinger Publishing.

Hall, Matthew. 2011. *Plants as Persons: A Philosophical Botany*. Albany, NY: SUNY Press.

Hart, John. 2007. "Catholicism." In *The Oxford Handbook of Religion and Ecology*, ed. Roger Gottlieb, 65–91. New York: Oxford University Press.

Jenkins, Willis. 2008. *Ecologies of Grace: Environmental Ethics and Christian Theology*. New York: Oxford University Press.

Kaza, Stephanie. 2008. *Mindfully Green: A Personal and Spiritual Guide to Whole Earth Thinking*. Boston, MA: Shambhala Publications.

Leopold, Aldo. 1989. *A Sand County Almanac and Sketches Here and There*. London: Oxford University Press.

McIntosh, Robert P. 1985. *The Background of Ecology: Concept and Theory*. New York: Cambridge University Press.

Merchant, Carolyn. 2007. *American Environmental History: An Introduction*. New York: Cambridge University Press.

Morton, Timothy. 2013. *Hyperobjects: Philosophy and Ecology after the End of the World*. Minneapolis: University of Minnesota Press.

Odum, Eugene P. 2000. "The Emergence of Ecology as a New Integrative Discipline." In *The Philosophy of Ecology: From Science to Synthesis*, ed. David R. Keller and Frank B. Golley, 194–203. Athens: University of Georgia Press.

Pierotti, Raymond. 2011. *Indigenous Knowledge, Ecology, and Evolutionary Biology*. New York: Routledge.

Richards, Robert J. 2002. *The Romantic Conception of Life: Science and Philosophy in the Age of Goethe*. Chicago, IL: Chicago University Press.

Rose, Deborah Bird and Libby Robin. 2004. "The Ecological Humanities in Action: An Invitation." *Australian Humanities Review* 31–32. http://www.australianhumanitiesreview.org/archive/Issue-April-2004/rose.html (accessed November 6, 2014).

Tucker, Mary Evelyn. 2003. *Worldly Wonder: Religions Enter Their Ecological Phase*. Chicago, IL: Open Court.

Worster, Donald. 1994. *Nature's Economy: A History of Ecological Ideas*, 2nd edn. New York: Cambridge University Press.

Zimmerman, Michael. 2009. "Interiority Regained: Integral Ecology and Environmental Ethics." In *Ecology and the Environment: Perspectives from the Humanities*, ed. Donald K. Swearer, 65–88. Cambridge, MA: Harvard University Press.

3 A geologian meets geophilosophers

Imagine a meeting between two parties. The first party consists of one person, Thomas Berry (1914–2009), an American Catholic priest who left the priest-hood to focus on his work as a cultural historian and an Earth scholar. Not a theologian, Berry is a geologian. "He coined the neologism, geologian, while flying over the Nile River, to describe himself, because theologian was too narrow" (Eaton, 2014: xiii). The second party consists of two people: Gilles Deleuze (1925–1995) and Félix Guattari (1930–1992), French theorists and co-authors with backgrounds in philosophy and psychoanalysis, respectively. In the last of their co-written works, Deleuze and Guattari (1994) propose a new kind of philosophy: a philosophy of Earth. Like Berry, they describe their work by coining a new word. For Deleuze and Guattari, their work is geophilosophy. What would a geologian and geophilosophers say to one another? What could their meeting contribute to a sense of ecological wisdom in an age of planetary interconnectedness?

Leaving aside the language barrier between Berry's English and the French of Deleuze and Guattari, one can imagine some of the discussions that would take place in a meeting between this geologian and these geophilosophers. They share much common ground, so they would have many similar reference points for their discussions. Born in the first half of the twentieth century, each of these three thinkers shares a similar historical context – a time of world wars, telecommunication, environmental crisis, computers, an acceleration of economic growth, increasing economic inequality, emancipatory social movements such as feminism and civil rights, and the articulation of new scientific fields such as quantum mechanics, relativity theory, molecular biology, chaos theory, evolutionary cosmology, and complex systems theory. Along with a historical context, Berry's thinking shares a common focus with Deleuze and Guattari: Earth. Both parties are concerned with the development of planetary thinking.

Despite their common context and their planetary aim, an actual meeting never took place. Berry never met Deleuze or Guattari, and neither Deleuze nor Guattari ever refer to Berry, and Berry never refers to them. The two parties appear to be entirely unaware of the work of the other, and likewise, people who bring one of the two parties into their own work rarely bring in the other. Why this lack of exchange? It is not simply due to the language barrier between French and English.

One of the reasons for this lack of exchange is that Berry and the people working with Berry's legacy are frequently engaged in studies of religious perspectives on ecological issues, whereas Deleuze, Guattari, and the people working with their geophilosophy are more frequently not concerned about religions or even hostile to religions. Another reason for the lack of exchange is stylistic. Deleuze and Guattari are notoriously difficult to read. They wrote in an experimental style that challenges most readers. In contrast, Berry's writing is deceptively accessible, using language that is so simple and easy that one might misunderstand his ideas as if they are too simple, lacking in academic details and scholarly refinement. Someone who prefers Deleuze and Guattari may think that Berry is too simplistic, not up for the task of dealing with the strange, complicated, and unprecedented challenges of planetary coexistence, and someone who prefers Berry might think that Deleuze and Guattari are unnecessarily complicated, playing smart word games that are not actually relevant to the real challenges facing the Earth community. However, rather than viewing their religious and stylistic differences as obstacles that prevent dialogue, one may view those differences as opportunities for a creative cross-fertilization of ideas.

Because no actual meeting took place, one can only speculate about what they might have said or done together. Would they have anything to say to each other about the planetary challenges facing humans today? Would they learn anything from one another? Would they disagree with each other frequently? Would they cooperate to enact a common vision? Of course, we will never know for sure. Nonetheless, it is possible to stage something like a meeting between these thinkers. It is possible to elaborate on the contrast between their conceptions of planetary coexistence. When that contrast comes into focus, one can understand how "Yes" could be the answer to all of those questions. Both parties would probably have much to say to each other about contemporary planetary challenges. They would probably learn from one another, disagree with one another, and cooperate to enact a shared vision of creative, mutually enhancing relationships between humans and the rest of the Earth community. This chapter draws out the contrast between Berry's work as a geologian and the work of Deleuze and Guattari as geophilosophers, including a consideration of the cultural contexts in which each party is situated, an overview of the planetary thinking advocated by each party, and a discussion of some possible points of connection whereby this geologian and these geophilosophers might facilitate the building of alliances across different cultures, different religions, and different ways of knowing.

Modern revolutions

The American context of Berry's thinking overlaps considerably with the French context in which Deleuze and Guattari worked, yet those contexts are also significantly different from one another. The similarities and differences between the geologian and the geophilosophers reflect the similarities and differences between the American Revolution (1765–1783) and the French Revolution (1789–1799).

Both of those revolutionary historical moments affirmed the power of the people. The rule of elite royals was called into question. Monarchy was challenged in favor of democracy. That affirmation of democracy led to the formation of the United States of America as an independent nation free of British monarchy. In France, it led to the formation of a democratic republic and the abolition of the French monarchy.

In these revolutions, people joined together in saying no to monarchy, saying no to oppressive political hierarchies that put some people in superior positions of power while others are relegated to inferior, subordinate positions without power, without a voice, without political representation. However, these revolutions are not simply anti-authoritarian. Along with saying no to oppressive political systems, they also said yes to freedom, equality, and community, or as the slogan of the French Revolution puts it, *liberté, égalité, fraternité* (liberty, equality, brotherhood). In other words, these revolutions were critical as well as constructive. They were critical of oppressive systems of power, and they worked toward the construction of new systems which redistribute power so that people can have more of a say in the decisions that affect their lives, more of a voice in their community, more representation in their government. Berry, Deleuze, and Guattari all share those revolutionary traits of their national histories. They all participate in the critique of oppressive authority and the construction of more democratic systems and more emancipatory ways of life. That revolutionary heritage thus provides an indication of the shared context in which Berry, Deleuze, and Guattari developed their approaches to planetary thinking. Furthermore, that revolutionary heritage also provides an indication of the differences between their approaches.

The difference between Berry's appreciation of religion and the more hostile attitude taken by Deleuze and Guattari repeats the difference between the attitudes toward religion in the American and French Revolutions. In the American Revolution, religions were seen as potential agents of social change. In that context, religions are seen as having power to mobilize people and help provide moral guidance for revolutionary activity. In contrast, religion in France during that period was seen as part of the established system of authority. The English had undergone a Puritan Revolution that weakened the political and moral authority of the Catholic Church, which meant that religion was not seen as synonymous with the oppressive authorities in power. In contrast, the Catholic Church still occupied a very dominant position in French society, which meant that a revolution against the oppressive status quo must also be a revolution against religion.

In the American Revolution, the search for democracy could be understood as some kind of Christian project. In the French Revolution, Christianity was the enemy, such that religion was seen as the problem, and reason was the prescribed solution. This did not entail a complete elimination of religion. The revolutionaries understood that the meaning-making practices of religion are a necessary part of society, so, instead of abolishing all religion, they replaced their inherited religion with a new religion, a humanistic religion dedicated to reason. The philosopher and religious scholar Mark C. Taylor (2009: 98) summarizes these contrasting attitudes toward religion.

> Whereas American revolutionaries understood their revolt as an extension of their [Christianity], the French Revolution was inseparable from the negation of Christianity. The ostensible overthrow of Christianity did not, however, mean the end of religion; while turning away from the Christian God, leaders of the Revolution embraced the religion of reason. This concession grew out of their recognition that, though historical forms of religion are inadequate, symbolic networks nonetheless remain necessary for establishing the meaning and purpose without which life becomes unbearable for many people. To meet these needs, they created a humanistic religion replete with rituals devoted to the goddess Reason staged in Nôtre Dame.

Modern America and France are both secular societies, letting worldly reason instead of premodern religion guide society. The American Revolution emphasized freedom of religion, opening up the door to religious pluralism, which allows for the practice of many different expressions of religion. Religious pluralism resists discrimination against religious traditions or against people who adhere to religious traditions. While secularism in America nurtured diverse religious expressions, the attitudes toward secularism in the French Revolution were less oriented toward religious pluralism, less concerned with freedom *of* religion and more focused on becoming free *from* religion.

Those contrasting attitudes toward religion are expressed quite clearly in the religious pluralism of Berry and the more anti-religious ideas expressed by Deleuze and Guattari. Berry celebrates all religious traditions, including the Confucian and Daoist traditions of East Asia, the Hindu and Buddhist traditions originating in South Asia, the biblical religions (Judaism, Christianity, and Islam), as well as the indigenous traditions of the world. Deleuze and Guattari focus more on philosophy, science, and art, with very little attention given to religion, and the attention that they do give religion is generally critical and antagonistic. However, as the remaining sections of this chapter indicate, the story gets more interesting than that. Berry is not without his own criticisms of religions, and Deleuze and Guattari are not without their appreciation for religions. Before turning to those sections, there is still more to say about the historical context in which our geologian and geophilosophers found themselves.

Postmodern differences

The revolutionary dynamics of the late eighteenth century in America and France indicate the modern context inherited by Berry, Deleuze, and Guattari. Along with their inheritance of modern developments of democracy, rationalism, and pluralism, these thinkers found themselves embedded in a new historical period, a postmodern era which criticized the notions of progress and reason that were guiding the modern era. In the postmodern era, it became apparent that the modern attempt to articulate a single story that is supposed to work for everyone does not actually work for everyone. The modern attempt to secure freedom from oppression was itself very oppressive. The modern story which said that the use of reason can make progress toward freedom did help some people attain freedom, but that story was also used to justify oppressive practices and systems that took away freedom, such as colonial expeditions to conquer foreign lands, the transatlantic slave trade, government and private control of shared resources (i.e., the enclosure of the commons), and missionary work to convert people to Christianity and out of non-Christian religions, which were considered superstitious or even satanic. Modern progress has provided some benefits for a few people at the expense of the suffering of many, and, along with human suffering, the so-called progress of modernity brought about the degradation and destruction of many habitats and populations of organisms, which were considered little more than fodder for the growing industrial civilization.

From the modern perspective, premodern stories are seen as oppressive or limiting because of their authoritarian politics (monarchy) and irrational superstitions (religion). From the postmodern perspective, the modern story is no less oppressive. In some sense, the modern story may be even more oppressive than the stories of ancient and medieval societies, particularly insofar as the modern story imposed itself upon the entire planet, spreading its ideals of progress and freedom around the world. This is not to say that a postmodern perspective implies that premodern and modern stories are completely wrong about everything. Postmodernism is a context from which the modernist claim to triumph over premodern authority and superstition is hard to believe. Modernists thought that their understanding of the world was superior to premodern ways of being in the world, but postmodernists do not exactly think that their understanding is superior to modern and premodern perspectives. Postmodernists find any grand story of the meaning of things doubtful.

Whether premodern, modern, postmodern, or otherwise, any attempt to tell a narrative that is supposed to make sense to everybody looks suspicious. Such grand stories – metanarratives – are so often used to justify forms of control or oppression that they are becoming increasingly difficult to believe. What about a transcendent God that controls everything and knows everything? It is doubtful. What about a rational individual that can find principles for making progress toward peace and prosperity for all? Doubtful. What about a postmodernism that can free everybody everywhere from the imprisoning chains of metanarratives? That, too, is doubtful. Every metanarrative is doubtful. That is the postmodern condition. Accordingly, the philosopher Jean-François Lyotard (1984: xxiv) describes postmodernism in terms of "incredulity toward metanarratives." Only a "little narrative" (*petit récit*) is believable anymore, a narrative that does not pretend to be valid for everyone at all times and places (p. 60). Postmodernism, then, is about people having their own truths according to their own contexts. There is no universal measure of true and false or right and wrong. Nothing is inherently better or worse than anything else, just different.

Postmodernism arose in the latter half of the twentieth century as people living in modern societies became increasingly aware that all stories have their limitations. Instead of trying to conquer the whole world with one meta-narrative, postmodernists would rather tell little stories that honor the unique differences of things, stories that focus on the complex texture of particular events in specific times and places. Postmodernism is the condition in which Berry found his path as a geologian. It is the condition in which Deleuze and Guattari became geophilosophers. Does this mean that they are postmodern thinkers? There is a yes and no answer to that question.

First, consider the yes.

Deleuze and Guattari are often considered postmodern, along with many other French philosophers in the second half of the twentieth century, including Lyotard, Jacques Derrida, Michel Foucault, and Jean Baudrillard. All of those thinkers are very critical of the modern concept of a free, rational, individual human. They indicate in various ways how the modern story fails to recognize that there are other ways of knowing outside the limits of the modern sense of reason, including emotional or affective ways of knowing as well as somatic or embodied ways of knowing. Deleuze and Guattari also criticize the modern story for failing to recognize the complex interconnectedness between humans and the natural world. Humans are always already entangled in dynamic material processes, which connect humans to Earth and to the evolving cosmos. Deleuze and Guattari (1983: 4) see humans not "as a king of creation, but rather as the being who is in intimate contact with the profound life of all forms or all types of beings, who is responsible for even the stars and animal life." They see the rational indivi-dualism of modernity as theoretically wrong, and, more than that, they see it as a destructive force that is turning earthly life into a collection of quantitative measurements, resources for exploitation and consumption.

Berry may also be considered to be postmodern, although he is generally not viewed that way. For instance, his work with the cosmologist Brian Swimme to articulate *The Universe Story* sounds like an attempt to construct a metanarrative (Swimme and Berry, 1992). However, as Stephen Dunn (2014) observes, Berry's storytelling honors different and disparate perspectives without promoting one perspective as superior to all different perspectives. The story of the universe is not simply a story of rational scientific evidence about the evolution of the universe from the Big Bang through the evolution of life on Earth. Along with scientific perspectives, Berry includes perspectives from religions, philosophies, and environmentalists: the theology of St. Thomas Aquinas, the wilderness preservation of John Muir, the environmental movement spurred on by Rachel Carson, Confucian values like sincerity (*ch'eng*), and much more. Unlike metanarratives, which homogenize differences and try to make everything and everyone fit within the same story, Berry's story of the universe is open to differences – different traditions, different cultures, and different ways of knowing. Furthermore, Berry may also be considered to be postmodern insofar as he is critical of the modern idea of the human as a rational individual disconnected from community and from the cosmos.

While it is true that Berry as well as Deleuze and Guattari may be considered to be postmodern, the question of whether they are postmodern also calls for a resounding no. They include postmodern critiques of modernism, but they do not involve themselves in one of the characteristic traits of postmodernism: relativism. This is not Einstein's theory of relativity. Relativism is the idea that truth is different for different contexts. There is no absolute truth. Everyone has their own story, their own truth. The benefit of postmodern relativism is that it does not force one story onto everybody. It is open to differences. The danger though is that you cannot tell others that they are wrong. You cannot tell others that their truth is restrictive or oppressive. You cannot stop cruelty, because perhaps what you call cruelty another person calls kindness.

> Does it follow that we are henceforth condemned to stand around like idiots in the face of the growth of the new order of cruelty and cynicism that is on the point of submerging the planet, with the firm intention, it seems, of staying? It is this regrettable conclusion that numerous intellectual and artistic milieus effectively seem to have reached, in particular those who invoke the fashion of postmodernism.
>
> (Guattari, 2013: 36)

At a moment in history when human actions are endangering and destroying the fabric of life on Earth, postmodern relativism cannot stop cruelty taking place. It produces a cynical attitude where nothing is worth believing in, and nothing is worth fighting for. Everything is relative. Deleuze and Guattari reject such relativism while also rejecting the absolutism that imposes its truth upon others. Truth is not made up on a whim, but neither is it imposed upon everyone from on high. Truth emerges in relationship with others, such that there is a "truth of the relative" without a "relativity of truth" (Deleuze and Guattari, 1994: 130). Similarly for Berry, truth is neither relative nor absolute. It is emergent – arising from the dynamic evolutionary processes of matter, life, and humanity. In other words, truth emerges in the relationships of community or communion that arise between different human and nonhuman participants in planetary coexistence.

Berry, Deleuze, and Guattari do not impose their planetary vision upon others like a metanarrative, but they do not thereby fall into relativism and give up their ability to resist the cruelty and cynicism destroying life on Earth. Indeed, precisely by becoming planetary, they avoid any system that would cruelly impose itself upon planetary coexistence (e.g., war, consumerism, metanarratives of progress, etc.), and they also avoid the cynicism of relativism, for which it is impossible to trust anyone or believe in anything. To be planetary is to restore "belief in the world" (Deleuze, 1989: 172). There are many ways to restore such belief. For instance, Deleuze considers the possibility that cinema can facilitate such restoration, whereas Berry indicates many ways in which science and religion can restore belief in this world. If this is postmodern, it is not a postmodern relativism. It is a restorative postmodernism, a postmodernism that recuperates biodiversity and cultural diversity, carefully integrating the finely textured differences that make up a vibrant Earth community. This restorative postmodernism may be more correctly described as "an integral postmodernist perspective" (Dunn, 2014: 242). Unlike modern individualists and postmodern relativists, a meeting between a geologian and geophilosophers indicates the possibility of affirming the intensity and vitality of planetary coexistence.

A clarification of terminology is important here. A restorative or integrative postmodernism is not after postmodernism. It arose at the same time as post-modernism – the latter half of the twentieth century. Postmodernism has many different facets, some of them more integrative than others, and some more rela-tivistic. One may think that a meeting of Berry with Deleuze and Guattari would produce something post-postmodern, but that is not a very helpful term. It does not make much sense to call something post-postmodern or post-post-anything. If the number three follows in a sequence after the number two, the number four would still be said to be after two, not after-after two. When a book that is written by a dead author is published, that is called a posthumous publication. If another book by that author is published a few years later, it would still be called post-humous, not post-posthumous. Furthermore, even the term postmodernism is quite misleading. Many postmodern thinkers were not trying to get beyond modernism. Such notions of progress and "beyond" are precisely the kinds of notions that postmodernists call into question. Less concerned with moving beyond anything, postmodernists generally express more concern for critiquing modernism and many of the processes related to modernization (e.g., coloni-zation, industrialization, and rational individualism). In that sense, the term "late modern" may be more appropriate than postmodern. However, Berry describes himself neither as a late modernist nor as a postmodernist. Deleuze and Guattari likewise do not use those terms. They speak of themselves as a geologian and geophilosophers. Their work is situated in the (post)modern contexts of the United States and France, but the scope of their work is wider than that. It is planetary.

A geologian

Berry did his earliest scholarly work as a historian, more specifically as a cultural historian and a historian of world religions. He wrote two noteworthy books con-tributing to the study of the religious worldviews of Hinduism and Buddhism (Berry, 1989, 1992). His work continued to develop, becoming more encompass-ing over time. Mary Evelyn Tucker, a student of Berry, notes this about him in her "Biography of Thomas Berry" (n.d.), observing that he extended his perspective as a cultural historian "to become a historian of the Earth." Berry was also a Catholic priest in the order of Passionists, which is not to say that he was a theo-logian. His transition from cultural historian to Earth historian led him to identify himself as a geologian.

Berry's focus is the whole Earth in all of its wondrous complexity and mystery. His work traverses disciplines of the sciences and humanities with the aim of cul-tivating vibrant expressions of planetary coexistence and overcoming the destruc-tive tendencies whereby humans objectify and dominate the Earth community.

Along with his own work, Berry has inspired many others, including scholars, activists, religious leaders, teachers, scientists, poets, and more. He has inspired transformation in the way that people feel, think, and act as creative participants in the evolutionary adventure of the universe. The relevance of his planetary thinking is indicated by his own work as well as by his influence on the works of others who are engaged in similar efforts to empower the emergence of a vibrant Earth community.

Berry's planetary thinking is evident in his conceptions of wisdom, humanity, Earth, the cosmos, story, and energy. Each of these conceptions will be discussed in later chapters. In this context, his work may be summarized with his notion of the "Great Work" – the work to undergo a transition away from the destructive presence of humans on Earth toward a mutually enhancing presence between humans and the rest of the Earth community (Berry, 1999: 4). The Great Work is the task of facilitating the composition of a vibrant planetary civilization. The destruction currently happening around the planet is, for Berry, an effect of certain ways of being that dissociate humans from one another and from their terrestrial context. The Great Work is the work of remedying that dissociation, bringing integration to the fragmentation of modern individualism. In short, the Great Work is to enact ways of being that empower participation in an integrative Earth community. "We are here to become integral with the larger Earth Community" (p. 48). The work of becoming integral is an immense task. It involves a reinvention of human nature (see Chapter 6). It is not about taking shorter showers, passing a few laws, and changing some light bulbs. Those are important in their own way, but the Great Work is much more comprehensive than that. It means creating new ways of being and knowing which respond to the entanglement of humans in the dynamics of planetary coexistence.

There is a religious dimension to the Great Work. For Berry, this religious dimension began in a childhood experience of a meadow. Berry experienced the meadow as a celebration of life, a celebration that evoked feelings of awe, wonder, and reverence for the meadow. The religious dimension of this experience is not to be found in religious institutions or in official doctrines. The religious dimension of Berry's experience of the meadow is to be found in the universe itself, specifically the "numinous dimension of the universe" (p. 14). The term "numinous" was coined by the German theologian and historian of religion Rudolf Otto, who uses the term to describe the sacred. For Otto, to say that the sacred is numinous is to say that it appears as wholly other from one's ordinary experience. The numinous is *mysterium tremendum et fascinans* – a mystery (*mysterium*) that becomes revealed in moments of "awe" which are characterized, on the one hand, by the horrible shuddering of "religious dread" (*tremendum*), and on the other hand, by fascinating wonder (*fascinans*) with the overwhelming majesty of that which is utterly unknown and ineffable (Otto, 1958: 5–32). The numinous dimension of the universe is the sacred, the wholly other mystery that shakes you to the core of your being while also exciting and inspiring you. For Berry (1999: 18), "the moments when the numinous dimension of the universe reveals itself" are "moments when the high meaning of existence is experienced."

Science, technology, design, policy, law, and economics are all necessary components of the Great Work, but the task of becoming integral with the Earth community requires more as well. It requires a restoration of a sense of the sacred. In other words, it requires a renewed sense of participation in "some numinous presence manifested in the wonderworld about us" (Berry, 1999: 20). Berry's understanding of a religious or sacred dimension of human–Earth relations follows in a long line of American nature writers that advocate for a spiritual or transcendental engagement with the natural world, including the preservationist John Muir and New England Transcendentalists like Ralph Waldo Emerson and Henry David Thoreau (p. 201). Berry's sense of a sacred universe is not only American, though. He is also deeply influenced by the French thinker Pierre Teilhard de Chardin (1881–1955), a paleontologist and a member of the Jesuit order of the Catholic Church. Teilhard made significant contributions to evolutionary science and to the dialogue between Christian and scientific perspectives.

For Teilhard, the evolving universe is sacred. The universe hosts the ongoing incarnation of the divine. In short, the universe is a "divine milieu" (Teilhard, 2001). This does not mean that the physical universe is simply identical to the spiritual reality of God. That would be pantheism – the position for which all (*pan*) is God (*theos*). Teilhard holds a more complex view, which is better described as panentheism: all (*pan*) is in (*en*) God (*theos*), and God is in all. Teilhard's panentheistic integration of religion and evolution continues to have a growing influence in the twenty-first century (Fabel and St. John, 2005). Berry expresses a similar view to Teilhard, saying that there are two distinct dimensions of reality. "The spiritual and the physical are two dimensions of the single reality that is the universe" (Berry, 2009: 49–50). Folded into one another, the spiritual and the physical are not collapsed into one another but neither are they separate. A key difference between Teilhard and Berry is that the former holds God as the primary sacred reality, whereas the latter claims that "the universe is the primary sacred reality" (p. 49). This reflects the difference between Teilhard's exclusively Christian focus and Berry's inclusion of multiple religious perspectives, including religions for which the numinous is not understood in terms of a transcendent creator God (e.g., Buddhism and Confucianism).

Drawing upon Teilhard's integration of science and spirituality, Berry's vision of a sacred universe has influenced numerous people working in diverse areas, including law and jurisprudence (Cullinan, 2011), poetry (Dellinger, 2011), cosmology (Swimme and Berry, 1992), and the field of religion and ecology (Grim and Tucker, 2014). What seems to be particularly compelling about Berry's work is not his scholarly attention to history or his critical analysis of the actions, institutions, and ideas spreading cruelty and destruction around the planet. What seems particularly compelling is the way in which he orients his attention and analysis toward a vision, a "dream of the Earth" (Berry, 1990). Berry's articulation of the Great Work of our current historical moment provides a sense of direction during a time of immense social and environmental upheaval. Berry's dream of mutually enhancing human–Earth relations is not a metanarrative to be imposed authoritatively upon others. It is a dream that empowers people to engage in the finely textured differences composing planetary coexistence. It is a dream that encourages people to renew their own thinking, feeling, and acting in relationship to the complex and wondrous world around them. "The dream drives the action" (Berry, 1999: 201). The dream of planetary renewal inspires people to change their lives, to bring positive transformation to their communities, and to restore their faith in the world.

Geophilosophers

Deleuze and Guattari spoke of themselves as geophilosophers only in the later years of their lives, after they had been writing together for approximately two decades. Prior to their work together, Deleuze and Guattari pursued very different paths, which began intersecting when they met in the wake of the protests and civil unrest of the May 1968 events in France. Their shared dreams of liberation led to a long-lasting collaboration which yielded multiple co-written works that have been highly influential in philosophy, sciences, arts, and politics (Dosse, 2010). Deleuze studied the European tradition of philosophy in its ancient, medieval, and modern periods. Guattari trained as a psychoanalyst under Jacques Lacan, who is famous for his radical interpretation of Freud's approach to psychoanalysis and for his rather complicated manner of writing. Deleuze wrote books on some prominent figures throughout the history of philosophy, including Benedict Spinoza, David Hume, Immanuel Kant, Friedrich Nietzsche, and Henri Bergson. Guattari worked in an experimental clinic – La Borde – and participated actively in anti-colonialist and communist political efforts.

Guattari was active in the political demonstrations in France in May 1968, which included marches, strikes, protests, and occupations, beginning with student protests against the rising tide of consumerism and capitalism. Deleuze and Guattari met one another in the wake of that brief revolutionary event. They began plotting a collaborative work that would provide theoretical tools for overcoming the cruelty and cynicism for which the world is nothing but a collection of commodities to be bought and sold, and humans are nothing but consumers. Throughout the subsequent decade, they wrote a two-volume work, *Capitalism and Schizophrenia*, the first volume of which was first published in 1972 – *Anti-Oedipus* – and the second – *A Thousand Plateaus* – in 1980 (with English translations first appearing in 1977 and 1987, respectively).

What does a mental disorder like schizophrenia have to do with capitalism? Schizophrenia for Deleuze and Guattari represents a way of being that slips out of the control of capitalism. Whereas capitalism treats you like a consumer, schizophrenia cracks open your subjectivity, making you think, feel, and act differently than what is prescribed by social norms and conventions. One who breaks free of the confines of a conventional identity is one who "scales the schizophrenic wall" (Deleuze and Guattari, 1983: 88). Noting this, Deleuze and Guattari propose a philosophical method which they call schizoanalysis. It is a way of undoing consumer subjectivity and constituting a new way of being that is more creative. It is a way of opening up possibilities to get outside of the confines of capitalism and produce complex connections with terrestrial and cosmic energies. Schizoanalysis goes by many names, including pop analysis, nomadology, and rhizomatics (see Chapter 4). Those names refer in different ways to methods of building networks with others to empower mutually enhancing relationships. That means building networks which resist the systems that are currently turning the whole world into a pile of property and resources which are worth nothing more than their monetary value.

Schizoanalysis is not identical to Berry's Great Work, particularly insofar as the former is relatively atheistic and the latter religious. Nonetheless, they share a criticism of consumerist subjectivity and a call for a reorientation of humans to their entanglement in the dynamic processes of Earth and the cosmos. This means reclaiming Earth from the territorial impulses that objectify it. It means letting Earth show up on its own terms. Accordingly, Deleuze and Guattari (1987: 39) want to know, "Who does the Earth think it is?" More is said about their conception of Earth in subsequent chapters (see Chapter 7). The effort of Deleuze and Guattari to reorient philosophy to Earth is particularly evident in their final work – *What is Philosophy?* – in which they propose "geophilosophy" (Deleuze and Guattari, 1994: 85).

In 1988, three years before the book was first published, Deleuze said in an interview that he and Guattari hoped to "produce a sort of philosophy of Nature, now that any distinction between nature and artifice is becoming blurred" (Deleuze, 1995: 155). In our current era of increasing planetary interconnectedness, the natural is entangled with the cultural, the organic with the technological, and the nonhuman with the human. Such an era calls for a new philosophy of nature, one which avoids binary categories that separate a subjective world of culture, technology, values, and human consciousness from an objective world of matter, life, facts, and nonhuman bodies. "Subject and object give a poor approximation of thought," and, according to Deleuze and Guattari (1994: 85), a better approximation is that "thinking takes place in the relationship of territory to the earth."

Earth is a dynamic and creative process where subjectivity and objectivity are indiscernibly mixed together. Nature and culture are inextricably intertwined. When Earth is defined, managed, or controlled, it is turned into territory. For Deleuze and Guattari, thinking is something humans do with Earth. Thinking happens as part of Earth, yet thinking and Earth get caught up in territories, which can become severely oppressive and destructive. The task of geophilosophy is to reorient thinking to the creative processes of Earth, to "deterritorialize" thinking, which means thinking outside of the territorial boxes of capitalism and consumer culture. Reconnecting to Earth also requires a sense of the cosmic evolution in which Earth is situated. Along with "the song of the earth," geophilosophy participates attentively in "the song of the universe"; that is, "the great Refrain" from which everything begins and in which everything ends (pp. 189–191).

Becoming an active participant in the great Refrain is not unlike participating in the dream of Berry's universe story. It can empower people to build networks of mutually intensifying relationships of planetary coexistence. The aim of geophilosophy is to facilitate a renewal of human–Earth relations, "*to summon forth*

a new earth, a new people" (p. 99). This renewal is not confined to the territory of
any particular discipline or way of knowing. Geophilosophy crosses disciplinary
boundaries. The applications of geophilosophy are far-reaching, including numerous ecological applications coming from arts, sciences, ethics, politics, and psychology (Herzogenrath, 2008, 2009; Dodds, 2011). A crucial part of geophilosophy
is that it does not confine itself within philosophy or within any academic discipline or field of study. It wanders outside of the official borders of philosophy,
never losing contact with the non-philosophical. "The non-philosophical is
perhaps closer to the heart of philosophy than philosophy itself, and this means
that philosophy cannot be content to be understood only philosophically or con-
ceptually, but is addressed essentially to non-philosophers as well" (Deleuze and
Guattari, 1994: 41). This sense of non-philosophy is influenced by the contemporary French thinker François Laruelle (p. 220, n. 5). His non-philosophy aims to
recuperate a sense of the undivided reality of the world, opening up possibilities
for a more ecological theory of nature, a theory which undoes the dualisms that
oppose nature to culture or nonhuman to human (Smith, 2013).

Geophilosophy engages multiple academic fields, and, more than that, it experiments with non-conceptual ways of knowing, including those that "belong to the
order of dreams, of pathological processes, esoteric experiences, drunkenness,
and excess" (Deleuze and Guattari, 1994: 41). Even though Deleuze and Guattari
are very critical of religions for treating spirituality like a matter of transcendent
authority, they nonetheless include a non-conceptual, numinous dimension in
geophilosophy, finding sources of knowledge in dreams, illness, secret religious
rituals, intoxication, and extreme states of being. Buried beneath their criticisms
of religion, there is a deep appreciation for the transformative power of spiritual
practices and symbols. Accordingly, there are numerous works that explore the
religious and theological dimensions hidden in Deleuze's philosophy (e.g.,
Bryden, 2001; Justaert, 2012; Ramey, 2012).

Furthermore, the experimental thinking of geophilosophy is never merely
human. It takes place amidst relations between human and nonhuman modes of
existence, which is to say, "one does not think without becoming something else,
something that does not think – an animal, a molecule, a particle" (p. 42).
Geophilosophy is about becoming different, becoming other, and thereby building
vibrant networks of planetary coexistence. The encounter with non-philosophy is
not just something that Deleuze and Guattari put in writing. It is something they
enacted through their collaboration as philosopher and non-philosopher,
respectively. Their commitment to collaborative thinking and their orientation
toward planetary renewal put them in a situation to be creative partners in dialogue
with Berry and others who work with religious approaches to the ecological
challenges of our current historical moment.

Postsecular possibilities

On the surface, it may appear that the geologian and geophilosophers would be
too different to provide any common ground for creative interaction. However,

they have more in common than their focus on Earth. Even though Deleuze and Guattari are critical of religions for propagating otherworldly aspirations and judgmental, authoritarian attitudes, they also harbor a deep appreciation for the non-conceptual ways of knowing grounded in religious symbols and experiences. Similarly, even though Berry takes an inclusive attitude toward all of the religious traditions of the world, he is also highly critical of any tendencies they exhibit that fail to honor the integrity of the Earth community. Rather than seeing Berry as religious and Deleuze and Guattari as secular or non-religious, they are all better described as postsecular. Their restorative postmodernism is not simply religious in the way that premodern societies were, but neither are they secular in the way that modern society attempted to be. The geologian and geophilosophers are postsecular insofar as their work is open to the symbolic and experiential knowledge of premodern religious worldviews while also being open to the rational knowledge of the modern secular worldview.

One thing which Berry could definitely agree on with Deleuze and Guattari is that religions should not be interpreted literally. They should be understood in terms of symbolic and experiential ways of knowing, not in the rational terms of literal facts. Berry's affirmation of religion is not an affirmation of a literal interpretation of religion but of the power of its stories and images. Similarly, Deleuze and Guattari criticize religion not for being literally inaccurate but for harboring authoritarian and otherworldly ethics. The mistake of believers and non-believers alike is to take religion literally and force it into a rational way of knowing. The medieval Jewish philosopher Moses Maimonides (1135–1204) makes this point by distinguishing between three different ways of interpreting the legendary tales contained in some Jewish scriptures. The first group includes those who follow the scriptures, believing in them as in a literal truth. Maimonides notes that this "first group is the largest one" (Maimonides, 1972: 407). Their error is that they do not understand science, and they fail to align their beliefs with what actually happens in the real world.

The second group likewise follow a literal interpretation of religious stories and images, except that they reject religions because so many of their stories and images cannot be literally true. Many new atheists today would fall in this second group, rejecting the existence of God, for instance, because they interpret God literally as a man in the sky or some kind of flying monster. Although both groups make the same mistake in failing to recognize the symbolic and metaphorical knowledge of religions, the second group make an additional mistake in thinking that they know better than the sages and teachers who initially communicated that symbolic and metaphorical knowledge. Berry, Deleuze, and Guattari would belong in the third group, which includes those who understand science and understand the indirect meanings and analogies communicated in religious ways of knowing.

> They know that the sages did not speak nonsense, and it is clear to them that the words of the sages contain both an obvious and a hidden meaning. Thus, whenever the sages spoke of things that seem impossible, they were

employing the style of riddle and parable which is the method of truly great thinkers.

(Maimonides, 1972: 409)

A meeting between a geologian and geophilosophers would not exclude those who speak of things that are literally impossible. It would be inclusive and hospitable toward riddles, parables, metaphors, images, and other ways of knowing.

A meeting between a geologian and geophilosophers would be a postsecular meeting in which religious and scientific ways of knowing can come together in the interest of working together to build mutually enhancing relationships between humans and all members of the Earth community. Similar postsecular meetings are taking place regularly in the Forum on Religion and Ecology, whose co-founders – Mary Evelyn Tucker and John Grim – are students of Berry. He passed on to them

> an abiding interest in the cosmologies embedded in the world religions, that is, the way in which these orienting narratives bind peoples, biodiversity, and place together. In addition, he had a prescient understanding of the significant challenges of the growing environmental crisis.
>
> (Grim and Tucker, 2014: 6)

Currently stationed at Yale, the Forum is a multi-religious and international organization dedicated to building connections among scholars, scientists, activists, advocates, religious practitioners, and policymakers, particularly with the aim of facilitating a deeper understanding of the ecological implications of the religious traditions of the world. The Forum emerged from a series of conferences between 1996 and 1998, the proceedings of which were published in a book series on Religion of the World and Ecology, which includes volumes on the ecological implications of Christianity, Judaism, Islam, Hinduism, Buddhism, Jainism, Confucianism, Daoism, Shinto, and indigenous traditions. Moreover, Berry attended many of those conferences, including the interdisciplinary conference on religious, scientific, and ethical perspectives on animals (Waldau and Patton, 2006). The series of conferences and books led to the development of the Forum website, which contains extensive links, references, news, and other resources for engaging in the field of religion and ecology, whether for research, education, personal development, activism, or outreach. The Forum includes philosophical and non-philosophical perspectives, and it empowers dialogue between religious and non-religious ways of knowing. In short, the Forum is a venue in which a geologian and geophilosophers could meet and collaborate in the emergence of mutually enhancing relationships of planetary coexistence.

Another important contribution to a postsecular approach to whole Earth thinking comes from Stephanie Kaza (2008), who coined the phrase "whole Earth thinking" to describe her approach to the integration of multiple ways of knowing to cultivate a flourishing Earth community. Kaza's whole Earth thinking is deeply informed by Buddhism, specifically by the tradition of Zen Buddhism, of which

Kaza has been a practitioner for most of her life (p. xiv). Along with Buddhism, she includes perspectives from environmentalism, psychology, and the study of complex systems, including the systems theory of Gregory Bateson, whose work contributed significantly to understandings of the connections between environmental systems, social and political systems, and systems of knowledge, mind, and subjectivity (p. 44). The integration of environmental, social, and subjective systems is a key component of whole Earth thinking. Furthermore, Kaza's Buddhist orientation provides a middle way between the religious approach taken by Berry and the more atheistic approach taken by Deleuze and Guattari. Buddhism is a religion, yet it is a religion with no transcendent Creator, and in that sense it could be considered atheistic. Buddhism does not find the sacred in a transcendent God or in an eternal self. Indeed, nothing is sacred.

"Vast emptiness, nothing sacred" (Addiss et al., 2008: 9). This is what is reported to have been said by the Buddhist monk named Bodhidharma, who brought what would eventually be called Chan (Zen in Japanese) to China from India, where Buddhism began approximately two and a half millennia ago. There is no sacred dimension independent from the mundane world, and there is no sacred thing independent from everything else. Everything is empty of independent existence. This suggests that all is entangled in interdependent relationships, which is a point also emphasized in systems theory, although Buddhism is not just a theory but a way of life that involves non-conceptual, numinous encounters with the relationships comprising the world. Nothing is sacred. Everything is empty. No thing is numinous. An experience of that emptiness is an experience of the intimate intertwining of things, an experience that awakens one's sense of care for all of the others with which one finds oneself connected. Gary Snyder (1990: 25), an important influence on Kaza's ecologically oriented Buddhism, sums this up with a Tibetan Buddhist saying: "The experience of emptiness engenders compassion." Moreover, the relevance of Buddhism to postsecular concerns for planetary flourishing is further indicated by the recent work of the leader of the Gelug sect of Tibetan Buddhism, the Dalai Lama (2011: 83), who calls for the integration of Buddhism with secular approaches to ethics for "our shared world."

The point of a meeting between a geologian and geophilosophers would not be about staying true to the visions of those thinkers, defending Buddhist territories over Berry's territory, or defending Berry's territory over the territory of Deleuze and Guattari. This relates to a Zen saying: "If you meet a Buddha, kill the Buddha" (Addiss et al., 2008: 49). The same goes for a geologian or geophilosophers. The point is certainly not to promote violence against anyone but to remember that the important work is not to focus your attention on the Buddha or on any leader or wise person, including Berry, Kaza, Deleuze, Guattari, etc. The point is to focus your attention on the things that those figures focused on. The Buddha was not focusing on himself but on liberating beings from suffering. Similarly, the point of a meeting between a geologian and geophilosophers would not be to focus on the territory of either party. The point is not to focus on their territories but on the same Earth toward which they directed their concerns.

One can imagine that a meeting between a geologian and geophilosophers would be an open, inclusive, and collaborative meeting, aiming to build connections with different perspectives in the interest of cultivating mutually enhancing human–Earth relations. It would not be without deep tensions, such as tensions between the religious worldviews of premodern societies and the secular, rational worldview of modern society, tensions between pluralistic and atheistic approaches to secularism, tensions between relativistic and restorative tendencies in postmodernism, and much more. The point of whole Earth thinking is not to avoid those tensions, but to engage them in productive ways. The friction generated by those tensions can create sparks to ignite new possibilities for building networks across differences and cultivating vibrant, flourishing expressions of planetary coexistence.

References

Addiss, Stephen, Stanley Lombardo, and Judith Roitman (eds). 2008. *Zen Sourcebook: Traditional Documents from China, Korea, and Japan.* Indianapolis, IN: Hackett Publishing.

Berry, Thomas. 1989. *Buddhism*. New York: Columbia University Press.

———. 1990. The *Dream of the Earth*. San Francisco, CA: Sierra Club Books.

———. 1992. *Religions of India*, 2nd edn. New York: Columbia University Press.

———. 1999. *The Great Work: Our Way into the Future*. New York: Bell Tower.

———. 2009. *The Sacred Universe: Earth, Spirituality, and Religion in the Twenty-first Century*. Ed. Mary Evelyn Tucker. New York: Columbia University Press.

Bryden, Mary (ed.). 2001. *Deleuze and Religion*. New York: Routledge.

Cullinan, Cormac. 2011. *Wild Law: A Manifesto for Earth Justice*, 2nd edn. Totnes, Devon: Green Books.

Dalai Lama XIV. 2011. *Beyond Religion: Ethics for a Whole World*. New York: Houghton Mifflin Harcourt Publishing Company.

Deleuze, Gilles. 1989. *Cinema 2: The Time-image*. Trans. Hugh Tomlinson and Robert Galeta. Minneapolis: Athlone Press.

———. 1995. *Negotiations, 1972–1990*. Trans. Martin Joughin. New York: Columbia University Press.

Deleuze, Gilles and Félix Guattari. 1983. *Anti-Oedipus: Capitalism and Schizophrenia*. Trans. Robert Hurley, Mark Seem, and Helen R. Lane. Minneapolis: University of Minnesota Press.

———. 1987. *A Thousand Plateaus: Capitalism and Schizophrenia*. Trans. Brian Massumi. Minneapolis: University of Minnesota Press.

———. 1994. *What is Philosophy?* Trans. Hugh Tomlinson and Graham Burchell. New York: Columbia University Press.

Dellinger, Drew. 2011. *Love Letter to the Milky Way*, 2nd edn. Ashland: White Cloud Press.

Dodds, Joseph. 2011. *Psychoanalysis and Ecology at the Edge of Chaos: Complexity Theory, Deleuze/Guattari, and Psychoanalysis for a Climate in Crisis*. New York: Routledge.

Dosse, François. 2010. *Gilles Deleuze and Félix Guattari: Intersecting Lives*. Trans. Deborah Glassman. New York: Columbia University Press.

Dunn, Stephen. 2014. "Afterword: Postmodern Suggestions." In *The Intellectual Journey of Thomas Berry: Imagining the Earth Community*, ed. Heater Eaton, 239–246. Lanham, MD: Lexington Books.

Eaton, Heather. 2014. "Introduction." In *The Intellectual Journey of Thomas Berry: Imagining the Earth Community*, ed. Heater Eaton, ix–xvii. Lanham, MD: Lexington Books.

Fabel, Arthur and Donald St. John (eds). 2005. *Teilhard in the 21st Century: The Emerging Spirit of Earth*. Maryknoll: Orbis Books.

Grim, John and Mary Evelyn Tucker. 2014. *Ecology and Religion*. Washington, DC: Island Press.

Guattari, Félix. 2013. *Schizoanalytic Cartographies*. Trans. Andrew Goffey. London: Bloomsbury Academic.

Herzogenrath, Bernd (ed.). 2008. *An [Un]Likely Alliance: Thinking Environment[s] with Deleuze|Guattari*. Newcastle upon Tyne: Cambridge Scholars.

——. 2009. *Deleuze|Guattari and Ecology*. London: Palgrave Macmillan.

Justaert, Kristien. 2012. *Theology after Deleuze*. New York: Continuum.

Kaza, Stephanie. 2008. *Mindfully Green: A Personal and Spiritual Guide to Whole Earth Thinking*. Boston, MA: Shambhala Publications.

Lyotard, Jean-François. 1984. *The Postmodern Condition: A Report on Knowledge*. Trans. Geoff Bennington and Brian Massumi. Minneapolis: University of Minnesota Press.

Maimonides, Moses. 1972. "Helek: Sanhedrin, Chapter Ten." In *A Maimonides Reader: Edited, with Introductions and Notes*, ed. Isadore Twersky, 401–423. Springfield, NJ: Behrman House.

Otto, Rudolf. 1958. *The Idea of the Holy*. Trans. J. W. Harvey. London: Oxford University Press.

Ramey, Joshua. 2012. *The Hermetic Deleuze: Philosophy and Spiritual Ordeal*. Durham, NC: Duke University Press.

Smith, Anthony Paul. 2013. *A Non-philosophical Theory of Nature: Ecologies of Thought*. New York: Palgrave Macmillan.

Snyder, Gary. 1990. *The Practice of the Wild*. Berkeley, CA: Counterpoint.

Swimme, Brian and Thomas Berry. 1992. *The Universe Story: From the Primordial Flaring Forth to the Ecozoic Era – A Celebration of the Unfolding of the Cosmos*. San Francisco, CA: HarperCollins.

Taylor, Mark C. 2009. *After God*. Chicago, IL: University of Chicago Press.

Teilhard de Chardin, Pierre. 2001. *The Divine Milieu*. Ed. Bernard Wall. New York: Harper Perennial Classics.

Tucker, Mary Evelyn. n.d. "Biography of Thomas Berry." http://www.thomasberry.org/Biography/tucker-bio.html (accessed December 3, 2014).

Waldau, Paul and Kimberly Patton (eds). 2006. *A Communion of Subjects: Animals in Religion, Science, and Ethics*. New York: Columbia University Press.

4 Integrating environments, societies, and subjects

A definitive trait of whole Earth thinking is a commitment to crossing the boundaries between different disciplines and different ways of knowing. Such boundary-crossing is a key ingredient in any efforts of whole Earth thinking to articulate comprehensive, inclusive, and relevant interpretations of the challenges facing planetary coexistence. For instance, issues around the invention and use of genetically modified organisms (GMOs) touch on numerous fields of study. While biology can present an understanding of the processes involved in genetic modification, it does not address the implications of patenting and selling GMOs. Those implications are matters for politics and economics. Integrating biology with politics and economics gives a more comprehensive picture of the many factors and competing interests involved in GMOs. However, those fields of study do not address ethical and theological questions about GMOs, questions about whether it is morally acceptable to manipulate the genetics of nonhuman life for the benefit of humans, questions about whether humans are acting too arrogantly – playing God – by intervening so deeply into the building blocks of life. It is a complex situation, which is to say, it is a situation with many parts weaving into one another and folding together (*complexere*: *com*, "with"; *plexere*, "folding" or "weaving"). Biological sciences give us one picture, social sciences like economics give us another, and fields like philosophy and religion give us pictures from the humanities. How can those pictures come together? Does anyone have the whole picture?

The situation resembles a well-known story that originated among the religions of South Asia (e.g., Hinduism, Jainism, and Buddhism). The story is told in many different ways, but the basic details are simple (Long, 2009: 117). A group of blind men come across an elephant, and each man touches a different part of the elephant and so thinks of the elephant in terms of that limited knowledge. One person touches the tail and thinks the elephant is a rope. Another touches the trunk and thinks it is a snake. Another grabs the leg and thinks it is a tree trunk. Another touches the side and thinks it is a wall. Another grabs an ear and thinks it is a fan. Another touches the tusk and thinks it is a spear. Each perspective is limited. How is it possible to figure out that it is an elephant? How can one attain knowledge of the whole? Does knowledge of the whole only come about through dialogue between the various perspectives? People mention this story to illustrate different problems, and the various versions of this story differ regarding the specific solution to those problems.

This chapter draws on the geologian Thomas Berry and the geophilosopher Félix Guattari to present some possible approaches to questions about how to integrate multiple, limited perspectives in order to practice whole Earth thinking. This is not to say that theirs are the only integrative visions. Quite the contrary: many integrative approaches to ecological and planetary questions have been expressed in recent decades. Indeed, there is an integrative or holistic impulse running through the entire history of ecological thought (see Chapter 2). More recently, approaches have emerged that aim to integrate premodern, modern, and postmodern ways of interpreting planetary coexistence. Two approaches are particularly noteworthy: the Integral Ecology of Sean Esbjörn-Hargens and Michael Zimmerman and the complex thought of Edgar Morin. Following an overview of their integrative visions, this chapter introduces a threefold approach derived from Berry and Guattari, who practice whole Earth thinking by weaving together environmental, social, and subjective facets of ecology.

Integral and complex

Esbjörn-Hargens and Zimmerman propose an "Integral" approach to ecology in their monumental work of that name, *Integral Ecology: Uniting Multiple Perspectives on the Natural World* (2009). In that book, they apply the Integral framework developed by the contemporary American writer and philosopher Ken Wilber. The work by Wilber that is most commonly associated with the term "Integral" (usually capitalized) is *Sex, Ecology, Spirituality*, which presents his Integral theory in the form of the "AQAL" model (pronounced *ah-qwul*), an "all-quadrant, all-level" map that accounts for physical, mental, and spiritual *levels* of reality, each of which has four different aspects, represented by four *quadrants*: individual and collective subjectivity ("I" and "We"), and individual and collective objectivity ("It" and "Its") (Wilber, 2000: 127–135). This framework allows for an integration of humanities and sciences to understand any phenomenon in the universe, from its evolving matter and life to the highest reaches of human consciousness. To sum up the framework very briefly, the all-quadrant and all-level map avoids oversimplifying things (i.e., reductionism) and makes it possible to bring together multiple contrasting and even contradictory perspectives on any issue. As the title *Sex, Ecology, Spirituality* suggests, Wilber applies his framework to ecological issues, including the ethical and religious dimensions of human–Earth relations.

Picking up where Wilber left off, Esbjörn-Hargens and Zimmerman (2009: 486) use Wilber's framework to explicitly articulate an Integral approach to ecology, which they describe as an "ecology of ecologies," which coordinates multiple perspectives on environmental issues and the natural world. Not unlike the example of the blind men and the elephant, they discuss the example of a tree, which appears differently from different perspectives. They claim that "there is simply no such thing as 'one tree'! Rather, there are different layers of trees enacted by each perceiver," including human perceivers like an artist, environmentalist, ecologist, or economist, as well as nonhuman perceivers like a bear, woodpecker, or beetle (p. 180). An Integral approach aims to coordinate the diversity of perspectives in order to implement comprehensive, effective, long-term solutions to the contemporary ecological problems. This means including biological and physical sciences, social sciences, and the humanities, overcoming the split between the objective world, which is studied by scientists, and the subjective world, which is studied by the humanities. An Integral approach avoids the object-versus-subject stance. In general, the Integral approach advocates for connection instead of polarization. For example, "Integral Ecology transcends the anthropocentrism versus anti-anthropocentrism duality" that poses human-centered values (anthropocentrism) in opposition to values centered on living organisms (biocentrism) or on whole ecosystems (ecocentrism) (p. 11). The Integral approach seeks to coordinate anthropocentric, biocentric, and ecocentric values. Imagine a polluted river: anthropocentric people may want to clean up the river because it is endangering the health of people who live along the river; biocentric people may want to clean it up because it is endangering the life that lives in and along the river; and ecocentric people may want to clean up the river because pollution damages the resilience and beauty of the ecosystem. Rather than arguing about which values are right, an Integral approach is like an "environmental pragmatism," facilitating the convergence of contrasting perspectives in order to take practical actions (Esbjörn-Hargens and Zimmerman, 2009: 554, n.57; Light and Katz, 1996).

For Integral Ecology, all perspectives are partially right, which means that no perspective is absolutely right. Responses to ecological problems call for the cooperation of as many perspectives as possible, including perspectives from the modern rationality of ecological science, from traditional religious worldviews, and from postmodern critiques of modern and traditional societies. Integral Ecology seeks inclusive dialogue between traditional, modern, and postmodern perspectives. No single perspective is the best. No perspective can provide the solution to the current planetary crisis. Indeed, "there is no single solution" to any crisis, in the same way that a tree or an elephant consists of multiple layers of meanings and interpretations disclosed to different perspectives (p. 339). Integral Ecology is even willing to work with perspectives which claim that the language of "crisis" is exaggerated and everything is actually getting better (e.g., more efficient technologies, more international cooperation, and better scientific understanding of ecology). The Integral approach also includes mystical or spiritual perspectives that see everything as always already perfect, such as a Christian mystic who experiences all as one with God, or a Tibetan Buddhist who experiences everything as a display of "Great Perfection" (Dzogchen). Embracing these apparently contradictory perspectives, Integral Ecology proposes this slogan for our era of planetary interconnectedness: "things are getting worse, are getting better, and are perfect" (p. 307).

Building networks across different perspectives, Integral Ecology is relevant to every discipline, theory, and method of ecological inquiry. Furthermore, there are many ways of developing integrative approaches to ecology. Incidentally,

Berry (1999: 98) describes his vision as an "integral Earth study." He calls for an "integral ecologist" to be a guide to situate humans in their planetary and cosmic contexts (Berry, 2009: 135). Esbjörn-Hargens and Zimmerman are not opposed to Berry's approach. They do not situate their approach as the only framework for integrating multiple ecological perspectives. They promote the emergence of "a variety of integral ecologies" (Esbjörn-Hargens and Zimmerman, 2009: 667). Integration "need not be contained within any single framework" (p. 540). Similarly, Stephanie Kaza makes the point that there are many ways to walk the path of whole Earth thinking, the green practice path. "There is no single green path: the path is determined by individual experiences, local needs, and personal motivation" (Kaza, 2008: xi). "No single model can even come close to capturing all that is going on" (p. 36). She draws upon the Buddhist concept of the Middle Way to indicate that the green practice path is diverse and always changing. "The Middle Way is about balance, moderation, and continuous reflection on what is appropriate. There is no single equation for what is right at any given time. Continuous reflection is key, for conditions and options are changing constantly" (p. 133). Kaza's vision of the green practice path is deeply influenced by Buddhism, but it is not exclusively Buddhist or even religious. It is open to all.

Anyone can walk the path of whole Earth thinking, regardless of whether they adhere to a specific religious tradition. An example of more non-traditional approaches to whole Earth thinking may be found in the approaches to ecology expressed by contemporary French theorists like Bruno Latour, Michel Serres, and Edgar Morin. Those thinkers and many twentieth-century French philosophers were capable of integrating humanities and sciences in a more effective way than in English-speaking academic contexts, where there is often a large gap between humanities and sciences (Crockett, 2014: 273). Reflecting the difference between modern American and French conceptions of religion (see Chapter 3), these French theorists do not focus on including traditional religions, at least not to the extent of American thinkers like Kaza or Integral theorists like Esbjörn-Hargens and Zimmerman. However, they do not reject religion in favor of modern rationalism and individualism. Rather, they aim to develop more complex ways of thinking that overcome simple oppositions between traditional and modern, religion and reason, humanities and sciences, and communities and individuals. For instance, one common thread among recent French ecological thought is the attempt to overcome the opposition between anthropocentric and non-anthropocentric perspectives, thus opening up possibilities for understanding the intertwining of humans with nonhumans, culture with nature, values with facts, and politics with science (Whiteside, 2002). Particularly noteworthy in this context is the work of Edgar Morin, whose ecological and planetary concerns are explicit throughout much of his work.

Morin's "complex thought" is outlined in detail in his immense six-volume work *La Méthode* [Method]. With the release of the second volume of that work, *La Vie de la Vie* [The Life of Life], Morin (1980: 77) began articulating his integrative approach to ecology, which he describes as general ecology. For Morin, general ecology engages more than just organism–environmental interactions.

General ecology extends to multiple interconnections between humans and the natural world, including present generations as well as the future of humanity and of all life on Earth. The human and social realms are inextricably entangled with biological and physical realms. Accordingly, there is no single discipline that can account for everything that general ecology studies. The method of Morin's complex thought is transdisciplinary, crossing the boundaries between various biological and physical sciences as well as social theory, anthropology, politics, psychology, and philosophy.

For Morin (1999: 114), complex thinking "endeavors to connect that which was separate while preserving distinctiveness and differences." It issues a "warning to the intellect, to beware of clarification, simplification, hasty reduction" (cited in Anselmo, 2005: 474). It is an "ecologized thinking," which conceives of the world's circuitous and recursive relations of interactions and retroactions, while also considering the "hologrammatic character" of these relations, according to which the whole (e.g., the planet) and the parts (e.g., humans) are internally interconnected, each being implicated within the constitution of the other (Morin, 1999: 130). Furthermore, Morin proposes a postsecular understanding of religion. His "gospel of doom" advocates for "an earthly religion of the third type" – a planetary religion which holds people together in their shared doom; that is, the shared limits of their planetary and finite context (p. 142). This planetary religion is critical of otherworldly salvation in traditional religions (e.g., Christian heaven or Buddhist nirvana), whereby people aim to escape this world of suffering, and it is also critical of the worldly salvation offered in modern secular contexts (e.g., Marxism, free market capitalism) (p. 141). For planetary religion, salvation lies in the efforts of "consciousness, love, and fellowship," which are not ways of avoiding our planetary limits in order "to escape doom," but are ways of facing our limits in order "to dodge the worst" and "to find out what is best" (p. 142).

Planetary, postsecular religion is one aspect of the "evolution toward a planetary consciousness" that has taken place throughout the past five centuries of modernization, colonialism, industrialization, world wars, and globalization, which together constitute what Morin calls "the Planetary Era" – an era of increasing interconnectedness between humans, organisms, and ecosystems across local, regional, national, international, and global scales (pp. 6, 24). On the one hand, that increasing interconnectedness has accompanied increasingly intense social and environmental crises, such as poverty, militarism, pollution, freshwater scarcity, and the loss of cultural and biological diversity. On the other hand, it has accompanied the emergence of planetary expressions of community and social cohesion, what Morin calls "planetary solidarity," which is not just a global solidarity of humans but a form of solidarity wherein human communities are intimately intertwined with one another and with the living and natural systems of the planet (p. 106).

Although such a "planetary union" has not been achieved, it is flashing up with increasing frequency and intensity as people bond together to resist violence and destruction and promote mutually enhancing relationships of peace, justice, and sustainability. Planetary union is possible, but not easy. It does not call for uncritical optimism. Planetary solidarity requires a monumental effort in the face of much uncertainty. It calls for a realistic approach that "*grounds itself in the uncertainty of the real*" (p. 108). This means that our solidarity as participants in "the complex web of the Planetary Era" does not entail that we humans have any mastery or control over ourselves or over the natural world (p. 146). Quite to the contrary, planetary solidarity is based on a shared recognition: "We are lost in the cosmos" (p. 133). We are lost, but not because we cannot find our way. We are lost because wandering is our way. We are cosmic nomads, "vagabonds of the unknown adventure," open to the uncertain and unpredictable possibilities that the future holds for planetary coexistence (p. 145).

Morin's openness to uncertainty and wandering is characteristic of much French theory in recent decades. For instance, the geophilosophers Gilles Deleuze and Félix Guattari describe their approach as a nomadology or nomad science, which wanders across the boundaries of academic disciplines and research methods, opening up academic territories to creative new connections (Deleuze and Guattari, 1987: 351). One cannot build new connections, networks, and alliances without facing the unknown, without wandering through uncertain challenges and opportunities. The framework of Integral Ecology provides one way of navigating that uncertainty. Morin's complex thought provides another, as does the nomadology or geophilosophy of Deleuze and Guattari. There is no specific or certain way to practice whole Earth thinking and seek ecological wisdom. "The wisdom-seeking process is not a single path nor a predictable path" (Kaza, 2008: 95).

Keeping in mind that there are multiple and unpredictable ways of thinking about the whole Earth, the remainder of this chapter introduces a threefold formula that may be used in many different approaches to whole Earth thinking. The formula is simple: environment, society, and subjectivity. An understanding of planetary coexistence calls for the integration of perspectives on environments, societies, and subjects. Variations of this threefold formula may be found in many places. For instance, the Indian activist and Jain monk Satish Kumar describes an ecological trinity of soil, soul, and society. Kumar's soil and soul correspond roughly to environment and subjectivity. "In a nutshell, we need to live a spiritual way of life and engage in the protection of the earth, enlightenment of the self and restoration of social justice" (Kumar, 2013: 141). A similar threefold formula may be seen in Wilber's (2000: 149) notion of the Big Three of "It/s" (environments), "We" (societies), and "I" (subjects). Wilber articulates very specific meanings for each of those three categories that can be somewhat restrictive in efforts to work outside of his theory. Similar but more open-ended approaches are presented by the geologian Thomas Berry and the geophilosopher Guattari.

Along with the geophilosophy he worked on with Deleuze, Guattari wrote in his own writings about an ecological philosophy or "ecosophy," which includes three different aspects or registers of ecological phenomena: environmental, social, and mental.[1] Perhaps influenced by Morin, Guattari (2000: 27) calls his ecosophy a "generalized ecology"; that is, an ecology which includes not only natural environments but also societies and the existential conditions that make up mind, knowledge, and subjectivity. It is an approach that opens ecology into cultural, planetary, and cosmic connections with the aim of addressing the multiple, interlocking crises taking place around the world, from income inequality to mass extinction, from immigration to global warming, from psychological depression to economic recession, from obesity to war.

> Thus the issue returns with insistence: how do we change mentalities, how do we reinvent social practices that would give back to humanity – if it ever had it – a sense of responsibility for its own survival, but equally for the future of all life on the planet, for animal and vegetable species, likewise for incorporeal species such as music, the arts, cinema, the relation with time, love and compassion for others, the feeling of fusion at the heart of the cosmos?
>
> (Guattari, 1995: 119–120)

This is not unlike Berry's vision of mutually enhancing human–Earth relations. Indeed, bearing in mind the contrast between a geologian like Berry and a geophilosopher like Guattari (see Chapter 3), one can find the threefold formula of Guattari's ecosophy in a different form in Berry's work.

In his presentation of *The Universe Story* with the cosmologist Brian Swimme, Berry proposes a cosmogenetic principle; that is, a principle that accounts for the evolutionary becoming (genesis) of the universe (cosmos). It is a threefold principle, for which all evolutionary processes are characterized by differentiation, subjectivity (or "autopoiesis," i.e., self-organization), and communion (Swimme and Berry, 1992: 71). These correspond approximately with Guattari's environmental, subjective, and social ecologies. Similarly, Berry's aim is to apply these three interlocking principles in a way that can facilitate an understanding of and response to the interlocking crises of planetary coexistence today: environmental, existential, and social crises. "Our present course is a violation of each of these three principles in their most primordial expression" (Berry, 1999: 163). To move from a destructive course to a path of mutually enhancing human–Earth relations, it is imperative that one understands these interrelated aspects of planetary coexistence. It is imperative that one understands environmental, social, and subjective ecologies.

Environmental

Environmental ecology is about the interconnected systems studied in biological and physical sciences. Swimme and Berry describe this ecological dimension in terms of differentiation. It covers the different observable and measurable characteristics of beings at all scales, from subatomic and microscopic to galactic and cosmic. "Some synonyms for differentiation are diversity, complexity, variation, disparity, multiform nature, heterogeneity, articulation" (Swimme and Berry, 1992: 71–72). The universe is an ongoing articulation of complexity; that is, an ongoing process of differentiation, beginning with the Big Bang approximately 13.8 billion years ago and proceeding through transformations and mutations into different forces (nuclear, electromagnetic, gravitational), particles, galaxies, stars, planets, bacteria, plants, fish, reptiles, mammals, and eventually me and you. In the universe described by Swimme and Berry, every being is unique: "to be is to be different" (p. 74). The universe is an ongoing production of new beings, new differences. In Deleuze's terms, the universe is an ongoing repetition of difference (Deleuze, 1994).

Environmental ecology studies the diversity of beings, mapping out their complexity, analyzing their unique structures. Moreover, the term "environment" can be misleading. It is not about one big thing called the environment, which surrounds the humans or organisms who live in the environment. Environmental ecology studies the various conditions that comprise all beings, including humans and nonhumans. That includes undeveloped or undomesticated natural areas as well as contexts with more human presence, ranging from rural contexts like farms and ranches to urban contexts like London and Tokyo. Whether human or nonhuman, everything can be seen as an assembly of different parts, and each assemblage connects to other assemblages to form parts of larger assemblages. Different theories and methods are more appropriate to some assemblages than to others. Physics, chemistry, biology, ecology, and geology each focus on a particular region or scale of beings. The point of environmental ecology is to understand different assemblages, describing their interactions with one another at multiple scales. For example, in looking at chemical pesticides, one would not just look at chemicals, but would also consider how chemicals relate to polluted ecosystems, how pollution in ecosystems relates to genetic mutations in organisms, how those genetic mutations indicate health risks for humans, how those health risks affect medical treatments and insurance plans, and so on. The connections are endless.

Imagine a densely populated city like San Francisco, situated in multiple nested assemblages, from the North American continent and the planet to our solar system, our galaxy (the Milky Way), and eventually to the cosmos as a whole. The city is an assemblage, and it contains many parts, each of which is itself an assemblage made up of other parts, such as a park, which itself contains many trees. Each tree is made up of cells, each of which is made up of molecules that are made up of atoms, which are themselves made up of subatomic particles. Buildings, roads, birds, sidewalks, beaches, people, gardens, cars, dogs, streetlights, bicycles, fog, buses, sea lions, and other assemblages in the city connect to one another and make connections outside of the city and into the cosmos. For instance, the city contains some buildings that generate electricity from solar panels on their roofs, and the solar panels are connecting to the sun – a powerful cosmic assemblage on which life on Earth depends. Environmental ecology sees interlocking assemblages everywhere, and each of them has various capacities for connecting with other assemblages, just as solar panels and trees have different capacities for connecting to the energy radiating from the sun.

Considering that the term "environment" is misleading because of its connotation as one big thing in which humans live, it is not necessary to use that term to describe this ecological perspective. Accordingly, Guattari (2000: 66) suggests that one could "rename environmental ecology *machinic ecology*," although that phrase is not necessarily less confusing. The term *machine* comes from complexity theories. For instance, Morin speaks of machines in his complex thought. For Morin (1999: 68), "every physical being whose activity includes work, transformation, production can be conceived as a machine," which means that birds, the sun, social institutions, technologies, and humans are all "machine-beings." Machines are not like literal machines – passive, inert, controllable objects. They are not mechanistic, but are dynamic, active, unpredictable assemblages, which are made up of interrelated parts and have capacities for affecting and being affected by other assemblages. Along these lines, the Deleuze/Guattari-inspired "assemblage theory" of Manuel DeLanda (2006) provides another way to articulate this perspective. There are multiple names for environmental ecology and many ways to practice it. The important point is to follow the differences of things and map out their complex networks. However, one must remember that it is impossible to exhaustively account for anything or any series of differences. Indeed, "each individual thing in the universe is ineffable," which means that "each thing remains as baffling as ever, no matter how profound our understanding" (Swimme and Berry, 1992: 74). The cutting edge of the unknown runs through every assemblage.

The dynamic processes of assemblages are radically open. Their functions are uncertain and unpredictable, which leads Guattari (2000: 66) to articulate "a principle specific to environmental ecology: it states that anything is possible – the worst disasters or the most flexible evolutions." Anything could happen. That principle is not just about a world "out there." It has serious implications for human existence. "Cosmic and human praxis" are brought together as environmental ecology engages in the unknown adventure of assemblages, from periods of organization, structure, and rigidity to periods of chaos, disequilibrium, and flexibility, which can produce destructive breakdowns and creative breakthroughs. The future of humanity and of life on Earth depends on our engagement in the diversity and complexity of beings. The involvement of human practices in environmental ecology points to an ethical component of ecosophy. Guattari calls for "an ecosophical ethics adapted to this terrifying and fascinating situation"; that is, an ethics capable of engaging in uncertainty and unpredictability, an ethics that knows how to act without knowing, an ethics that carefully and cautiously recognizes that anything is possible (p. 67). It is an ethics capable of dealing with situations in which one is not capable, unprecedented and dangerous situations like a nuclear meltdown or global warming. This is similar to what the Romantic poet John Keats (1990: xi) calls "Negative Capability," which means that one is "capable of being in uncertainties, mysteries, doubts, without any irritable reaching after fact and reason." This ethical approach extends throughout social and subjective ecologies as well.

Social

Social ecology is about the expressions of collective meanings and values investigated in cultural studies and social sciences. If environmental ecology focuses on complexity, social ecology focuses on community. Swimme and

Berry (1992: 72) offer numerous terms that express this dimension of things, including "communion, interrelatedness, interdependence, kinship, mutuality, internal relatedness, reciprocity, complementarity, interconnectivity, and affiliation." To be is to be different, yet differences are always involved in relationships with other differences. Environmental phenomena are always involved in some kind of social coexistence. Along with explicit differences, there is also a relational dimension to existence. "To be is to be related" (p. 77). Community is a basic aspect of reality. Nothing exists completely independently.

The existence of every single being depends on the relations and communications it has with everything around it, extending to the whole cosmos. Accordingly, Deleuze (1990: 180) claims that to be is to participate in a "unique event in which all events communicate with one another," raising "a single voice for every hum of voices and every drop of water in the sea." To be is to be in communication with the cosmos. "Nothing is itself without everything else" (Swimme and Berry, 1992: 77). An integrative approach to ecology must not view the world merely as "a collection of objects," for it is also "a communion of subjects" (Berry, 1999: 16). In Guattari's (2000: 62) terminology, social ecology studies collective subjectivity, including social struggles, media, economic institutions, and efforts to raise awareness – "sudden mass consciousness-raising," as Guattari puts it, "always remains possible."

Returning to the above example of chemical pesticides, the social perspective would ask not just about the chemistry, ecology, and health issues involved in pesticide use but would consider the cultural values, economic processes, political powers, and types of communication that lead to the production and use of chemical pesticides. Similarly, social ecology would add to the above analysis of San Francisco, asking questions about the subjective dimension of all of the assemblages mapped by environmental ecology. What are the cultures and subcultures in the city? What languages are spoken (including nonhuman communication systems)? How do the city's human and nonhuman residents relate to one another in terms of friendship, kinship, political alliances, financial obligations, and employment? How do people participate in media, arts, religions, and entertainment? While environmental ecology would notice that there are humans in San Francisco, social ecology would consider how resources and opportunities are distributed differently for people across lines of race, gender, age, ethnicity, and economic class. While environmental ecology would notice that there are dogs in the city, social ecology would notice the differences between dogs employed as service animals, stray dogs, and dogs that are companions (i.e., "pets").

Social ecology is often associated with the enduring legacy of Murray Bookchin, who developed a theory of social ecology that critiques the unjust and unsustainable conditions of capitalism, which reduces the shared world to a heap of properties and commodities (Light, 1998). For the current model of capitalism, anything valuable can be reduced to monetary value. That means that the communion of subjects can be reduced to a mere collection of objects. Responses of social ecology to the objectification of the inhabitants of habitats of Earth can take many forms. Social ecology is not necessarily socialist. It can take many forms, including democratic, libertarian, and anarchist. The important point is that it criticizes the attempt to let trade and markets run the world. It criticizes the ways in which capitalism has taken power away from people and put it in the hands of corporations, turning people from citizens into consumers. Capitalism has become increasingly pervasive throughout the last century, expanding beyond national territories and spreading around to become something like a global empire (Hardt and Negri, 2001). Furthermore, capitalism has deepened the extent of its reach by turning ideas into property (intellectual property) and even turning the basic building blocks of life into property (patenting the genetic makeup of GMOs). Today's capitalism is a global biocapitalism, and it is running up against its limits in the ecological crisis to which its rapacious consumption is contributing (Žižek, 2008: 357, 421).

Like Bookchin and other social ecologists, Guattari (2000: 31) is highly critical of global capitalism, which he calls "Integrated World Capitalism." The task of social ecology is to reclaim the eroded subjectivities of groups, institutions, organizations, nationalities, and cultures. This means calling into question "the whole of subjectivity and capitalistic power formations," thus opening up ecology beyond its association with "a small nature-loving minority" and "qualified specialists" of environmental science and policy (p. 52). Ecology is not just about scientific inquiries into the natural world, and it is not just about loving the great outdoors or appreciating the beauty of nature. Ecology is also about the "existential Territories" that make up the shared meanings and values of group subjectivity (p. 33).

Extending far beyond environmental scientists and nature lovers, ecology touches upon issues of international trade, government regulations, languages, church groups, families, social media, funding, arts, research institutions, films, environmental non-governmental organizations (NGOs), traditions, and much more. Cultural renewal is at stake. Social ecology takes on the challenge of "reconstructing the modalities of 'group-being'" (p. 34). Guattari gives the example of rock music, which brings people together across national boundaries, functioning like "a sort of initiatory cult" that provides young people with some kind of cultural identity, some musical means for obtaining "a bare minimum of existential Territories" in a world where existential or psychological well-being is eroded by consumerism and individualism (p. 33). Along these lines, the emerging field of ecomusicology is one among many interdisciplinary areas of inquiry that has much to contribute to social ecology (Allen and Dawe, 2015). Political ecology, ecological economics, religion and ecology, media ecology, ecofeminism, environmental justice, and environmental sociology are among some of the other approaches that would be relevant to the task of reinventing group subjectivity and reclaiming the communion of subjects.

The point of social ecology is not to find some general recommendation or one-size-fits-all answer that is supposed to work for everyone who applies it. The point is to try things out for oneself in one's own social settings, from intimate personal relationships to participation in religious, education, political, and economic institutions. "Instead of clinging to general recommendations we would be implementing effective practices of experimentation, as much on a microsocial level as on a larger institutional scale" (Guattari, 2000: 35).

Subjective

Along with their complexity (environmental) and community (social), all beings have their own singularity, which is not reducible to any measurement or observable difference, or to any relationship or connection. I am not just an assemblage, and I am not just a bundle of relationships or a node in a network. I am a singular being, an actually existing individual with my own value and meaning. I am a subject. Some different words for this aspect of the world are "self-manifestation, sentience, self-organization, dynamic centers of experience, presence, identity, inner principle of being, voice, interiority" (Swimme and Berry, 1992: 72). Another term is autopoiesis, which is used in sciences to refer to the capacity for self-production or self-organization (*auto*, "self"; *poiesis*, "production").

> Autopoiesis refers to the power each thing has to participate directly in the cosmos-creating endeavor. . . . Autopoiesis points to the interior dimension of things. Even the simplest atom cannot be understood by considering only its physical structure or the outer world of external relationships with other things. Things emerge with an inner capacity for self-manifestation.
>
> (Swimme and Berry, 1992: 75)

To be is not only to be different and be related. To be is to be subjective.

The task of reclaiming a communion of subjects is not only about the reclaiming of communion but also the reclaiming of subjectivity. The current planetary crisis involves a loss of relationship and a loss of subjectivity as humans and nonhumans have been reduced to a pile of property, as if the world is nothing but resources. If it is not the same as complexity and community, what, then, is subjectivity? You can think about it grammatically. A subject of a sentence is the agent, the actor – the one that performs an action (the verb). In contrast, the object of a sentence is that which receives action or that toward which an action is directed. To objectify something is to deprive it of the agency of subject. Feminist resistance to the objectification of women aims to reclaim the multiple forms of female and feminine agency. Some forms of political ecology aim to reclaim the agency of nonhumans, arguing that all beings are "actors" (Latour, 2004: 86). This goes against the modern philosopher René Descartes (1994: 51), who famously defines subjective existence in terms of a thinking ego: "I think, therefore I am." Subjectivity is not located primarily in thinking. It can be found in all forms of agency and self-organization, which always emerge with "the real Territories of existence," not in some thinking ego that is separate from its body, its community, and its environment (Guattari, 2000: 35).

To say that something is an actor is to say that it has a singular existence, an individual agency that is connected to – but not reducible to – its complexity as a system (environmental ecology) and its community in relationships with others (social ecology). Guattari speaks of this as the mental dimension of ecosophy. It is more than a rational or intellectual dimension. It includes emotional, aesthetic, ethical, spiritual, and perceptual capacities of subjectivity. This ecological dimension includes all of the processes that go into making a subject, similar to what the social theorist Gregory Bateson refers to as an "ecology of ideas" or "ecology of mind" (Guattari, 2000: 54; Bateson, 2000). It covers all aspects of "subjectification," opening up possibilities to radically transform oneself and one's experience, to radically reinvent one's sense of the world, including one's sense of time, imagination, knowledge, embodiment, and even "the 'mysteries' of life and death" (Guattari, 2000: 35).

Returning to the example of San Francisco, along with the complexity and community of the city, ecosophy would study the different kinds of agency or sub-jectivity expressed by the city's human and nonhuman residents. How and when do people feel empowered, free, depressed, anxious, happy, sad, and angry? Do dogs have enough space to play, or are their actions restricted by the trappings of urbanization? Do birds have enough opportunities to sing, or is their singing con-fused by the preponderance of interfering noises, from traffic to ring tones? How and when do people find meaning in their lives? What ideas do people have about themselves, their society, and their environment? Mental ecology studies these questions, and, more than that, it aims to transform subjects, including the develop-ment of innovative practice to open up possibilities for relatively autonomous forms of agency, which is to say a free, creative, and self-reliant subjectivity "that can articulate itself appropriately in relation to the rest of society" (p. 59).

Existential transformation is thus a necessary component of any comprehen-sive response to the current planetary crisis. Ecological issues are never simply issues of the natural environment, nor are they completely reducible to problems of politics and economics. While science, technology, policy, and community-building are necessary for developing a globally coordinated response to contem-porary planetary problems, they are not sufficient. Ecological issues are always entangled with the singularity of actually existing individuals, the agency whereby each being exists as itself and persists in its being over time. Subjectivity must be taken into account. "The demands of singularity are rising up almost everywhere" (p. 31). That is even more accurate now than when Guattari first said it over twenty-five years ago. Human and nonhuman actors are rising up and refusing to be taken for granted, refusing to be exploited like a repository of resources, refus-ing to be reduced to a collection of objects. Even the planet's climate is refusing to be reduced to an object, as it increasingly becomes apparent that it is an actor in its own right and not simply a background against which humans can play out their lives.

By expanding ecology beyond environmental perspectives to include social and mental ecologies, ecology becomes more capable of facilitating a transition away from practices that treat the world like nothing but a collection of objects and toward practices for recuperating community and agency, reclaiming a com-munion of subjects. For an integrative vision of ecology, "the question becomes one of how to encourage the organization of individual and collective ventures, and how to direct them towards an ecology of resingularization" (p. 65). Such resingularization restores subjectivity and community, but not in a way that negates the importance of differentiation. To attend to the singularity of all of human and nonhuman participants in planetary coexistence is to facilitate the integration of subjects into one Earth community and to facilitate the complexity and ongoing differentiation of every member of that community. "Individuals must become both more united and increasingly different" (p. 69). An integrative vision of ecology honors the unity and difference that make up planetary coexistence.

By weaving together "the tangled paths of the tri-ecological vision," one can develop an integrative approach to ecology that faces the uncertainty and unpredictability of our current historical moment while empowering efforts to create liberating modes of planetary coexistence for environments, societies, and subjects (p. 67). Such an integrative vision is a radical revision of the values guiding human individuals and communities. An integrative revision is necessary for the flourishing of life on Earth. Indeed, it may be necessary even for the continued existence of the human species. "There is at least a risk that there will be no more human history unless humanity undertakes a radical reconsideration of itself" (p. 68). As humans find themselves in an era of increasing planetary interconnectedness, it is more crucial than ever that we learn to think in complex ways, integrating environmental, social, and subjective ecologies in the interest of cultivating a vibrant Earth community. One of the reasons that this chapter juxtaposes the approach of Berry (and Swimme) and Guattari (and Deleuze) is to highlight that there is not just one way to participate in whole Earth thinking. There are many ways to practice complex thinking and to integrate multiple ecological perspectives. There are many sources for the practice of ecosophy. There are many roots to ecological wisdom.

Note

1   Arne Naess, a founding figure in the deep ecology movement, describes his approach as "ecophilosophy" and "ecosophy" (1989: 36). Guattari's ecosophy does not draw on Naess, although their work does exhibit some overlapping points (Bogue, 2009).

References

Allen, Aaron and Kevin Dawe (eds). 2015. *Current Directions in Ecomusicology: Music, Nature, Environment*. New York: Routledge.

Anselmo, Annmaria. 2005. "Vico and Hegel: Philosophical Sources for Morin's Sociology." *World Futures* 61(6): 470–480.

Bateson, Gregory. 2000. *Steps to an Ecology of Mind*. Chicago, IL: University of Chicago Press.

Berry, Thomas. 1999. *The Great Work: Our Way into the Future*. New York: Bell Tower.

——. 2009. *The Sacred Universe: Earth, Spirituality, and Religion in the Twenty-first Century*. Ed. Mary Evelyn Tucker. New York: Columbia University Press.

Bogue, Ronald. 2009. "A Thousand Ecologies." In *Deleuze|Guattari and Ecology*, ed. Bernd Herzogenrath, 42–56. London: Palgrave Macmillan.

Crockett, Clayton. 2014. "Entropy." In *The Future of Continental Philosophy of Religion*, ed. Clayton Crockett, B. Keith Putt, and Jeffrey W. Robbins, 272–281. Bloomington: Indiana University Press.

DeLanda, Manuel. 2006. *A New Philosophy of Society: Assemblage Theory and Social Complexity*. London: Continuum.

Deleuze, Gilles. 1990. *The Logic of Sense*. Trans. Constantin V. Boundas. New York: Columbia University Press.

——. 1994. *Difference and Repetition*. Trans. Paul Patton. New York: Columbia University Press.

Deleuze, Gilles and Félix Guattari. 1987. *A Thousand Plateaus: Capitalism and Schizophrenia*. Trans. Brian Massumi. Minneapolis: University of Minnesota Press.

Descartes, René. 1994. *Discourse on the Method*. Trans. George Heffernan. Notre Dame: University of Notre Dame Press.

Esbjörn-Hargens, Sean and Michael Zimmerman. 2009. *Integral Ecology: Uniting Multiple Perspectives on the Natural World*. Boston, MA: Integral Books.

Guattari, Félix. 1995. *Chaosmosis: An Ethico-Aesthetic Paradigm*. Trans. Paul Bains and Julian Pefanis. Bloomington: Indiana University Press.

——. 2000. *The Three Ecologies*. Trans. Ian Pindar and Paul Sutton. London: Athlone Press.

Hardt, Michael and Antonio Negri. 2001. *Empire*. Cambridge, MA: Harvard University Press.

Kaza, Stephanie. 2008. *Mindfully Green: A Personal and Spiritual Guide to Whole Earth Thinking*. Boston, MA: Shambhala Publications.

Keats, John. 1990. *The Love Poems of John Keats: In Praise of Beauty*. Ed. David Stanford Burr. New York: St. Martin's Press.

Kumar, Satish. 2013. "Three Dimensions of Ecology: Soil, Soul and Society." In *Spiritual Ecology: The Cry of the Earth*, ed. Llewellyn Vaughan-Lee, 129–141. Point Reyes, CA: The Golden Sufi Center.

Latour, Bruno. 2004. *Politics of Nature: How to Bring the Sciences into Democracy*. Trans. Catherine Porter. Cambridge, MA: Harvard University Press.

Light, Andrew (ed.). 1998. *Social Ecology after Bookchin*. New York: Guilford Press.

Light, Andrew and Eric Katz (eds). 1996. *Environmental Pragmatism*. New York: Routledge.

Long, Jeffery D. 2009. *Jainism: An Introduction*. London: I.B. Tauris.

Morin, Edgar. 1980. *La Méthode, II: La Vie de la Vie*. Paris: Éditions du Seuil.

——. 1999. *Homeland Earth: A Manifesto for the New Millennium*. Trans. Sean M. Kelly and Roger LaPointe. Cresskill: Hampton Press.

Naess, Arne. 1989. *Ecology, Community and Lifestyle*. Trans. Donald Rothenberg. Cambridge: Cambridge University Press.

Swimme, Brian and Thomas Berry. 1992. *The Universe Story: From the Primordial Flaring Forth to the Ecozoic Era – A Celebration of the Unfolding of the Cosmos*. San Francisco, CA: HarperCollins.

Whiteside, Kerry H. 2002. *Divided Natures: French Contributions to Political Ecology*. Cambridge, MA: MIT Press.

Wilber, Ken. 2000. *Sex, Ecology, Spirituality: The Spirit of Evolution*, 2nd revised edn. Boston, MA: Shambhala Publications.

Žižek, Slavoj. 2008. *In Defense of Lost Causes*. New York: Verso.

5   Roots of ecological wisdom

Many religions speak of wisdom: *hokmah* in Judaism, *'aql* in Islam, and *prajña* in Hindu and Buddhist traditions. Philosophers likewise have a lot to say about wisdom. Indeed, the very term "philosophy" (*philosophia*) designates a "love" (*philia*) of "wisdom" (*sophia*). The pursuit of wisdom seems to be one of the benefits of including philosophical and religious perspectives into an understanding of contemporary ecological issues. Yet, there is something boring about wisdom. The repeated sayings, maxims, and proverbs associated with wisdom often sound very profound but upon closer inspection they are often very vague, and they are just as vulnerable to counterarguments, reversals, and refutations as any other claim.

Sometimes wise sayings only sound wise because of the tone or the authority of the person saying them. When you take away the authority, the emphatic tone, or the charisma, wisdom starts to look more common, more banal. This is a point that the contemporary philosopher Slavoj Žižek (1997: 71–72) makes in his discussion of the "inherent stupidity of proverbs":

> Let us engage in a mental experiment by way of trying to construct proverbial wisdom out of the relationship between terrestrial life, its pleasures, and its Beyond. If one says, "Forget about the afterlife, about the Elsewhere, seize the day, enjoy life fully here and now, it's the only life you've got!" it sounds deep. If one says exactly the opposite ("Do not get trapped in the illusory and vain pleasures of earthly life; money, power, and passions are all destined to vanish into thin air – think about eternity!"), it also sounds deep. If one combines the two sides ("Bring Eternity into your everyday life, live your life on this earth as if it is already permeated by Eternity!"), we get another profound thought. Needless to add, the same goes for its inversion: "Do not try in vain to bring together Eternity and your terrestrial life, accept humbly that you are forever split between Heaven and Earth!" If, finally, one simply gets perplexed by all these reversals and claims: "Life is an enigma, do not try to penetrate its secrets, accept the beauty of its unfathomable mystery!" the result is, again, no less profound than its reversal: "Do not allow yourself to be distracted by false mysteries that just dissimulate the fact that, ultimately, life is very simple – it is what it is, it is simply here without reason and

rhyme!" Needless to add that, by uniting mystery and simplicity, one again obtains a wisdom: "The ultimate, unfathomable mystery of life resides in its very simplicity, in the simple fact that there is life."

If that is wisdom, then wisdom is basically an empty display of authority, whether it is the authority of a charismatic teacher or sage, or the authority of a tradition. It maintains the authority of the traditions or the leaders who propagate wise sayings, but it does not empower people to participate in the dynamics of planetary coexistence. That kind of wisdom would confuse instead of deepen an understanding of ecological problems.

The easy reversal or refutation of proverbs, maxims, and other pithy sayings is a symptom of the banality of wisdom. Appeals to charisma, authority, and simple sayings are no substitute for thinking. In that sense, claims to wisdom should always be subject to question and criticism. However, there is another sense of wisdom, one which is distinct from proverbs. It is one which empowers people to participate in the complexities of existence. Although many people claim that their idioms and catchphrases express wisdom, and many slogans are marketed as truths, this kind of wisdom is not to be found in short statements about how to live your life. Nor is this kind of wisdom a collection of ideas about how to live your life.

Wisdom in this sense is a practice of changing one's life. It is an example of what the philosopher Peter Sloterdijk (2012: 6) refers to as "the life of practice": "it seems contemplative without relinquishing characteristics of activity and active without losing the contemplative perspective. Practice, or exercise, is the oldest form of self-referential training with the most momentous consequences." Through the thoughtful and active work of training or exercise (*askesis*), the practitioner becomes transformed. In this sense, wisdom is best understood as a transformative exercise or as an ascetic practice to intensify and deepen one's thinking, feeling, and acting. Depending on the specifics of the training program, the practitioner can develop more capacities, cultivate virtues, learn skills, build relationships, and more. This is the real meaning of wisdom for philosophical and religious practitioners. It is not about sayings and slogans, or about appeals to authority and charisma.

Wisdom is about practice. It is a contemplative way of being in the world, an attentive and careful way of transforming one's relationships to oneself, society, and the natural world. Today, as wisdom-seekers find themselves situated in the context of worldwide ecological crises, and as environmental advocates find themselves in need of integrative visions, contemplative traditions and ecology are beginning to converge in developing practices of ecological wisdom. Douglas Christie refers to such practices in terms of "contemplative ecology" (Christie, 2013). For Christie, ecological wisdom is not to be found in just one religious tradition or in just one way of knowing. Contemplative ecology brings together transformative practices from multiple ways of knowing, including the perspectives of Christian contemplatives, monks, and theologians while also including perspectives from other religious traditions, and from poets, naturalists, and scientists.

In the current era of increasing planetary interconnectedness, it is important not only to encourage people to seek ecological wisdom, but also to seek dialogue with multiple sources of wisdom. In dialogue, contrasting approaches to wisdom can forge alliances with one another and facilitate cross-cultural and cross-disciplinary responses to the interlocking environmental, social, and existential crises of the planetary era. Multiple sources of ecological wisdom can come together with a shared interest in cultivating an integrative vision of ecology and facilitating mutually enhancing human–Earth relations. In short, diverse practices of ecological wisdom can nurture the development of whole Earth thinking and empower vibrant modes of planetary coexistence. In Stephanie Kaza's (2008: 85) account of the multiple sources of wisdom for whole Earth thinking, she notes that there are two ways to seek wisdom: (1) the systematic way, which involves following plans, committing to schedules, and studying regularly, and (2) the serendipitous way, which involves remaining open to changing circumstances and learning from what presents itself. Depending on your personal dispositions and the opportunities available to you, either the systematic or serendipitous way could be most suitable to you, or any combination of the two. The important thing is to recognize that your existence is situated in a whole ecosystem of traditions.

You live in a wisdom ecology, where multiple lineages of contemplative practice converge. "It is crucial to see yourself as part of an open system of wisdom transmission, flowing across time through generations and across space through networks of communication" (p. 86). There is no single path toward wisdom on which you might walk. "The wisdom-seeking process is not a single path nor a predictable path" (p. 95). To really engage in the training practices of wisdom is to completely immerse oneself in a complex network of wisdom sources, realizing that you are not a follower, and wisdom is not simply a road. Gary Snyder (1990: 161) makes this point while reflecting on the sense of the "way" (*Dao*) expressed in the ancient Chinese tradition of Daoism:

> The actuality of things cannot be confined within so linear an image as a road. The intention of training can only be accomplished when the "follower" has been forgotten. The way is without difficulty – it does not itself propose obstacles to us, it is open in all directions.

This chapter is about finding oneself in an open system of diverse sources of ecological wisdom, specifically in light of the approaches to wisdom expressed in the geophilosophy and ecosophy of Gilles Deleuze and Félix Guattari and in the work of the geologian Thomas Berry. Deleuze and Guattari provide tactics for crossing boundaries between multiple ways of knowing, and Berry complements their approach with his fourfold wisdom, which includes sources of wisdom from indigenous traditions, women, classical religious and philosophical traditions, and contemporary sciences. Whether training systematically, serendipitously, or both, the approaches to wisdom expressed by the geologian and geophilosophers can empower transformative practices of wisdom that integrate contrasting ecological perspectives and cultivate mutually enhancing human–Earth relations.

Tangled roots

Charles Darwin concludes *The Origin of Species* with a contemplative description of the interconnectedness of the life inhabiting a bank.

> It is interesting to contemplate a tangled bank, clothed with many plants of many kinds, with birds singing on the bushes, with various insects flitting about, and with worms crawling through the damp earth, and to reflect that these elaborately constructed forms, so different from each other, and dependent upon each other in so complex a manner, have all been produced by laws acting around us.
>
> (Darwin, 1991: 408)

That image has inspired many interpretations and analyses related to evolutionary theory, and it has been influential in the development of ecological sciences, specifically the concept of ecosystems (Hagen, 1992). The open ecosystem of diverse sources of wisdom may perhaps also be thought of like Darwin's tangled bank. The sources of wisdom are not isolated and independent from one another. They emerged in relationship to one another. Christian and Muslim interpretations of wisdom draw on Jewish sources; philosophers, artists, scientists, and theologians have influenced one another for thousands of years; Zen Buddhist practices bring together elements of multiple traditions, including Hinduism, Daoism, and Shinto (the tradition of the Ainu people, who are indigenous to Japan). Even if one tries to follow only one path on the way to wisdom, there is no single path that is not entangled with some other path, either throughout historical developments or through contemporary communication.

The ecosystem of wisdom traditions is a tangled bank. To use another image, if the sources of wisdom may be thought of as roots of wisdom, one could say that the roots of wisdom are tangled, like the root systems of tubers and bulbs, which grow in knotty systems, horizontal networks in which roots and shoots are sent out from the nodes. For Deleuze and Guattari, this would mean that wisdom is rhizomatic. They adapt the term "rhizome" from plant sciences to describe entangled, open systems, which are more complex than the vertical hierarchies of trees, where roots, trunk, branches, and leaves are neatly organized (Deleuze and Guattari, 1987: 6). Ginger, bamboo, crabgrass, and violets are examples of rhizomes, but for Deleuze and Guattari the term can apply to any system insofar as it is more entangled and complex than may be captured in a hierarchy or neatly ordered organization.

To say that the roots of wisdom are tangled like rhizomes is not to say that all of the sources of wisdom are the same. There are many points of overlap and similarity between different wisdom traditions, but the tangled traditions, lineages, and practices nonetheless retain their difference and multiplicity. The concept of the rhizome thus stands in contrast to the idea that beneath the surface differences between traditions there is one underlying wisdom – a "perennial philosophy," which is always the same but takes on different expressions in different traditions (Huxley, 2009). Rhizomatic networks exhibit connection with difference, consistency with multiplicity. Furthermore, rhizomes can take on stable structures, and they can also explode structures and open up possibilities for the creation of new structures. For instance, Christianity may be considered to be a relatively stable structure, but it has also undergone revolutionary transitions where old structures were broken or divided, such as the Great Schism in the eleventh century, when Eastern Orthodox Christianity split from the Church of Rome, and the Roman Church underwent another schism in the sixteenth century during the Protestant Reformation. Every approach to wisdom has its stabilizing and destabilizing moments, or as Deleuze and Guattari describe the situation, every rhizome has lines of segmentarity (territorialization; stabilizing) and lines of flight (deterritorialization; destabilizing). Stability and order are no better or worse than destabilization and transformation. Different contexts call for different configurations of stabilizing and destabilizing activity. Sometimes it is time to settle down and build, and at other times situations call for change and revolution.

The task of rhizomatic wisdom is to practice finding the most creative mixtures of order and transformation, structure and fluidity, closure and openness. This is the "wisdom of the plants" (Deleuze and Guattari, 1987: 11). It is also the wisdom of nomads, who are adept at making themselves at home while crossing multiple territories. Accordingly, rhizomatics is closely related to what Deleuze and Guattari call nomad science or "nomadology" (p. 351). Nomadology wanders outside of the official territories of different fields of study, opening up possibilities for new alliances and connections between multiple ways of knowing and multiple environments, societies, and subjects. Rhizomatics and nomadology also go by the name "pop analysis," which is a method for analyzing events that elude official standards, proper definitions, and authoritative interpretations (p. 24). What Deleuze and Guattari (1986: 26–27) call "pop" ("pop music, pop philosophy, pop writing") is an "escape for language, for music, for writing," an escape from any standards that exclude minorities and homogenize differences, an escape from the "oppressive quality" of any system that aims to be a master over others. Whether in philosophy, science, art, or some other mode of expression, pop analysis articulates open, entangled systems that have profound potentials for creative transformation.

A common thread in rhizomatics, nomadology, and pop analysis is the idea of crossing boundaries to build complex and creative networks. The movement of boundary-crossing may be described as "a transversal movement" (Deleuze and Guattari, 1987: 25). Transversal thinking "tends to be achieved when there is a maximum communication among the different levels and, above all, in different meanings" (Guattari, 1984: 18). Transversal thinking could be described like interdisciplinary or transdisciplinary thinking. There is no single way to participate in transversal thinking. The point is to engage with the networks in which one is involved and find opportunities to make creative connections.

There is no simply right way or wrong way to do it. The point is to experiment with making connections in a way that opens up creative possibilities for the Earth community. Rhizomatic wisdom – the wisdom of the plants – is grounded in terrestrial coexistence. The wisdom loved by philosophers must be an eco-logical wisdom (ecosophy), which is to say, a grounded, terrestrial wisdom (geophilosophy). If wisdom does not serve this world, it just becomes another abstract form of wisdom, another philosophy that serves oppressive standards and authorities. If it does not serve immanence, it is no better than the pithy wisdom that Žižek (1997: 71) describes as "inherent stupidity." Geophilosophers like Deleuze and Guattari (1994: 44) "carry out a vast diversion of wisdom; they place it at the service of pure immanence," at the service of Earth.

Crossing boundaries between multiple, entangled ways of knowing in order to cultivate creative connections in the service of Earth, the geophilosophy of Deleuze and Guattari resonates with Berry's approach to wisdom. However, Deleuze and Guattari tend to homogenize the creative possibilities of religious practices by referring to all religions as imperialistic or authoritarian (p. 89). In contrast, Berry presents a more inclusive vision of the sources of ecological wisdom, crossing boundaries between four sources of wisdom, which tangle together in various ways: (1) indigenous traditions; (2) classical religious and philosophical traditions; (3) the ways of knowing embedded in feminist per-spectives and the experiences of women, and (4) contemporary sciences. Those four traditions comprise the tangled roots of "a fourfold wisdom," which can "guide us into the future" as we reinvent ourselves and deepen our engage-ment with the complexity, community, and subjectivity of the Earth community (Berry, 1999: 176). Attaining this fourfold wisdom is an integrative practice. It is an "integral interpretation of experience," a transversal interpretation that emerges from a "primordial experience" of intimacy with the Earth community (Berry, 2009: 147). The remainder of this chapter provides a brief overview of each of the tangled roots of the fourfold wisdom. The point here is not to be exhaustive but to provide some entryways into creative engagements with integrative practices of ecological wisdom.

Indigenous traditions

There is not just one indigenous source of wisdom. Indigenous traditions are multiple and diverse, and they are never simply static but always change over time. Preceding the historical emergence of philosophy, science, and classical religions, indigenous traditions represent the oldest forms of ecological know-ledge, often called the traditional ecological knowledge (TEK) (see Chapter 2). Indigenous ways of knowing have been demonstrated to be quite capable of facilitating sustainable relationships between humans and their place. No tradition is free of problems or limitations in its ecological knowledge. There is no "ecological noble savage" (Buege, 1996). No one is perfect or ecologically inno-cent. At the very least, by eating to live you are inevitably complicit in some harm to another living being.

Without idealizing or romanticizing indigenous traditions, one can nonetheless appreciate those traditions as sources of practices for cultivating integrative visions of human–Earth relations.

> As the years pass it becomes ever more clear that dialogue with native peoples here [in the United States] and throughout the world is urgently needed to provide the human community with models of a more integral human-presence to the Earth.
>
> (Berry, 1999: 180)

What distinguishes indigenous wisdom from other sources is its sense of pro-found intimacy between all human and nonhuman participants in a place. As Berry notes, that intimacy is experienced through a unique sensitivity to the pres-ence of the sacred – "that numinous presence that is pervasive throughout the universe" (p. 178). The sacred is immanent, showing up in diverse fascinating and terrifying displays in the multifarious events of the natural world. A religious ecology in which sacred power is immanent in all things may be described as animism. Deriving from the Latin word for "soul" (*anima*), the term "animism" can refer to any view of the world in which some powers of agency, subjectivity, and personhood are distributed throughout all things – human and nonhuman – and are not located solely in humans or in some transcendent real separate from this world (Harvey, 2006).

Indigenous sources of wisdom may be found in practices of intimate participa-tion in the complexity, community, and subjectivity of places. Although there are increasing numbers of texts available that describe native perspectives (autobiog-raphies, anthropological research, novels, religious studies), native sources of wisdom are primarily oral- and place-based. Indigenous ways of knowing were not passed on primarily through writing.

> A native wisdom was passed down through the generations, a wisdom carried in the lives of the people, in their thoughts and speech; in their customs, songs, and rituals; in their arts, their poetry; and in their stories not in any written form. In a special manner this wisdom is carried by the sacred person-alities: the elders.
>
> (Berry, 1999: 177)

Those elders include men and women, leaders and healers (or, in somewhat restric-tive, outdated terms, "chiefs" and "shamans"). With stories, rituals, and symbols, elders mediate relationships between the diverse human and nonhuman members of a community. Wisdom in this context is a practice of engaging in one's ecological community. It is a practice of place-making. The anthropologist Keith Basso (1996: 121) describes wisdom in the context of the Western Apache, reporting a memor-able expression of one of the elders in that community: "Wisdom sits in places."

Wisdom is not just in books or in your head. Wisdom is not just in humans. Wisdom is an ecological practice of intimate participation in place. That wisdom is relevant today for many reasons. Consider the following three reasons. First, it is important to preserve and recuperate indigenous sources of wisdom so that indigenous communities have knowledge for practicing sustainable ways of life. That benefits the people in those traditions as well as the ecological communities they inhabit, and robust ecological communities are indirectly beneficial for the stability of planetary systems like climate, biodiversity, and the hydrological cycle. Second, this wisdom is also relevant insofar as it provides an external critique of late modern civilization. In the margins of that civilization, indigenous traditions have a unique perspective from which to criticize the reduction of wisdom to ideas in the human head and pithy sayings about life, and from which to criticize the displacement and destruction of intimate human–Earth relations for the sake of the narrow-minded values of individualism, consumerism, and corporate globalization. Third, this wisdom is relevant not only for indigenous peoples and their ecological communities, and not only for critical perspectives on modernism. It is also relevant for providing constructive perspectives that can support the efforts of non-natives to recuperate a sense of intimate participation with their place in the Earth community. This is a crucial point. Native traditions communicate practices that can empower non-natives to intimately intertwine with their place. For natives and non-natives, indigenous wisdom provides practices for "becoming native to this place" (Jackson, 1994).

Of course, non-natives cannot simply decide to become native. It is not like choosing from items at a buffet, picking up some modern habits along with a few pieces of indigenous wisdom. It is not like changing a pair of pants, as if you could just put on an indigenous lifeway and walk around in it for a while. It is an ongoing, intergenerational commitment to place-based knowledge. Gary Snyder (1990: 191) describes this knowledge as a commitment to "reinhabitation: moving back into a terrain that has been abused and half-forgotten – and then replanting trees, dechannelizing streambeds, breaking up asphalt." As a practice of wisdom, reinhabitation

> grounds and places you in your actual condition. You know north from south, pine from fir, in which direction the new moon might be found, where the water comes from, where the garbage goes, how to shake hands, how to sharpen a knife, how the interest rates work.
>
> (Snyder, 1990: 190)

Concepts of reinhabitation and becoming native are part of the movement of bioregionalism, of which Snyder is an advocate (see Chapter 1). Bioregionalism is about bringing place into history, so that places and ecological communities (bioregions) are treated like actors on the world's stage and not relegated to a background against which humans play out their cultural dramas (p. 44). Bioregionalism emerged as a movement in the United States in the 1970s with environmental and political efforts to bring decision-making back to local communities, back into place, so that decisions about human–Earth relations are not managed by corporations and governments, but are negotiated by the communities which live with the effects of those decisions. Deeply influenced by indigenous traditions, bioregionalism recognizes that the wisdom needed to cultivate mutually enhancing human–Earth relations does not sit in books or in the ingenuity of individual humans. The wisdom needed to cultivate a vibrant planetary coexistence is to be found in renewed intimacy with one's place in the Earth community.

Feminisms

No two people have the exact same experience of something. Every perspective is unique. Similarly, every contemplative practice is unique. The way to wisdom is not precisely the same for everybody. However, throughout history, some of the differences between multiple ways of knowing have been erased. Some approaches to wisdom have been marginalized or excluded from civilization, such as the marginalization of indigenous perspectives in modern societies. Throughout the past 5000 years, women have been systematically marginalized and excluded from societies around the world. The social system of patriarchy is the norm for many people. In that system, women are considered to be essentially subordinate to men, as if they are inherently less intelligent or less capable than men and, indeed, less human. Men are seen as having the full subjectivity of humanity, while women are viewed more like objects with no agency of their own. For instance, in patriarchal societies women have been excluded from voting and from other forms of political participation, such that political agency is distributed only among males (more specifically, males of a particular age, race, and socioeconomic class, such as adult, white, landowning males in the early history of the United States).

The twentieth century saw widespread movements of women (with some male allies) seeking the empowerment of women and the dismantling of sexist hierarchies that reduce women to a collection of objects. In short, there is not simply one feminism. There are multiple feminisms, many women's movements. Some of these movements focus on the struggle for rights, such as voting rights (women's suffrage), rights to education and employment, and reproductive rights. They facilitate the full participation of women in society beyond the notion of women's work, which is always and only housework (e.g., cleaning, childcare, and meal preparation). Along with attaining rights and opportunities, these movements also focus on opening up the very idea of "woman" to multiple expressions of gender and sexuality, such that there is no single essence or universal definition that applies to all women in all times and places.

Ecofeminism is the movement that focuses most explicitly on the ecological implications of patriarchy and sexism, whereas many scholars of environmental ethics argue that a key problem in the global ecological crisis is the anthropocentric attitude whereby humans focus primarily or exclusively on what is valuable to them, with little or no concern for the values of organisms and ecosystems. Ecofeminists add to this by arguing that the problem is not the centering of value upon the human (*anthropos*) but more specifically upon the male human (*andros*), with the values of women marginalized along with the values of life and nature. "This centering of men on themselves, to the detriment of women, the home, and the family as well as the Earth and everything on the Earth, is identified as *androcentrism*" (Berry, 1999: 181). The problem is not simply anthropocentrism but androcentrism.

The solution to androcentrism is not to replace it with a centrism that privileges women (gynocentrism). That would just be a reversal of the same "logic of colonization"; that is, the same pattern of binary oppositions that are used as justification for domination (Plumwood, 1993: 43). The solution is to dismantle rigid hierarchies (e.g., men/women, humans/nature, white/color, and reason/emotion) and open them up to multiple, dynamic possibilities for cultivating mutually enhancing relationships instead of relationships of violence and exploitation. In other words, the solution is to decolonize gender and sexuality. This calls for the wisdom of women. It calls for the voices of women to be heard on their own terms and not in terms of sexist hierarchies. It calls for a profound recognition of the uniqueness of women's experiences throughout history. "Out of their historical experience an immense store of wisdom is available to women for influencing the course of the future in its every aspect" (Berry, 1999: 183). Many efforts are already underway to include the historical experiences of women in the history of religions (Ruether, 2005), the history of sciences (E. F. Keller, 1995), and in the history of human–Earth relations (Merchant, 1990).

As with indigenous wisdom, including the wisdom of women has many benefits. It benefits women and their communities, because empowered women have more opportunities to care for themselves, their societies, and the natural environment. It contributes to critical perspectives on interlocking systems of domination that exploit and oppress beings based on sex and gender (sexism), skin color (racism), species (speciesism), socioeconomic status (classism), age (ageism), and ability (ableism). Furthermore, along with benefiting women and their communities, and along with providing critical perspectives on oppressive power relations, the wisdom of women supports the efforts of all genders and sexes to cultivate mutually enhancing human–Earth relations. As Deleuze and Guattari (1987: 277) put it, "becoming-woman" includes practices for all people to undo oppressive hierarchies and participate in the creative processes or "becomings" that connect humans to the universe: becoming-animal, becoming-molecular, becoming-intense, becoming-imperceptible, and becoming-cosmic. All efforts to ground a terrestrial wisdom can benefit from including the wisdom of women.

This role of the wisdom of women in facilitating mutually enhancing human–Earth relations is evident in Anna Peterson's discussion of some shared characteristics of feminist and ecofeminist perspectives on ethics. "Ecofeminism, like other forms of feminist philosophy, holds relationality up as a guide for ethical action and an ideal to be sought" (Peterson, 2001: 146). Ecofeminism shifts ethics away from principles, rules, and calculation, turning instead toward a sense of care for relationships. Along with the focus on relationality, many (eco)feminist theories attend to the "contextual-bodily" dimension of human thinking, feeling, and acting (p. 140). In other words, relationships do not take place in the same way for all people. They change depending on one's context and one's own bodily experience. This means that knowledge is always place-based and embodied. Every perspective is partial. Even the most objective scientific facts must be understood not as absolute universals but as "situated knowledges" (Haraway, 1991: 183). That does not make facts less true. It simply does away with the notion that knowledge comes out of nowhere. Knowledge comes from bodies in ecological and social contexts.

Along with a focus on relationality and contextual-bodily knowledge, ecofeminist ethics is often oriented around narrative. Formal arguments and abstract interpretations talk about problems as if they were still pictures, detached from the relationships and contexts of moving bodies. A narrative approach to ethics is about making decisions based on "an ongoing story rather than a snapshot, as it were, that tells nothing about the characters and their problems outside the moment in which a decision is required" (Peterson, 2001: 141). Narrative is a crucial component of ecological wisdom (see Chapter 9). Peterson notes that, for many feminists and ecofeminists, relationality, contextual-bodily knowledge, and narrative come together in an integrative conception of the human person, such that stories and experiences embedded in relational contexts are understood as the source and moral compass of human nature. In other words, relationships are "both a goal or moral behavior and a constitutive dimension of humanness" (p. 149). Moreover, these characteristics of ecofeminist perspectives overlap with the place-based ways of knowing that are prominent in indigenous traditions, specifically insofar as those ways of knowing focus on relationships, embodiment, context, and narrative. Accordingly, there are fruitful opportunities for collaboration between these approaches to wisdom, which does not only mean collaboration between native people and women. All people engaged in bioregionalism or ecofeminism can collaborate, working together to practice care for relationships (Plumwood, 1993: 186).

Classical traditions

During the ancient and medieval historical periods, the dominant approaches to wisdom were those articulated in classical traditions of philosophy and religion. During these periods, the animistic wisdom of indigenous traditions and the relational wisdom of women's experiences were marginalized and suppressed in favor of new approaches to wisdom. These new approaches were less place-based and relationally oriented and more focused on universal principles, written texts, formal rules, and rationality. For instance, philosophy, Buddhism, Confucianism, and Christianity all approach wisdom through the experiences of excellent role models – paradigmatic individuals like Socrates, the Buddha, Confucius, and Jesus (Jaspers, 1962). These religions are not restricted to particular places. They can travel anywhere that their texts and teachings can travel. For example, although the Bible refers to particular places, it is not based in place. You can pick it up and take it with you, and it will still make sense. The transportability of the

Bible enabled the Jewish tradition to survive at times when place-based living was relatively impossible, times of wandering, slavery, or dispersion (i.e., diaspora).

It seems that these traditions have severe limitations for ecological wisdom: their patriarchy, their suppression of animism, their detachment from place through literacy, and their detachment from community through a focus on paradigmatic individuals. What can classical traditions contribute to an ecological wisdom? For Berry, the contributions of classical traditions to the fourfold wisdom may be found in their sense of wisdom as aligning the individual self with the larger community of beings. In these traditions, "the fulfillment of the human" is to be found "in the larger functioning of the universe" (Berry, 1999: 193). Berry mentions examples of this in Hinduism, Buddhism, and Confucianism. In Hinduism, that wisdom (*prajña*) may be found in conceptions of the unity of one's deepest self (*atman*) with the ultimate reality of all existence (*brahman*). Wisdom may be attained through meditation and ritual, and it takes on many symbolic forms, such as images of deities like Ganesha and Saraswati. In Buddhism *prajña* is a practice of discerning the true nature of every being, its "Buddha Nature" which harbors potential for liberation from suffering. This discernment is sometimes represented with the Bodhisattva of wisdom, Manjushri, who is often depicted holding a sword that he uses for cutting through illusion to attain truth. In Confucianism, wisdom may be found in the idea of "One Body" expressed by the Neo-Confucian thinker Wang-Yang Ming, for whom all humans and non-humans should be cared for in order to realize the unity of humanity, forming one body with all beings.

Every tradition harbors contemplative practices for aligning one's individual self with the Earth community and with the entire cosmos. Following the methods used in the field of religion and ecology, classical religious traditions may be retrieved, re-evaluated, and reconstructed to draw out their ecological wisdom while remaining critical of the limiting and oppressive traits of those religions (Grim and Tucker, 2014: 86). For instance, in Christie's (2013: 190) contemplative ecology, he recovers biblical expressions of wisdom as *hokmah* (Hebrew) and *sophia* (Greek), which represent "the feminine creative principle through whom the world is birthed." Wisdom is the "enlivening force sustaining" the world (p. 189). This recovery makes it possible to re-examine wisdom, re-evaluating the notion that wisdom is a collection of abstract knowledge or pithy sayings. Such a notion prevents wisdom from promoting ecological concern. In contrast, Christie reconstructs the relational and contextual dimension of wisdom as the creative power that fosters the world's emergence.

A relational and contextual sense of wisdom, along with the feminine gender of *hokmah/sophia*, provides support for feminist theological efforts to recuperate feminine images of divine creativity (Johnson, 2002). Furthermore, Christie reconstructs the notion of wisdom to align it with indigenous approaches to wisdom. The indigenous understanding that "wisdom sits in places" may be found in the focus of early Christian monks on meditating in and on a particular place (*topos*), such as a cell, a desert, or a mountain cave (Christie, 2013: 128). This contributes to a sense of concern for ecological issues, including environmental problems related to the destruction of places and bioregions, social problems related to displacement and homelessness, and existential problems related to experiences of homesickness and a lack of a sense of belonging. Along these lines, it is clear that wisdom is not a view from nowhere, surveying things from above the fray, detached from the messiness of worldly affairs. It is not something that humans can possess and master. Quite to the contrary, wisdom comes through deep encounters with suffering, and it is never mastered with certainty but always remains "beyond the grasp of human beings" (p. 279).

Of all the classical traditions, the ungraspable and unattainable aspect of wisdom is particularly emphasized in philosophy, which positions itself in contrast to religions, always questioning the knowledge inherited from religious myths, symbols, and rituals. Philosophy emerged in ancient Greece among thinkers who attempted to interpret the world based on their own experience and their use of rational speech (*logos*) rather than accepting the status quo and uncritically believing what society and tradition deem true. While some philosophers maintain that they possess *sophia*, like the ancient sophists, a consistent theme throughout the entire history of philosophy is that a philosopher never fully attains wisdom but is always seeking it, desiring it, in love (*philia*) with *sophia*. This point is often attributed to Socrates, who is reported to have been told by a priestess (the Delphic oracle) that he is the wisest person in Athens. In one of Plato's dialogues, Socrates reflects on his claim, noting his disbelief that he is the wisest. Based on conversations with other Athenians, Socrates concludes that, if he is wiser than others, it is precisely because he knows that he does not know everything. One conversation left him thinking, "I *am* likely to be a little bit wiser than he in this very thing: that whatever I do not know, I do not even suppose I know" (Plato, 1998: 70).

Like other classical traditions, philosophy has benefits and limitations for ecological wisdom. Its limitations include patriarchy and other forms of the logic of colonization, a reliance on abstract principles instead of situated knowledge, a focus on individuals apart from their relationships, and the exclusion of non-rational ways of knowing (e.g., symbol, narrative, emotion, and embodiment). The ecological benefits of philosophy may be found in its commitment to questioning authority and encouraging people to think for themselves. Critical questioning attitudes are of the utmost importance for contemporary struggles to transform the status quo and undo the destructive attitudes, values, and beliefs guiding individuals and societies. Furthermore, there are thinkers and lineages in philosophy that aim to bring wisdom down to Earth and integrate humans into terrestrial existence. Consider the words of the nineteenth-century German philosopher Friedrich Nietzsche.

> Stay loyal to the earth. . . . May your bestowing love and your knowledge serve towards the meaning of the earth! Thus I beg and entreat you. . . . Lead, as I do, the flown-away virtue back to earth – yes, back to body and life: that it may give the earth its meaning, a human meaning!
>
> (Nietzsche, 1969: 102)

An Earth-based philosophy is what Deleuze and Guattari call geophilosophy. It does not follow the wisdom of human reason or the wisdom of authoritative texts or charismatic leaders, but the "wisdom of the plants": "Follow the plants" (Deleuze and Guattari, 1987: 11). Geophilosophy follows the wisdom of bodies moving in dynamic relationships and contexts. It is aligned with ecological wisdom (ecosophy) in thinking transversally. It crosses boundaries to create concepts *"to summon forth a new earth, a new people,"* which is to say, it creates concepts for integrating environments, societies, and subjects into vibrant modes of planetary coexistence (Deleuze and Guattari, 1994: 99). Deleuze and Guattari note that wisdom, whether philosophical or religious, is often expressed with notions that rely on escapist fantasies of otherworldly transcendence and often perpetuate imperialistic authorities and hierarchies (p. 89). Nonetheless, classical traditions hold much promise for the development of ecological wisdom. Retrievals, re-evaluations, and reconstructions of these philosophical and religious ways of knowing can empower contemplative practices for cultivating mutually enhancing human–Earth relations.

Sciences

Without contemporary scientific perspectives, ecological wisdom would not be very ecological. It is important to remember that the term "ecology" emerged from a scientific context in the nineteenth century as an extension of biological sciences to include the study of whole systems of the organism–environment relationships that comprise the evolutionary struggle for existence (see Chapter 2). Contemporary sciences have unique contributions to make toward ecological wisdom. As with indigenous traditions, feminist perspectives, and classical traditions, sciences are not without limitations, yet they hold much promise for developing practices that cross environmental, social, and subjective boundaries in ways which connect humans to their place and to the cosmos.

It is important to note that there is not one science, one model or paradigm to cover all scientific inquiry (Kuhn, 2012). Contemporary sciences are not the same as the early modern sciences of the seventeenth century, which are themselves quite different from ancient and medieval sciences, although they do share a common lineage and shared points of reference. Furthermore, the scientific tradition that began in ancient Greece is only one lineage among others, such as yoga, traditional Chinese medicine (TCM), and traditional ecological knowledge, which Gregory Cajete (1999) calls "native science." Berry honors those traditions in his fourfold wisdom, but the specific scientific contributions to ecological wisdom that Berry has in mind reflect the state of scientific knowledge in the twenty-first century, and not ancient, medieval, early modern, yogic, or traditional sciences. The scientific perspectives that Berry has in mind consider themselves distinct from philosophical, religious, and traditional ways of knowing.

In the ancient world, science and philosophy were not separated but were considered as two dimensions of the same study of the natural world. Science included any pursuit of knowledge about things. Indeed, the word "science" derives from the Latin *scientia*, which translates the Greek word for knowledge, *episteme*. Whereas science refers to the pursuit of knowledge, philosophy is a particular pursuit of knowledge which aims to understand the first sources and causes of things, the ultimate principles of reality, value, and knowledge. One could not practice science without involving philosophy, and one could not practice philosophy without involving science. Then, in the modern period, scientific perspectives increasingly distinguished themselves from philosophy and from what were considered superstitious pseudo-sciences such as alchemy and astrology. Philosophy, religion, and traditional ways of knowing include evidence from tradition and testimony and from many kinds of experience, including non-rational experiences of intense emotion, imagination, and ecstatic vision. In contrast, the method of modern sciences focuses on a narrow range of observable evidence that allows for unprecedented access to the quantifiable characteristics of the universe.

Modern science viewed the world like a calculable collection of objects, in short, a mechanistic universe. While that view ignores subjectivity, quality, and mystery, its practical applications in technological developments are undeniable (Berry, 1999: 191). The modern scientific view of the universe provided the knowledge that made possible the mechanistic technology of the Industrial Revolution. Modern science is complicit in immense destruction throughout the Earth community, which is not to say that it has not provided some benefits to some members of the human population. Despite the limitations of modern science, the experimental method of repeatable tests and observations granted a unique status to scientific inquiry, opening up the possibility for the ongoing articulation of increasingly intricate and comprehensive forms of scientific knowledge. As the trial-and-error process of hypothesizing, testing, and observing continued, the mechanistic paradigm began to crack.

Beginning in the nineteenth century and proceeding through the present day, the scientific view of the world as a calculable collection of separate, passive, inert objects has been giving way to a paradigm oriented around complex and communicative networks of active, dynamic, and self-organizing systems. This could be called postmodern or late modern science. This is the scientific approach that Berry considers part of the fourfold wisdom. It includes scientific developments such as the evolutionary theory, genetics, and ecology that began in the nineteenth century and many sciences that emerged in the twentieth century, including quantum and relativity theories of physics, evolutionary cosmology, chaos theory, and complex systems theory.

This period of scientific developments has facilitated the articulation of the interconnected and evolutionary dynamics of the universe, or, as Berry puts it, the "unity of the universe" (interconnected) and "the emergent nature of the universe" (evolutionary) (Berry, 1999: 192). To be is to be interconnected and to emerge over time; nothing is completely alone, and everything changes. Furthermore, those scientific developments have facilitated an articulation of the connections between human intelligence and the rest of the cosmos. Rather than seeing human subjective faculties as alien or unprecedented in a universe with no agency, contemporary sciences are finding varied forms of agency in nonhumans. For instance, biosemiotics studies agency and meaning in all kinds of living systems (Barbieri, 2008). Similarly, cognitive ethology studies the intelligences manifest in animal behavior (Allen and Bekoff, 1997). Indeed, self-organizing (autopoetic) dynamics may be found even in nonliving systems such as stars, galaxies, and atoms (Swimme and Berry, 1992: 75). In short, the universe is less like a collection of objects and more like an interdependent network of actors – a communion of subjects.

The wisdom of science is found in contemporary engagements with the emergent complexity and agency of all beings, from the microscopic and quantum levels of existence to the intergalactic and cosmic levels. This is relational and contextual wisdom, affirming that all existence is situated in complex networks. It is also narrative wisdom. In an evolutionary framework, the universe has a temporal structure like a narrative. As Brian Swimme and Mary Evelyn Tucker (2011: 6) put it, "the universe is unfolding and has a story – a beginning, a middle (where we are now), and, perhaps in some unimaginable future, an end." The story of our universe began approximately 13.8 billion years ago, with the Big Bang, and it is unfolding toward an uncertain future. It is a story with innumerable actors coming and going, relationships are constantly being created and broken, and new events keep happening. It is a story that situates human beings in the ongoing emergence of a communion of subjects.

Alongside indigenous traditions, feminist perspectives, and the philosophical and religious ways of knowing embedded in classical traditions, the scientific account of the universe story provides wisdom for the current era of planetary interconnectedness. "The story of the universe becomes the epic story of our times" (Berry, 1999: 193). Although the scientific account of the universe is not a religious story, it is not without some numinous dimension, some wholly other mystery that provokes tremendous awe and wonder in all those who contemplate its immensity. "This immense journey evokes wonder from scientists and non-scientists alike" (Swimme and Tucker, 2011: 4). Along with an integrative vision of the universe as a communion of subjects, each of the tangled roots of the fourfold wisdom encourages a sense of wonder, a sense of intimate participation in the uncertainty, ineffability, and mystery of the cosmos. Moreover, the fourfold wisdom is but one way to contemplate the tangled ecosystem of diverse lineages and traditions of wisdom. It is but one way of articulating practices for cultivating a sense of intimate participation in the environments, societies, and subjects of the world, a sense of what Tucker (2003) calls "worldly wonder." Berry (1999: 166) observes that "a widespread awakening to the wonder of the Earth" is taking place in the twenty-first century.

In our time of crisis, roots and shoots of ecological wisdom are growing around the planet. The widespread awakening of ecological wisdom is changing everything. It is changing lives, reorienting people to their bodies and places, compelling people to build mutually enhancing relationships with one another and with the whole Earth community.

References

Allen, Colin and Marc Bekoff. 1997. *Species of Mind: The Philosophy and Biology of Cognitive Ethology*. Cambridge, MA: MIT Press.

Barbieri, Marcello (ed.). 2008. *Introduction to Biosemiotics: The New Biological Synthesis*. Dordrecht: Springer.

Basso, Keith. 1996. *Wisdom Sits in Places: Landscape and Language Among the Western Apache*. Albuquerque: The University of New Mexico Press.

Berry, Thomas. 1999. *The Great Work: Our Way into the Future*. New York: Bell Tower.

——. 2009. *The Sacred Universe: Earth, Spirituality, and Religion in the Twenty-first Century*. Ed. Mary Evelyn Tucker. New York: Columbia University Press.

Buege, Douglas J. 1996. "The Ecological Noble Savage Revisited." *Environmental Ethics* 18(1): 71–88.

Cajete, Gregory. 1999. *Native Science: Natural Laws of Interdependence*. Santa Fe, CA: Clear Light Publishers.

Christie, Douglas E. 2013. *The Blue Sapphire of the Mind: Notes for a Contemplative Ecology*. New York: Oxford University Press.

Darwin, Charles. 1991. *The Origin of Species*. Amherst: Prometheus Books.

Deleuze, Gilles and Félix Guattari. 1986. *Kafka: Toward a Minor Literature*. Trans. Dana Polan. Minneapolis: University of Minnesota Press.

——. 1987. *A Thousand Plateaus: Capitalism and Schizophrenia*. Trans. Brian Massumi. Minneapolis: University of Minnesota Press.

——. 1994. *What is Philosophy?* Trans. Hugh Tomlinson and Graham Burchell. New York: Columbia University Press.

Grim, John and Mary Evelyn Tucker. 2014. *Ecology and Religion*. Washington, D.C.: Island Press.

Guattari, Félix. 1984. *Molecular Revolution: Psychiatry and Politics*. Trans. Rosemary Sheed. New York: Penguin Books.

——. 1995. *Chaosmosis: An Ethico–Aesthetic Paradigm*. Trans. Paul Bains and Julian Pefanis. Bloomington: Indiana University Press.

——. 2000. *The Three Ecologies*. Trans. Ian Pindar and Paul Sutton. London: Athlone Press.

Hagen, Joel. 1992. *An Entangled Bank: The Origins of Ecosystem Ecology*. New Brunswick, NJ: Rutgers University Press.

Haraway, Donna. 1991. *Simians, Cyborgs, and Women: The Reinvention of Nature*. New York: Routledge.

Harvey, Graham. 2006. *Animism: Respecting the Living World*. New York: Columbia University Press.

Huxley, Aldous. 2009. *The Perennial Philosophy*. New York: HarperCollins.

Jackson, Wes. 1994. *Becoming Native to This Place*. Lexington: University Press of Kentucky.

Jaspers, Karl. 1962. *Socrates, Buddha, Confucius, Jesus: The Paradigmatic Individuals*. Trans. Ralph Manheim. San Diego, CA: Harcourt Brace & Company.

Johnson, Elizabeth A. 2002. *She Who Is: The Mystery of God in Feminist Theological Discourse*. New York: The Crossroad Publishing Company.

Kaza, Stephanie. 2008. *Mindfully Green: A Personal and Spiritual Guide to Whole Earth Thinking*. Boston, MA: Shambhala Publications.

Keller, Evelyn Fox. 1995. *Reflections on Gender and Science*. New Haven, CT: Yale University Press.

Kuhn, Thomas. 2012. *The Structure of Scientific Revolution*, 50th anniversary edn. Chicago, IL: University of Chicago Press.

Merchant, Carolyn. 1990. "Gender and Environmental History." *The Journal of American History* 76(4): 1117–1121.

Nietzsche, Friedrich. 1969. *Thus Spoke Zarathustra: A Book for Everyone and No One*. Trans. R.J. Hollingdale. New York: Penguin Books.

Peterson, Anna L. 2001. *Being Human: Ethics, Environment, and Our Place in the World*. Berkeley: University of California Press.

Plato. 1998. *Apology of Socrates*. In *Four Texts on Socrates: Plato and Aristophanes*, revised edn, ed. and trans. Thomas West and Grace Starry West, 63–97. Ithaca, NY: Cornell University Press.

Plumwood, Val. 1993. *Feminism and the Mastery of Nature*. New York: Routledge.

Ruether, Rosemary Radford. 2005. *Integrating Ecofeminism, Globalization, and World Religions*. Lanham, MD: Rowman & Littlefield.

Sloterdijk, Peter. 2012. *The Art of Philosophy: Wisdom as Practice*. New York: Columbia University Press.

Snyder, Gary. 1990. *The Practice of the Wild*. Berkeley, CA: Counterpoint.

Swimme, Brian and Thomas Berry. 1992. *The Universe Story: From the Primordial Flaring Forth to the Ecozoic Era – A Celebration of the Unfolding of the Cosmos*. San Francisco, CA: HarperCollins.

Swimme, Brian and Mary Evelyn Tucker. 2011. *Journey of the Universe*. New Haven, CT: Yale University Press.

Tucker, Mary Evelyn. 2003. *Worldly Wonder: Religions Enter Their Ecological Phase*. Chicago, IL: Open Court.

Žižek, Slavoj. 1997. *The Abyss of Freedom*. Ann Arbor: University of Michigan Press.

6 Reinventing the human

Humans today find themselves within a planetary context. It no longer makes sense to imagine that humans live on Earth as if on a stage. Humans are living inside Earth, dwelling amidst its air, water, land, and life. We are active participants in Earth's processes, as is evident in human-generated (anthropogenic) phenomena such as global climate change, species extinction, pollution, toxic waste, deforestation, mountaintop removal, hydroelectric dams, and urbanization. Humans are not on top of Earth in a hierarchal sense either. Although humans have planetary impacts, we are by no means in charge or in control of the situation. We have some limited power to act and to affect planetary conditions, but we are vastly outnumbered by nonhuman beings of all shapes and sizes that also act. Their actions affect planetary conditions in ways that are difficult to calculate and predict.

Planetary problems are too complex to control. Consider climate change. The climate is conditioned by the chemical makeup of the atmosphere, and the atmosphere is too large to immediately impact. It takes time, and it requires the coordination of many factors worldwide, including the ways in which people eat, drive, and fly, the ways in which people make things, use them, and throw them away, and all of the ways in which people use energy. To complicate things further, climate change is caused by the burning of fossil fuels, which are foundational for the global market economy, providing it with the energy source it needs in order to maintain infinite or at least indefinite growth. This means that to some extent the climate crisis is a problem of the dominant paradigm (i.e., capitalism) driving the global economy (Klein, 2014). Changing the planet's atmosphere and the global economy are immense challenges on ecological, economic, psychological, and political levels. It is too big to grasp, too much to control. We are too deeply inside of it to find a position from which to control it. Such is human existence within a planetary context.

Human actions always produce unintended and unexpected consequences, and as those actions are becoming increasingly planetary in scale, the consequences are endangering more lives (including future generations) and putting the whole Earth community at risk. Is this what it means to be human? Do we belong to a species that is essentially a destructive presence on Earth, committing species suicide along with "biocide" and "geocide" (Berry, 1999: 74)?

"Does it follow that we are henceforth condemned to stand around like idiots in the face of the growth of the new order of cruelty and cynicism that is on the point of submerging the planet, with the firm intention, it seems, of staying" (Guattari, 2013: 36)? The multiple paths of ecological wisdom indicate that the answer to each of those questions is no. Being human does not simply mean endangering and destroying the Earth community, and we are not condemned to stand idly by and let it happen.

We are enmeshed in multiple sources of ecological wisdom that can facilitate a shift away from the life-negating, destructive patterns of human existence and toward more integrative, life-affirming ways of being in the world. This is the task of the geophilosophy of Gilles Deleuze and Félix Guattari (1994: 109), "*to summon forth a new earth, a new people,*" facilitating a renewal of humanity and a rejuvenation of planetary coexistence. This is the question of ecosophy for Guattari. How are we to "give back to humanity – if it ever had it – a sense of responsibility for its own survival, but equally for the future of all life on the planet," and even "for incorporeal species such as music, the arts, cinema, the relation with time, love and compassion for others, the feeling of fusion at the heart of the cosmos" (Guattari, 1995: 119–120)?

Thinking of the whole Earth community, becoming responsible for planetary coexistence: this is perhaps the greatest transition humanity has undergone since our species first emerged approximately 200,000 years ago. In any case, it is surely the greatest task facing humans today. It is the magnum opus of our current era. Thomas Berry (1999: 3) describes this task as the "Great Work" of our time: "to carry out a transition from a period of human devastation of the Earth to a period when humans would be present to the planet in a mutually beneficial manner." Such a task involves a radical renewal of human existence. It calls for us to undertake practices "to reinvent the human," to create new ways of being that care for the whole Earth community (p. 159). Humans are not on Earth to dominate, master, possess, and exploit. "We are here to become integral with the larger Earth Community" (p. 48).

An integrative reinvention of the human means more than rethinking a few ideas, making some new laws, or becoming a vegetarian. While those are not bad things to do, more is called for. Berry outlines multiple aspects involved in the reinvention of the human. Reinventing the human means rethinking the very nature of humanity, rethinking humans "at the species level" (p. 160). Furthermore, such reinvention must take place "with critical reflection" (p. 159). Critical thinking and discernment is crucial for thinking across multiple layers of environmental, social, and subjective dimensions of the human species. Not all reinventions are as effective as others in facilitating mutually enhancing human–Earth relations. Critical reflection provides means for distinguishing between different ways of being human in a planetary context.

To transform humans at the species level requires that humans situate themselves within the ecological dynamics of the Earth community (p. 161). Accordingly, a reinvention of the human cannot take place without understanding the complexity, community, and subjectivity of Earth (see Chapter 7).

The reinvention that Berry calls for also situates humans in the "*time-developmental context*" of the evolving universe (p. 162). To reinvent the human thus requires an understanding that the universe is not a giant container or background but is an unfolding, creative, and interconnected process (see Chapter 8). Finally, Berry says that the work of reinvention is activated "by means of story and shared dream experience" (p. 159). Non-rational ways of knowing embedded in narrative and imagination are necessary components of whole Earth thinking (see Chapter 9). The remainder of this chapter elaborates on the reinvention of the human, providing an overview of the emergence of the human species as a planetary presence, a discussion of critical reflections on humanity, humanism, and anthropocentrism, and an introduction of some ways of imagining the integration of the human species into its ecological and cosmic contexts.

Becoming human

The current scientific understanding of the evolution of the human species is relatively new. It has been approximately one and a half centuries since the release of Charles Darwin's application of his theory of evolution to humans, *The Descent of Man*, in 1871 (Darwin, 2004). Since then, scientific accounts of the evolutionary journey of the human species have become more intricate, reflecting increasing amounts of evidence and the development of more thorough methods and more nuanced theories. While many facts still remain to be known, there is a consensus among many scientists (e.g., anthropologists, archaeologists, geneticists, paleontologists) about some of the basic outlines of the evolutionary emergence of the human species. That evolutionary story has challenged long-held notions and provoked new ideas about the relationship of humans to other animals and the place of humans in the natural world. Accordingly, an understanding of some of the details of human evolution provides a context for critical reflection on the meaning of human existence.

The human species is approximately 200,000 years old. That marks the emergence of anatomically modern humans, *Homo sapiens sapiens* (one of but a few subspecies of *Homo sapiens*). Humans did not appear out of nothing. Characteristically human traits like upright posture and large brains developed gradually over time. Humans share some characteristics in various degrees with other species in the *Homo* genus, which emerged earlier over the course of the preceding two million years. The *Homo* genus itself shares important characteristics with primates that first appeared a few million years before them.

> Our current best evidence suggests that something of profound importance took place five to seven million years ago in Africa. . . . A new line of energetic apes emerged that would, over the next several million years, bring forth massive brains and learn to dwell in a world saturated with dreams.
>
> (Swimme and Tucker, 2011: 81)

The story begins with apes not much different than chimps living in forests somewhere around the center of the African continent. At the time, the climate was becoming drier, and food was becoming scarce. Some of the apes left the forests and headed for the open terrain of nearby savannahs. As early as four million years ago, there is evidence that the apes acquired capacities for walking on two feet (bipedalism). That would have facilitated their movement in open spaces. Also facilitating their movement was their expanding brain size, which accompanied increasing capacities for using tools.

Along with bipedalism and increased brain size, another important trait in the emergence of humans is "behavioral flexibility" (p. 84). Due perhaps to their brains or some genetic change, humans have an astounding openness to the world, like a childlike state of wonder, which is so amazed and awestruck that instinctual responses are muted and habits inhibited. All young mammals exhibit some behavioral flexibility relative to the mature members of their species. Holding onto immature traits (neoteny) for longer periods of time increases behavioral flexibility. One of the unique traits of humans is our indeterminately extended neoteny. We can be childlike our entire lives, always learning, playing, wondering, and trying new things. That openness provides the conditions for the "cumulative culture" or "collective learning" that characterizes human culture, where each generation can accumulate the knowledge of previous generations, add to it, and pass it along to future generations (Christian, 2011: 146–147). Collective learning involves the ongoing process of reflection, which means more than just thinking or communicating. It means thinking about thinking, communicating about communication. Reflexivity is evident in human uses of symbolic expressions like images and stories (Swimme and Tucker, 2011: 87). Humans can exteriorize thoughts and feelings in symbolic forms, and those symbols can then affect thoughts and feelings, which are then expressed with symbols, and so on. The reflexive process of cultural accumulation has made it possible for human civilization to undergo radical transformations while humans have remained anatomically identical.

Humans did not leave Africa until close to fifty thousand years ago (p. 83). Since then, humans have gradually distributed themselves around the planet, spreading symbols and cumulative culture as they traversed the planet's many terrains, making marks that we can still find today, from cave paintings to musical instruments, from tools to burial sites. A particularly radical transformation began approximately ten thousand years ago with the invention of agriculture, which includes plant and animal husbandry as well as practices of domestication (Christian, 2011: 207). This transformation involved a transition away from the less sedentary lives of nomads, gatherers, and hunters, leading the way to the development of cities and the stratified social systems associated with cities, where divisions between genders and classes are often very rigid. This is not to say that the Agricultural Revolution was a disaster. It also provided a surplus of food to stabilize and even grow the human population, which was only in the low millions at the time, nowhere near the current population, which is over seven billion and growing.

With the material conditions provided by agriculture, cities and eventually empires began to emerge around the planet. Cities have always been hubs of learning, catalyzing the development of cumulative culture. As cities continued to develop and empires continued to expand, new technologies and new ways of thinking developed as well, including writing, the phonetic alphabet, and classical traditions of philosophy and religion, science and mathematics, and enduring architectural achievements like the pyramids of Egypt and the Parthenon of Athens. Agriculture was not the sole cause of this creative explosion of culture, but it was a material condition without which there would not have been sufficient energy (e.g., food, fodder, and fuel) for this cultural explosion. Another revolution began with the widespread use in the modern era of another energy source: fossil fuels, particularly oil. Beginning in the eighteenth century, the Industrial Revolution supported increases in the human population and in rates of resource consumption. It enabled humans to become an increasingly planetary presence, mostly through ecological devastation. Powered with fossil fuel, industrial technology enabled the clear-cutting of forests, massive irrigation and damming projects, the building of highways, mining projects, and concentrated animal feeding operations (CAFOs, i.e., factory farms), all the while using the atmosphere as a dumping ground for carbon dioxide and other by-products emitted through the burning of fossil fuels.

Between their industrial technology and their ideals of progress and the mastery of nature, "modern humans transformed the planet into a bundle of resources" (Swimme and Tucker, 2011: 100). Through cumulative culture and the discovery of powerful energy sources, the symbolic consciousness of human beings has become intimately intertwined with the whole Earth community. The Holocene epoch that began around the time of the invention of agriculture is now ending. The Anthropocene is beginning, an epoch in which planetary systems are affected by human decisions.

> Because of the power of symbolic consciousness to amplify our control, humans have begun to alter the very functioning of what was previously an entirely wild selection process in nature. We have crossed over into an Earth whose very atmosphere and biosphere are being shaped by human decisions. . . . We have thus radically altered the evolutionary dynamics of Earth.
>
> (Swimme and Tucker, 2011: 101)

This transformation is so radical that it is occasioning a mass extinction of species (p. 102). Life on Earth has not seen this radical an alteration since the last mass extinction event, when the dinosaurs went extinct around sixty-five million years ago.

A planetary human is emerging. It is not anatomically different from the first humans, or from the humans of agricultural or early industrial societies. It still has the same bipedalism, big brain, and behavioral flexibility. However, the environmental, social, and subjective conditions of the human species have changed dramatically. Through the ongoing learning process of cumulative culture and the development of large-scale, complex societies, humans have become an Earth-shaping force that is endangering their own future and the future of all life on Earth. It is too late to avoid the Anthropocene. We cannot undo what has been done or unlearn what we have learned. The human species is planetary, intimately entangled with the whole Earth community. If humans ever thought that they were in control of the natural world or were the most important kind of being in the universe, it is impossible to think that anymore, because the human can no longer be neatly separated from the rest of the planet.

Critical reflection

As the human species is undergoing a transition into a planetary phase, it is imperative to use critical reflection to discern the difference between creative, life-affirming responses to this transition and responses that propagate destruction and devastation to humans and the rest of the Earth community. For Berry, critical reflection includes scientific and technical knowledge (Berry, 1999: 161). While those forms of knowledge are surely necessary for cultivating mutually enhancing human–Earth relations, the range of their critical thinking is relatively narrow. Deleuze and Guattari point to further sources of critical reflection, which are often grouped together into a philosophical movement called critical theory (Schrift, 2014; Simons, 2010). There are many variations of critical theory, but they have in common a shared concern for drawing upon sciences and humanities to express resistance to oppressive social systems and to empower the emancipation of the oppressed and exploited.

Some feminist theorists use critical theory to question and transform patriarchal power systems. Some critical theorists draw upon Karl Marx to analyze inequalities and injustices in the functioning of the supposedly "free" markets of capitalism. Critical theorists often challenge the basic values of modernism, arguing that individualism alienates people from their communities and rationalism reduces everything to a mere object. Along those lines, many critical theorists may be called postmodern. They may also be called postcolonial insofar as they inherit a planet thoroughly worked over by colonialism, and they often challenge the oppressive power relations of new forms of colonialism (neocolonialism), like a corporation based in the United States imposing its activities upon other countries. Many critical theorists may also be described as postsecular. They generally do not adhere to religious traditions in any strict sense, yet they are also critical of the secularism of modern society for privileging rational knowledge to the exclusion of other ways of knowing. With postmodern, postcolonial, and postsecular perspectives, critical reflection can contribute to a reinvention of the human that overcomes systems of alienation, inequality, exclusion, and domination. Furthermore, drawing from scientific and technical knowledge and from critical theory, posthumanist perspectives may be added to this list.

Posthumanism comes after the humanism of classical and modern traditions. In many ways, the perspectives in those traditions focus on the meanings and values of human existence to the exclusion of nonhuman modes of terrestrial existence.

In other words, those traditions contain relatively anthropocentric perspectives, including metaphysically anthropocentric perspectives, which view humans as having unique value that sets them apart in the universe, and ethically anthropocentric perspectives, for which humans are the only or primary recipients of ethical concern. This is not to say that there are not sources in classical traditions for cultivating mutually enhancing human–Earth relations. They contain profound sources of ecological wisdom (see Chapter 5). Nonetheless, they also harbor anthropocentric tendencies. Even Buddhism, which many environmentalists consider ecologically friendly due to its emphasis on the interdependent connectedness of all beings, may be considered anthropocentric or at least "weakly anthropocentric" insofar as it includes a focus on one's personal quest for liberation, which may exclude ecological concerns (Sahni, 2008: 88).

The eighteenth-century German philosopher Immanuel Kant exemplifies a modern sense of humanism. For Kant, only humans have value in themselves, apart from the values that others attribute to them. Each human is an end in itself, not simply a means to an end. Accordingly, humans have direct duties to respect the values of other humans and not treat humans as if they are just objects. Animals, plants, rivers, forest, fungi, biodiversity, and the atmosphere do not have value in themselves. They are only objects, means to whatever ends humans may assign to them. The only duties humans have toward nonhumans are indirect duties: "animals must be regarded as man's instruments," yet "we have duties toward the animals because thus we cultivate the corresponding duties toward human beings. . . . Our duties towards animals, then, are indirect duties toward mankind," and similarly, "duties toward inanimate objects" are "indirectly duties towards mankind" (Kant, 1963: 240–241). In other words, animals or rivers should only be respected because it is good practice for ensuring that one respects humans. It is not directly wrong to physically abuse a dog. It is only indirectly wrong because it cultivates a habit that could lead one to beat a human.

Reflecting the cynicism and malaise of the twentieth century, some proponents of existentialism described themselves in terms of humanism, holding that humans are the only and lonely source of value and meaning in a world that is essentially valueless and meaningless (Sartre, 2007). In that case, the only way that you have any duties to other beings – human or nonhuman – is by deciding for yourself as an individual whether other beings have value. From the classical humanism of paradigmatic individualism like Confucius, the Buddha, and Socrates to the modern humanisms of Kant and existentialists, posthumanism resists any attempts to grant the human species an exclusively central or exceptional significance as opposed to the rest of the cosmos, whether as the main recipient of concern or as the primary or only source of meaning in the universe. Posthumanism resists all forms of human exceptionalism, which is relatively synonymous with anthropocentrism, speciesism, human chauvinism, and human narcissism.

Whether classical or modern, humanisms cannot account for the complex connections entangling humans with the environmental, social, and subjective dimensions of the Earth community. Posthumanism resituates the human species within its ecological and cosmic contexts. This is not the same as transhumanism. Both posthumanism and transhumanism are critical of humanisms, but transhumanists aim to transform the human species in a way which transcends the human condition through technological enhancements that increase human potential and bypass limitations like aging, sickness, and bodily death. Although they agree in their critical stance toward humanism, "posthumanism is the *opposite* of transhumanism," with the latter intensifying human exceptionalism while the former "opposes the fantasies of disembodiment and autonomy, inherited from humanism itself" (Wolfe, 2010: xv).

With critical reflection, posthumanism signifies a transition. It is a transition to a rejuvenated sense of the world, an integrative participation in the cosmos. Through critical reflection, humans can reinvent themselves to become "integral with the process" of the unfolding cosmos and experience "the universe with the delight of our postcritical naiveté" (Berry, 1999: 116). This transition to a post-critical condition is not a transhumanist transition away from embodiment and material conditions. It is a transition toward a more intimate engagement in ecological relationships, an engagement that does not erase or transcend the human but resituates human nature into wild nature, such that humans find the natural world while also finding themselves. This is similar to the point that Gary Snyder (1990: 74) makes regarding posthumanism.

> The "post" in *posthumanism* is on account of the word *human*. The dialogue to open next would be among all beings, toward a rhetoric of ecological relationships. This is not to put down the human: the "proper study of mankind" *is* what it means to be human. It's not enough to be shown in school that we are kin to all the rest: we have to feel it all the way through. Then we can also be uniquely "human" with no sense of special privilege. . . . When humans know themselves, the rest of nature is right there.

This entails that one cease being anthropocentric, but not simply in order to become non-anthropocentric instead.

Whole Earth thinking is not about putting the human species down in order to lift up nonhuman nature. It criticizes anthropocentrism not just for positioning the human in a superior position relative to the rest of the universe. It criticizes the very distinction that opposes the human to the natural world or opposes anthropocentrism to non-anthropocentrism. Posthumanism opens up possibilities to reinvent the human in a way that integrates the human into planetary and cosmic communion. Neither anthropocentric nor non-anthropocentric, a cosmically connected human is anthropocosmic.

Becoming anthropocosmic

Since the 1970s, with the emergence of environmental ethics, deep ecology, ecofeminism, and other environmentally oriented movements and schools of thought, many scholars and activists became engaged in projects to criticize anthropocentrism and construct non-anthropocentric models to guide human thinking, feeling, and acting. However, non-anthropocentrism has its own limitations, as may be seen in the two predominant alternatives to anthropocentrism: biocentrism and ecocentrism (Gudorf and Huchingson, 2010: 4–15). Biocentrism and ecocentrism have supported efforts to attend to the values intrinsic to individual living organisms (biocentrism) and to whole ecosystems (ecocentrism). However, they also have tendencies to relegate human issues to the periphery of ethical and political concern, marginalizing social problems like sexism, racism, and poverty. Basically, whenever something is given the special privilege of a "central" position, other beings become peripheral, subordinate, marginalized. Anthropocentric perspectives attend to human existence while ignoring or exploiting nonhuman organisms and ecosystems, and non-anthropocentric positions have the reverse problem – caring for nonhumans while ignoring human interests and even becoming anti-human or misanthropic.

The problem of anthropocentrism does not just require a new form of centrism, where something other than humans gets the special privilege of being at the center. Mutually enhancing human–Earth relations require a reinvention of the human which criticizes the false dichotomy separating humans from the rest of the natural world, a reinvention that recuperates the intimate intertwining of *anthropos* and *kosmos*. Such a reinvention would carry out a transition from anthropocentric and anthropocosmic ways of being in the world. Despite the predominance of anthropocentrism in classical and modern traditions, anthropocosmic perspectives may be found in the ecological wisdom of philosophical, scientific, and religious interpretations of humanity. As Grim and Tucker (2014: 56) observe, "anthropocosmic views of the human as emerging from out of the processes of nature provide new orientations for mutually enhancing human–Earth relations of participation rather than domination."

Interpreted anthropocosmically, the human species is entangled in complex interrelations with the rest of the natural world. Our species is unique, but it is not separate from the cosmos. Along similar lines, some feminists and environmental philosophers have developed concepts of the self as an ecological self; that is, a relational or connective self, which is not separate from the natural world (separative self), yet it is not simply "at one with" or continuously identical to the natural world either (Keller, 1986). Along these lines, Val Plumwood (1993: 179) criticizes the ecological self of deep ecology, which aims for a complete merger of self and cosmos, uncritically reversing the problem of the self/world "hyperseparation" and thereby perpetuating a "false choice" between continuity (unity) and difference (separation). The relational self is "a complex, interacting pattern of both continuity and difference" with the rest of the world (p. 67). "We need to understand and affirm both otherness and our community in the earth" (p. 137).

Becoming anthropocosmic means participating in the uniqueness and connectedness of humans in relationship to the natural world. It is about finding oneself entangled in complex networks that extend to multiplicities of other humans and nonhumans. The geophilosophy of Deleuze and Guattari points to such a view. They discuss the connective fibers of the cosmos. "A fiber stretches from a human to an animal, from a human or an animal to molecules, from molecules to particles, and so on to the imperceptible. Every fiber is a Universe fiber" (Deleuze and Guattari, 1987: 249). Humans are not separate from cosmic processes. We are not isolated things inside of a cosmic container. Seeking ecological wisdom, we realize that we are participants in the creative processes of cosmic complexity, community, and subjectivity. "We are not in the world, we become with the world. . . . We become universes. Becoming animal, plant, molecular" (Deleuze and Guattari, 1994: 169). Perhaps that is what it means to be human. "Perhaps that is why we are here – to drink so deeply of the powers of the universe we become the human form of the universe. Becoming not just nation-state people, but universe people" (Swimme and Tucker, 2011: 112–113).

An important philosophical contribution to an anthropocosmic interpretation of human existence comes from the twentieth-century French philosopher Gaston Bachelard. He is particularly important because, in his analysis of poetic images of intimate spaces, he explicitly proposes an "anthropo-cosmology" (Bachelard, 1994: 47). To understand the intimate relationships that humans experience with the world around them, one must understand the connective tissue between humans and the cosmos. Bachelard considers a diverse array of anthropocosmic images expressed in poetry and literary images, including images of intimate spaces at multiple scales, from nests and shells, to drawers and houses, and even to the immensity of the whole cosmos. Cosmic immensity is not simply an exterior, an outside, which exists somewhere else, over there. Immensity is intimately interwoven into each actor in the evolutionary epic of the universe. It is "*inner immensity*," "intimate immensity" (183–185).

In much the same way that your early childhood relationships with your parents shape your identity and continue to condition your experience throughout your life, intimate relationships with places shape all humans and condition our sense of the world. Along with "parental complexes," there are "anthropocosmic complexes" that affect who we are (Bachelard, 1971: 123). The intimacy of anthropocosmic complexes can be lost, whether collectively as with shared values of anthropocentrism, or individually as in personal experiences of alienation, displacement, and homesickness. The "anthropocosmic ties" connecting humans with the cosmos can become slack, frayed, and undone, leaving the human feeling like a lonely subject set over against the rest of the cosmos, which becomes nothing but an object (Bachelard, 1994: 4). For Bachelard, experiences of poetic imagination can tighten and retie intimate interconnections between humans and the myriad habitats and inhabitants with which they share space. Similarly, for Deleuze and Guattari (1994: 169), it is through contemplative vision that humans can integrate into the creative process of the cosmos: "we become with the world; we become by contemplating it."

Images, visions, and symbols for tying humans together with the cosmos may also be found in religious traditions. The academic field of religious studies can contribute much to a transformation of human existence through a recovery of the vast sources of anthropocosmic symbolism found in religious traditions. This point is expressed by the historian of religions, Mircea Eliade (1991: 36).

> Still with the aid of the history of religions, man might recover the symbolism of his body, which is an anthropocosmos. What the various techniques of the imagination, and especially poetic techniques, have realised in this direction is almost nothing beside what the history of religions might promise. . . . By regaining awareness of his own anthropocosmic symbolism – which is only one variety of the archaic symbolism – modern man will obtain a new existential dimension.

Anthropocosmic experiences can be occasioned by contemplating images and narratives that envision correspondences between the human (microcosm) and macrocosmic entities like a mountain, a river, the sun, and the whole universe. Your eyes are stars, your body is a mountain, your veins are rivers, and your house is the cosmos. Becoming anthropocosmic, the human becomes "a living cosmos open to all the other living cosmoses" (Eliade, 1970: 455).

The recovery of anthropocosmic perspectives has been taken up by many scholars in the field of religion and ecology. Although Berry never uses the term "anthropocosmic," he finds such a vision in Hindu images of the human as a microcosm ("microcosmos") and the cosmos as a macro-human ("macranthropos"): "We are each the cosmic person, the *Mahapurusha*, the Great Person of Hindu India, expressed in the universe itself" (Berry, 1999: 175). As an example of someone who explicitly uses the term, Tu Weiming (1985) discusses an "anthropocosmic" vision in the Confucian worldview. He finds it expressed in the Confucian concept of a fundamental "unity of Heaven and humanity" (*tianrenheyi*), which envisions human existence emerging out of a series of overlapping concentric circles, like a ripples on the water after a stone is thrown into a pond. To be human is to participate in overlapping spheres of human community, terrestrial environment, and the cosmos as a whole. Tu (2001) emphasizes the ecological wisdom of this anthropocosmic vision, which he sees as contributing to an "ecological turn" in contemporary Confucianism and in Chinese models of development oriented toward ecological cultures.

Adding to this Confucian perspective, James Miller (2001: 279) claims that another Chinese religious tradition also has an "anthropocosmic vision," which affirms "the mutual implication of human beings, their social systems, and their natural environment." Miller observes that there is an anthropocosmic vision in the ancient Chinese religion of Daoism, for which humans and the natural world are conceived of as participants in one dynamic process, one "path" or "way" (*Dao*). Daoist and Confucian perspectives are quite different, like yin and yang, with Daoists tending toward spontaneity and immersion in nature, and Confucians tending toward systematic plans, education, and self-cultivation. Their different approaches converge in recognizing anthropocosmic connectivity. From Confucian or Daoist perspectives, one would not have to choose between caring for human health (anthropocentrism) and caring about planetary systems. They are intertwined. They are aspects of the same path. Climate change is a problem affecting the integrity of the atmosphere and, therefore, also a problem for my human existence.

One might suppose that such perspectives, while easily found in East Asian traditions, is not so easily found in theistic traditions like Judaism, Christianity, and Islam, where human–Earth interdependence can become eclipsed by the high importance placed on human relations with the divine. However, as William Chittick (2002: 149) notes in his account of the anthropocosmic perspectives in the Islamic philosophical tradition, an anthropocosmic vision "is normative for the human race" and is not exclusive to any particular tradition. The transition from anthropocentric to anthropocosmic ways of being in the world is crucial for the entire human species as we reinvent ourselves in an era of planetary interconnectedness.

> We are cracking open the shell of our anthropocentric selves and our particular religious traditions to move toward more expansive religious sensibilities that embrace both Earth and universe. New configurations of tradition and modernity will emerge, and with them will come retrieval of texts, reconstruction of theologies, renewal of symbols and rituals, and re-evaluations of ethics, and, most importantly, a revivified sense of wonder and celebration.
>
> (Tucker, 2003: 52)

Along with anthropocosmic perspectives in religion and philosophy, "a reformulated anthropocosmic perspective is now being rediscovered amid scientific ecology and evolution" (Grim and Tucker, 2014: 44). Ecology and evolution both envision interconnections between humans and the rest of the natural world. Evolution imagines these connections across massive time-scales, crossing the evolution of humans, primates, mammals, animals, the first life on Earth, the formation of the solar systems, and the Big Bang. Ecology focuses on connections between species and their environmental conditions, connecting humans to the air, sunlight, water, land, and entire community of life on Earth. Situated in an ecological and evolutionary context, the opposition between humans and the cosmos gives way to anthropocosmic connectivity.

Early modern science tended toward a view of the world as an inert machine obeying predictable laws, leaving human subjects feeling isolated and alone in an unfeeling universe. The scientific developments of the twentieth century changed things. Inquiries into quantum physics, relativity theory, systems theory, and evolutionary cosmology have rendered the early modern mechanistic view of the universe obsolete, opening the way for a more integrative view, wherein humans are seen as active participants enmeshed in a creative and interconnected cosmos (Hollick, 2006). Challenging the restriction of subjectivity and self-directed (autonomous) agency to humans, analyses of complex systems have provided evidence that there is self-organizing (autopoietic) activity at all scales of existence, atoms and stars, cells and organisms, ecosystems and cities.

Studying the diverse array of self-organizing systems throughout the universe, the complex systems researcher Stuart Kauffman (1995) envisions human subjects "at home in the universe." Similarly, the anthropologist Terrence Deacon (2011) has contributed to an understanding of the process of emergence, whereby the subjectivity of the human mind developed out of the self-organizing dynamics inherent in the physical, chemical, and biological systems of terrestrial existence. It is becoming increasingly difficult to maintain the view that the material world is a collection of passive, inert, meaningless objects. Scientific knowledge of creative emergence, complexity, and self-organization in matter, life, and humans suggests that the cosmos is much more like a communion of subjects than a collection of objects. Such scientific knowledge contributes to the recognition that human existence is always already entangled with intimate immensity. Contemporary sciences thus cross paths with philosophical and religious approaches for which becoming human means becoming anthropocosmic.

Drawing upon ecological wisdom embedded in philosophy, religion, and science, one can participate in the reinvention of the human at the species level, maintaining a critical attitude toward anthropocentric and humanistic perspectives while retying the anthropocosmic threads that can orient human thinking, feeling, and acting toward the cultivation of mutually enhancing human–Earth relations. Reinventing the human, becoming anthropocosmic, humans are opening up to a new understanding of themselves as a species as well as a new understanding of Earth and the cosmos. Finding ourselves, we find the world. "When humans know themselves, the rest of nature is right there" (Snyder, 1990: 74).

References

Bachelard, Gaston. 1971. *The Poetics of Reverie: Childhood, Language, and the Cosmos*. Trans. Daniel Russell. Boston, MA: Beacon Press.
———. 1994. *The Poetics of Space*. Trans. Maria Jolas. Boston, MA: Beacon Press.
Berry, Thomas. 1999. *The Great Work: Our Way into the Future*. New York: Bell Tower.
———. 2009. *The Sacred Universe: Earth, Spirituality, and Religion in the Twenty-first Century*. Ed. Mary Evelyn Tucker. New York: Columbia University Press.
Chittick, William. 2002. "The Anthropocosmic Vision in Islamic Thought." In *God, Life and the Cosmos*, ed. Ted Peters, Muzaffar Iqbal, and Syed Nomanul Haq, 125–49. Burlington, VA: Ashgate.
Christian, David. 2011. *Maps of Time: An Introduction to Big History*. Berkeley: University of California Press.
Darwin, Charles. 2004. *The Descent of Man*. London: Penguin Classics.
Deacon, Terrence. 2011. *Incomplete Nature: How Mind Emerged from Matter*. New York. W.W. Norton.
Deleuze, Gilles and Félix Guattari. 1987. *A Thousand Plateaus: Capitalism and Schizophrenia*. Trans. Brian Massumi. Minneapolis: University of Minnesota Press.
———. 1994. *What is Philosophy?* Trans. Hugh Tomlinson and Graham Burchell. New York: Columbia University Press.
Eliade, Mircea. 1970. *Patterns in Comparative Religion*. Trans. Rosemary Sheed. Cleveland, OH: World Publishing.

——. 1991. *Images and Symbols: Studies in Religious Symbolism*. Trans. Philip Mairet. Princeton, NJ: Princeton University Press.

Grim, John and Mary Evelyn Tucker. 2014. *Ecology and Religion*. Washington, DC: Island Press.

Guattari, Félix. 2013. *Schizoanalytic Cartographies*. Trans. Andrew Goffey. London: Bloomsbury Academic.

Gudorf, Christine E. and James E. Huchingson. 2010. *Boundaries: A Casebook in Environmental Ethics*, 2nd edn. Washington, DC: Georgetown University Press.

Hollick, Malcolm. 2006. *The Science of Oneness: A Worldview for the Twenty-first Century*. New York: O Books.

Kant, Immanuel. 1963. *Lectures on Ethics*. Trans. Louis Infield. Indianapolis, IN: Hackett Publishing.

Kauffman, Stuart. 1995. *At Home in the Universe: The Search for Laws of Self-organization and Complexity*. Oxford: Oxford University Press.

Keller, Catherine. 1986. *From a Broken Web: Separation, Sexism, and Self*. Boston, MA: Beacon Press.

Klein, Naomi. 2014. *This Changes Everything: Capitalism vs. the Climate*. New York: Simon & Schuster.

Miller, James. 2001. "Envisioning the Daoist Body in the Cosmic Economy of Power." *Daedalus* 130(4): 265–282.

Plumwood, Val. 1993. *Feminism and the Mastery of Nature*. New York: Routledge.

Sahni, Pragati. 2008. *Environmental Ethics in Buddhism: A Virtues Approach*. New York: Routledge.

Sartre, Jean-Paul. 2007. *Existentialism is a Humanism*. Trans. Carol Macomber. New Haven, CT: Yale University Press.

Schrift, Alan D. (ed.). 2014. *Poststructuralism and Critical Theory's Second Generation*. New York: Routledge.

Simons, Jon (ed.). 2010. *From Agamben to Žižek: Contemporary Critical Theorists*. Edinburgh: Edinburgh University Press.

Snyder, Gary. 1990. *The Practice of the Wild*. Berkeley, CA: Counterpoint.

Swimme, Brian and Mary Evelyn Tucker. 2011. *Journey of the Universe*. New Haven, CT: Yale University Press.

Tu, Weiming. 1985. *Confucian Thought: Selfhood as Creative Transformation*. Albany: State University of New York Press.

——. 2001. "The Ecological Turn in New Confucian Humanism: Implications for China and the World. *Daedalus* 130(4): 243–264.

Tucker, Mary Evelyn. 2003. *Worldly Wonder: Religions Enter Their Ecological Phase*. Chicago, IL: Open Court.

Wolfe, Cary. 2010. *What is Posthumanism?* Minneapolis: University of Minnesota Press.

7 Emerging Earth community

Humans inhabit a planet, a moving body, which is rotating on its axis while orbiting the sun. That may seem obvious, but it has taken a long time for our species to come to this knowledge. Out of the 200,000 years that our species has existed, only in the past 500 years have humans entered "the Planetary Era"; that is, the era in which humans discover that "Earth *is* a planet" (Morin, 1999: 6).[1]

Especially after the scientific contributions of Copernicus and Galileo in the sixteenth and seventeenth centuries, it became increasingly widespread and accepted knowledge that humans do not live on a stationary foundation but on moving ground, an orb flying through space. Prior to that, Earth was not considered to be a planet.

The astronomers of ancient societies observed that some celestial bodies move over time, while others seem motionless. For instance, to an observer in the Northern Hemisphere, the North Star appears motionless, while other stars look as if they are rotating around Earth, in the same way that the sun appears to rise and set. The movements of the stars are sufficiently stable to provide reliable guidance for travelers and seafarers. Some of the moving stars have an erratic movement, as if they are wandering outside of a fixed path. For ancient Greek astronomers, a wandering star was called a "planet" (*planetes*), because its primary activity is "to wander" (*planasthai*). For example, if you are on Earth looking at the planet Mercury, it will occasionally appear to wander. A few times a year, it appears over the course of a few weeks to stop, move backward (retrograde), and then start moving forward again. Current astronomical knowledge understands that Mercury and other planets do have fixed paths (orbits), and they only appear to wander because our perspective is moving: we see planets orbiting the sun while we ourselves are orbiting the sun.

The ancient Greeks did not believe that Earth was a planet. Earth was thought of as a motionless center around which stars and planets moved. Of course, there are always outliers who envision things differently. Aristarchus of Samos is such an outlier. He developed a sun-centered (heliocentric) model of astronomy over 2000 years ago, although it was dismissed in favor of Ptolemy's Earth-centered (geocentric) model, which was finally displaced after the relatively recent work of Copernicus. Accordingly, Aristarchus is sometimes described as the "Copernicus of Antiquity," although admirers of the ancient world may prefer to describe Copernicus as the "Aristarchus of the Renaissance" (Gassendi, 2002: 114). In any case, Aristarchus and Copernicus were both adventurous thinkers who were willing to challenge accepted opinions in their efforts to express the truth about our planetary context.

Today, it is relatively common knowledge that Earth revolves around the sun. Indeed, with increasingly intricate maps, models, and measurements humans have more detailed knowledge of Earth than ever before, including knowledge of Earth's origins and evolution. Yet, at the same time we are realizing that we inhabit a planet, we are also coming to realize that human actions are unraveling the evolutionary fabric of planetary coexistence. With ever-more humans using industrial technology and seeking unending economic growth, human actions are undoing planetary systems, contributing to a mass extinction of species, destabilizing the climate, acidifying the oceans, polluting waterways, and spreading non-biodegradable plastic, Styrofoam, and radioactive material around the planet. One of the species that humans are putting at risk is the human species. To degrade or destroy planetary systems like biodiversity, atmosphere, and freshwater is to foul our own nest. To put it another way, it is like cutting a branch off of a tree while you are sitting on it. You and the branch will hit the ground together. For instance, as sea-levels rise due to global warming, many coastal ecosystems will be damaged, and humans too will be impacted, such as citizens of island nations who must evacuate their entire population. Along with climate refugees and environmental immigration, environmental problems like pollution and toxic waste also cause human health problems, such as increased risk of cancer and other diseases. The environmental justice movement and the field of environmental health address multiple ways in which humans are negatively impacted by environmental harm (Rolston, 2012: 8, 33).

We know that we inhabit a planet, but it is not clear what that means. We do not yet know what to think about our place in the whole Earth. In other words, we know that we inhabit a planet, but not all of us are thinking about it or acting like it. Many personal decisions and social institutions do not account for the evolutionary and ecological dependence humans have in relationship to Earth. Failing to recognize their dependence, humans thereby fail to recognize that it is in their best interest to cultivate beneficial relations with the Earth community. Cultivating vibrant modes of planetary coexistence is not optional for humans. It is a matter of survival. As the geologian Thomas Berry (1999: 3) claims, the work of fostering "mutually beneficial" relations with Earth is the "Great Work" of our time. Human existence depends on it. "Thinking about the earth," as Kaza (2008: 64) describes the situation, "is no longer something you do now and then; it has become a way of life." The future of humanity and of all life on Earth demands that humans stop acting as if they are living in an infinite storeroom of resources and start acting like participants in the evolutionary and ecological relationships of Earth.

Becoming creative participants in the emerging Earth community instead of dominators is a matter of becoming anthropocosmic instead of anthropocentric, reinventing the human species by rejuvenating connections between humans,

Earth, and the universe (see Chapter 6). By rejuvenating connections with the Earth community, the planet itself appears to change. No longer appearing like a bunch of resources to be used and consumed, Earth appears differently, like something new. A reinvention of the human is also a renewal of Earth, a renewed participation in Earth's ongoing emergence. Accordingly, for the geophilosophers Gilles Deleuze and Félix Guattari, the philosophical work of creating concepts aims for the renewal of people and the planet. "The creation of concepts in itself calls for a future form, for a new earth and people that do not yet exist" (Deleuze and Guattari, 1994: 108).

Along with philosophical perspectives, religious, scientific, and political perspectives recognize the importance of facilitating participation in the emergence of a vibrant Earth community. This is indicated by the website Emerging Earth Community (EmergingEarthCommunity.org). As the "About" section of the site says, "Emerging Earth Community is an effort to broaden understanding of the complex nature of current environmental concerns so as to respond with longer term perspectives and goals." Connecting visitors to multiple endeavors of two students of Berry, Mary Evelyn Tucker and John Grim, the site is a hub that brings together religious perspectives, represented by the Forum on Religion and Ecology (co-founded by Tucker and Grim), scientific perspectives, represented in the multimedia *Journey of the Universe* project (written by Tucker and the cosmologist Brian Swimme), and ethical and political perspectives, represented by the most negotiated international document in history: the Earth Charter, to which Tucker was a contributor. Adhering to the integrative vision of three ecologies, this chapter draws upon those philosophical, religious, scientific, and ethico-political sources to describe the environmental, social, and subjective facets of the emerging Earth community.

Terrestrial complexity

The *Journey of the Universe* project brings together perspectives from sciences and humanities to articulate the evolutionary epic – a complex, multilayered narrative connecting humans, Earth, and the cosmos. Furthermore, as Swimme and Tucker (2011: ix) say in the *Journey of the Universe* book, the project is grounded in Berry's vision of the Great Work. With a website, book, film, and conversation series, the project provides diverse paths from which one can enter into a deeper participation with the universe and cultivate mutually enhancing relations between humans and the whole Earth community. In their account of the evolution of Earth, Swimme and Tucker provide an accessible summary of contemporary scientific understandings of Earth. For those understandings, Earth is not merely an object. It is a dynamic, complex system that has been evolving since it formed approximately four and a half billion years ago, around the same time as the sun.

Swimme and Tucker use the image of "Earth as an egg" (p. 39). Deleuze (1994: 251) invokes this image as well: "The world is an egg." Earth, an organism, the cosmos, and every other assemblage may be thought of as an egg in the sense that it harbors multiple potentials for becoming something, an actually existing individual. Earth is not a static system but an intense process of individuation, an assemblage with potentials branching out in numerous directions: becoming a mountain, becoming a river, becoming bacteria, becoming a volcano, becoming marsupial, becoming tundra, becoming alligator, becoming human, and so much more. As a cauldron of transformative potential, Earth is like an egg in its basic geological structure. Just as an egg has shell on its outside with egg-white underneath and a yolk in the core, Earth has an exterior shell (the crust) with a layer underneath it (the mantle) and a molten center (the core). Although the crust may make the egg look like a stable, balanced system, it is concealing an intense, swirling process of transformation. "The whole Earth is a great tablet holding the multiple overlaid new and ancient traces of the swirl of forces" (Snyder, 1990: 29)

Underneath Earth's crust is a chaotic process, a "seething disequilibrium" (Swimme and Tucker, 2011: 39). The combined presence of extreme heat, gravity, and decaying radioactive elements inside of Earth produces a convection current, a churning movement that pushes magma from the core into the mantle and onto the surface (becoming crust) while also pulling crust back into the magma (becoming mantle) and toward the center of the planet (becoming core). Earth organizes itself through this seething and churning process, remaining in "the zone between chaos and rigidity," never becoming completely rigid and fixed into strata and never collapsing into complete disorder and disequilibrium (p. 41). In the terminology of Deleuze and Guattari (1987), Earth may be understood as a creative tension between stratification (rigidity; territorialization) and destratification (chaos; deterritorialization). An important implication of this tension is that terrestrial existence is creative and self-organizing (autopoietic), always making, unmaking, and remaking patterns. Even before life emerged, Earth stratified, destratified, and restratified itself into numerous combinations.

Living organisms exist on strata that are different from the physical and chemical strata of inorganic matter. Strata may also be considered as levels or spheres. Organisms are part of the biosphere (life-sphere), whereas the strata of inorganic matter are located in the spheres of rock (lithosphere), water (hydrosphere), and air (atmosphere). The biosphere is unique among the other spheres, and furthermore, among living organisms there are many different strata, from the simple cells that emerged from the intense seething and churning of the planet approximately four billion years ago to cells with nuclei (two billion years ago) and then eventually to more complex forms of life, including plants, fungi, fish, reptiles, birds, and mammals (Swimme and Tucker, 2011: 48).

Life on Earth is diverse among itself and different from physical and chemical phenomena. There can be atoms without the existence of organisms, but an organism cannot exist without atoms. A lizard and a stone occupy different strata. One may seem more complex than the other. Nonetheless, the "matter is the same on all the strata" (Deleuze and Guattari, 1987: 45). "Earth's life is a manifestation of the deep patterning of the universe, referred to as self-organizing dynamics" (Swimme and Tucker, 2011: 48). Matter is self-organizing on all strata. Living organisms did not get their capacity for self-organization from nowhere. Their capacity emerged from the material universe. From atoms and whirlpools to stars and galaxies, all matter harbors creative potentials for self-organization, potentials for producing new structures out of the tensions that take place at the edge where rigidity and chaos meet. The production of order and organization out of the fluctuations of chaotic systems is one of the groundbreaking scientific discoveries of the twentieth century, providing evidence for an inherently creative universe, radically different from the mechanistic universe envisioned by early modern science (Prigogine and Stengers, 1984).

There is an important lesson here for a "geology of morals" (Deleuze and Guattari, 1987: 39). Neither stratified nor destratified systems are inherently good or bad. What is important is whether stratification or destratification cultivate mutually enhancing modes of planetary coexistence or destroy the conditions of planetary coexistence. For instance, pollinator insects and flowers have developed a mutually enhancing relationship over time. Consider the example of a wasp and an orchid (10). The insect and flower have a symbiotic relationship, benefiting one another mutually. The wasp gets nutritional benefits from the orchid's pollen, and the spread of the pollen by the wasp facilitates the reproduction of the orchid. They deterritorialize one another, each using the other's territory for its own, yet in the process they build a new mutually intensifying territory – a co-evolutionary alliance.

A similar mutual benefit may be seen in the relationship between humans and flowering plants. In contrast to gymnosperms like pine trees and redwoods, which produce naked (*gymnos*) seeds (*spermoi*), flowering plants are angiosperms, which means that they contain their seeds within a vessel (*angeion*). An apple, for example, is a vessel for the seeds of the apple tree. The vessels allow the seeds to travel further than they would otherwise. An animal might eat an apple and deposit the undigested seeds miles away. Some seeds have hooks or burs with which to transport their genetic material. Dandelions contain their seeds in tiny parachutes that float away when you blow on them. Combining compelling storytelling with scientific understanding, the naturalist Loren Eiseley describes how the evolution of flowering plants allowed the diversity and abundance of plant species to increase dramatically. "A plant, a fixed, rooted thing, immobilized in a single spot, had devised a way of propelling its offspring across open space" (Eiseley, 1957: 69).

This evolutionary development facilitated the spread of plants around the planet. With more flowers transforming the sun's light into energy (photosynthesis), more energy was available for mammals, which emerged in the Mesozoic Era around the same period as flowering plants. Following the extinction of the dinosaurs approximately sixty-five million years ago, some species of angiosperms and mammals survived the extinction event. Along with beneficial relations between pollinator insects and some flowering plants, mammals and flowering plants also went on to develop mutually beneficial relationships: mammals helping angiosperms reproduce by carrying their seeds in or on their bodies, and plants providing an abundant energy source for mammals. While populations of flowering plants exploded, the number and size of mammals increased. Those mammals include the primate ancestors of humans, who would not have had the energy necessary for their evolutionary emergence without angiosperms.

The mutually beneficial relationships that may be seen between some species may also be seen on the macro scale of the whole planet. All life on Earth (the biosphere) is entangled in a co-evolutionary relationship with Earth's atmosphere. The oxygen in the atmosphere exists because of photosynthesizing organisms, which obtain energy by absorbing carbon dioxide and sunlight, releasing oxygen as a by-product. Photosynthesizing organisms began populating the planet within millions of years after the first living cells emerged around four billion years ago. As a result, the atmosphere became oxygenated, creating an oxygen crisis that began suffocating life on Earth. Life adapted, and organisms developed capacities for breathing (respiration), which involves breaking down oxygen and turning it into energy, expelling carbon dioxide as a by-product. Organisms changed the atmosphere by releasing oxygen, and the oxygenated atmosphere in turn changed organisms, and then breathing organisms changed the atmosphere by absorbing oxygen and emitting carbon dioxide. Life changes the atmosphere, which changes life, which changes the atmosphere, and so on. The biosphere and the atmosphere thus developed a co-evolutionary relationship. The living and nonliving strata of Earth interconnect into one complex planetary system, which some call Gaia.

The chemist James Lovelock and the microbiologist Lynn Margulis worked together in the 1970s to develop what became known as the Gaia hypothesis or Gaia theory, which is more generally referred to in terms of Earth systems science (Schneider et al., 2004; Harding, 2006). The name Gaia refers to an Earth goddess in ancient Greek mythology, but the point of Gaia theory is not that Earth is divine or sacred. The point is that Earth is a self-regulating, self-organizing system, such that changes in one part (e.g., the biosphere) are regulated by changes in other parts (e.g., the atmosphere), thus maintaining relative stability (homeostasis) amidst the chaotic fluctuations of Earth's evolution. This picture is further complicated by the emergence of human beings, whose consciousness and culture has developed into a planetary presence (see Chapter 6).

The atmosphere, biosphere, lithosphere, and hydrosphere of the planet are now joined by the sphere of human intelligence and culture, which is often referred to as the noosphere – a sphere of mind (*nous*). To understand the complexity of Earth's environments thus requires an integrative analysis of the multiple strata of planetary coexistence, including strata of ethical values, ideas, cultures, and traditions, strata that cannot be understood from scientific perspectives alone but also require the theories and methods from the humanities. Along these lines, what is called for is an "integral Earth study," which would investigate complex as well as the community and subjectivity distributed across "the five macrophase components of the Earth" – atmosphere, hydrosphere, lithosphere, biosphere, and noosphere (Berry, 1999: 90).

An integral Earth study is another way of saying whole Earth thinking. It is of the utmost importance for the future of humanity and the whole Earth community. It provides ways of understanding and responding to the destabilization of planetary systems that is occurring due to the incredible increase in human population and consumption. Is this destratification simply destroying the conditions for life on Earth, or is it opening up possibilities for the development of mutually enhancing relations between humans and the whole Earth community?

Earth community

The relational and interdependent dynamics of Earth point toward social ecology and the role of community in planetary coexistence. Forms of community may be found in the intergenerational relationships whereby organisms reproduce and care for their offspring. Swimme and Tucker (2011: 77) observe that such "parental care" is a shared theme among many perspectives of "feminine wisdom," including religious figures such as Mary the mother of Jesus, the Chinese Bodhisattva of compassion Kuan Yin, and Oshun, the goddess of love, intimacy, and freshwater in the West African tradition of Yoruba. In the study of animal behavior (ethology), parental care involves all behaviors that a parent directs toward the well-being of its offspring. This is very pronounced in the worlds of mammals, where mothers spend considerable time – weeks and even years – attending to the members of their next generation, protecting, nurturing, and teaching.

Mammals did not invent parental care. Mammalian senses of community emerged out of previous forms. For instance, some reptilian mothers protect and care for their eggs. Although it is not with the same intensity of mammals, reptiles nonetheless exhibit parental care. Swimme and Tucker go on to consider the parental care expressed in plant life (p. 78). A conifer, like a Douglas fir, spends considerable amounts of energy on producing cones, which only function to produce offspring, with no function for the tree that produces them. A relational concern is present, at least in a germinal or larval form, in the intergenerational activities whereby organisms reproduce, including the reproductive activities of bacteria and fungi. To live is to be enmeshed in networks of care. Is a molecule a network of care? Perhaps that would be going too far. In any case, even at the molecular level, existence is always already coexistence. Nothing can exist without dependence on the other beings around it, and those beings are themselves dependent on others. "Nothing is itself without everything else" (Berry, 1999: 181).

Humans have developed particularly complex networks of care. Following the Agricultural Revolution, human communities extended to the sizes of cities and eventually empires. During the past 500 years, humans have extended their sense of community even further, beyond the boundaries of cities, states, and nations, covering the entire globe. Entering the Anthropocene, the human community is now a planetary presence. So far, the process of becoming planetary has been extremely destructive. Morin (1999: 8) refers to this period of time as "the Planetary Iron Age," and as he understands it, this is the period of time "in which we still find ourselves." Historically, the Iron Age refers to the period of human societies approximately 2000 to 3000 years ago, leading up to and including the emergence of classical religious and philosophical traditions. In ancient Greek mythology, images of an Iron Age were generally used to represent a period of time that is dominated by greed and war. In both senses, the past 500 years have been a Planetary Iron Age. It is a period of time dominated by war and greed (e.g., colonialism, militarism, industrialization, and consumerism), and it is also a time in which new traditions are emerging that are integrating sources of ecological wisdom to reinvent the human and cultivate a flourishing Earth community.

The future remains uncertain. It is unclear whether domination or care will be the main pattern of planetary coexistence. So much harm and destruction has already taken place that it is unclear whether humans will even have an opportunity to make a transition toward mutually enhancing human–Earth relations. The consensus among scientists is that life on Earth is currently undergoing a mass extinction event (Kolbert, 2014). It is the sixth mass extinction in the history of the planet, the previous of which was the Cretaceous extinction, which brought about the end of the dinosaurs and of the whole Mesozoic Era. Now, the current era (Cenozoic) is coming to an end. How will humans respond to this transition? This is our Great Work.

> Our own special role, which we will hand on to our children, is that of managing the arduous transition from the terminal Cenozoic to the emerging Ecozoic Era, the period when humans will be present to the planet as participating members of the comprehensive Earth community. This is our Great Work and the work of our children.
>
> (Berry 1999: 7–8)

The arrival of what Berry imagines as the Ecozoic is not impossible, but it is by no means guaranteed.

If humans maintain the current path of destruction, the end of the Cenozoic will mark a transition toward a planet where biodiversity, ecosystem stability, and human well-being become increasingly degraded and destroyed by the globally dominant "extractive economy," which views everything and everyone as resources (p. 138). If humans survive such a destructive transition out of the Cenozoic, they will inhabit a technologically dominated planet where to be is to be managed and controlled, exploited for the benefit of government and corporate elites. Care and relational intimacy will have given way to "the Technozoic, a future of increased exploitation of Earth as resource" (Swimme and Berry, 1992: 15). This is not to say that technology is the problem. The Technozoic is a way of referring to perspectives oriented toward anthropocentric calculation and control, which are evident in some forms of technological domination, and they may also be found in the greed and manipulation that characterize consumer culture and the economic system of corporate globalization (p. 250).

For the Deleuzian political philosophers Michael Hardt and Antonio Negri (2009), the tension between domination and mutually enhancing relations may be described as a tension between empire and the commonwealth of the multitude.

Empire is the name for the global extractive economy and its accompanying media, security, and governance. The multitude is the name for all people in their radical multiplicity, including multiple personalities, genders, ages, abilities, traditions, and cultures. The commonwealth is the shared world, the global commons, the Earth community, and it also refers to the network of intimate social relationships whereby humans participate in rather than dominate the Earth community. Those are relationships of care and mutuality. Along those lines, Hardt and Negri develop a political concept of love to energize the multitude to resist empire and reconstitute the commonwealth (p. 179).

A notable aspect of philosophers like Hardt and Negri or Deleuze and Guattari is that they work together. Their efforts to create concepts that empower the multitude are joint efforts. Both pairs have co-authored multiple books together. A crucial feature of an Earth community of mutually enhancing relationships is precisely that it emerges by building relationships, and writing together is one way of doing that. Berry's work with Swimme, Swimme's work with Tucker (Journey of the Universe), and Tucker's work with Grim (The Forum on Religion and Ecology) exemplify this practice of creative collaboration in the emerging Earth community. Furthermore, for collaborative efforts to cultivate mutually enhancing human–Earth relations, a particularly significant document is the Earth Charter, which is the most thoroughly negotiated international document in history. It presents a vision of shared values and principles for a planetary civilization grounded in peaceful, just, and sustainable relationships between humans and the whole Earth community.

The Earth Charter was drafted by a diverse group of scientists, scholars, political leaders, religious leaders, and others. Since it was issued in June 2000, the Earth Charter has been endorsed by many individuals and more than 4500 organizations, including universities, governments, religious groups, and non-governmental organizations. The Earth Charter articulates a planetary vision grounded in principles of human rights, democratic political participation, social and economic equity, nonviolence, respect for life, and ecological integrity. The "Preamble" provides an overview of the scope and aim of the document:

> As the world becomes increasingly interdependent and fragile, the future at once holds great peril and great promise. To move forward we must recognize that in the midst of a magnificent diversity of cultures and life forms we are one human family and on Earth community with a common destiny. . . . Towards this end, it is imperative that we, the peoples of Earth, declare our responsibility to one another, to the greater community of life, and to future generations.
>
> (Grim and Tucker, 2014: 200)

The values articulated in the Earth Charter are relevant to everyday practices, activism, and advocacy, and they have significant implications for transforming ethics, religions, governance, international law, and social movements, orienting them toward the emergence of a flourishing Earth community (Westra and Vilela, 2014; Grim and Tucker, 2014: 156).

Planetary subjects

One of the implications of the vision of mutually enhancing human–Earth relations is that human and nonhuman beings have value, and not just economic or monetary value. They have value on their own terms. They have their own singular capacities and abilities, their own self-organizing dynamics; in short, their own subjectivity. What is the subjectivity of Earth? How is Earth an actor or agent, a self-organizing assemblage? "Who does the Earth think it is" (Deleuze and Guattari, 1987: 39)? What are terrestrial beings on their own terms, each according to its unique singularity? These may seem like questions of only theoretical significance. However, they have direct ethical and political implications. For instance, Berry (1999: 5) argues that a flourishing Earth community is one in which "every being has rights," and the rights of each kind of being depend on its unique traits: "Trees have tree rights, insects have insect rights, rivers have river rights, mountains have mountain rights."

Understanding the subjectivity distributed across the planet makes it possible to orient law and jurisprudence toward mutually enhancing human–Earth relations (Cullinan, 2011). More generally, it makes it possible to orient all aspects of human individual and social activity toward "an ecology of resingularization"; that is, toward the recuperation of the subjectivity of all participants in planetary coexistence (Guattari, 2000: 65). Recuperating subjectivity means respecting and empowering the capacities of things to determine and organize themselves. Rather than treating something like an object in your world, you treat it as if it has its own perspective. A raccoon is not just a thing in your world. You exist in its world, perhaps as a visitor or trespasser on its terrain. Do not only consider what things mean to you. Consider what you may mean to them. Moving beyond anthropocentrism does not mean that you stop experiencing yourself as a unique center of value in the world. It means that you also experience nonhumans as centers of value in their own right. As Gaston Bachelard (1994: 171) says in his analysis of anthropocosmic images, even an "evening lamp on the family table is also the center of a world."

For Berry, and for Deleuze and Guattari, all material beings harbor subjective capacities. All strata of Earth and of the universe exhibit self-organizing dynamics. Human subjectivity is not the origin or the standard of all subjectivity. It is unique, but not specially privileged. As Gary Snyder (1990: 22) puts it, "each creature is a spirit with an intelligence as brilliant as our own." Each planetary creature is an actor playing a role, communicating its part in the Earth community. The world is thus not a passive background to human subjectivity. Humans are immersed in an active, attentive, communicative world.

> The world is watching: one cannot walk through a meadow or forest without a ripple of report spreading out from one's passage. The thrush darts back, the jay squalls, a beetle scuttles under the grasses, and the signal is passed

along. Every creature knows when a hawk is cruising or a human strolling. The information passed through the system is intelligence.

(Snyder, 1990: 20–21)

To be is to be intelligent, to be discerning. Everything that exists exercises capacities for affecting and being affected by other beings. Each being has unique intelligences. There is not just one kind of intelligence. Beyond cognitive and verbal intelligence, there are somatic, migratory, predatory, social, and emotional kinds of intelligence. Consider the bonding intelligence of atoms or the nuclear intelligence of stars.

Perhaps it is not surprising that some humans hold on to anthropocentric perspectives and claim that human intelligence makes us too special to be just an animal or just another participant in a communion of multiple human and non-human subjects. As Snyder (1990: 17) conjectures, "other animals might feel they are something different than 'just animals' too." No animals are just animals. Each species and each individual has its own singular existence, its own subjectivity. If Earth is to be viewed as a storehouse, it is not a storehouse of objects that have no value apart from their economic use as resources. Earth may be understood as a storehouse of the creative, interdependent, self-organizing dynamics of the unfolding cosmos (see Chapter 8). Like an egg, it is a storehouse for the emergence of subjectivity, which exhibits intelligence and discerning wisdom as well as relational care and compassion.

In Japanese Buddhism, a Bodhisattva is imagined as just such a storehouse. The name of the Bodhisattva Jizo means "earth storehouse" or "earth womb," not in the sense of a container for resources but in the sense of a matrix for wisdom and compassion, especially compassion for the suffering of children (Kaza, 2008: 13). Far from treating terrestrial beings like objects, Jizo is concerned about the suffering of all beings, which implies that beings have some kind of agency or subjectivity that makes them capable of suffering. The figure of Jizo indicates the possibility of committing oneself to the cultivation of a flourishing Earth community, in which all beings become emancipated subjects, liberated from suffering. In other words, Jizo indicates the possibility of becoming "a concerned earth citizen" (p. 61). In that context, the whole Earth appears as a matrix for the ongoing emergence of subjects entangled in relationships of complexity and community. It is an awe-inspiring vision. Caring for the emerging Earth community, one develops "a sense of awe for the earth as a miraculous whole" (p. 26). Awe for the whole Earth opens out onto wonder for the whole cosmos, an evolving communion of subjects.

Note

1   Because Earth is a planet, I mention Earth throughout this work as a proper noun, capitalized with no article (no "a" or "the"). This is the standard grammar for referring to planets. Thus, it is incorrect to refer to Jupiter as jupiter, the jupiter, or the Jupiter. It is Jupiter. Many works cited throughout this book speak of Earth as earth, the earth, or the Earth. I have maintained those spellings whenever using direct quotations. The point here is not to control grammar. The point is to draw attention to the fact that Earth is one among other planets in a solar system.

References

Bachelard, Gaston. 1994. *The Poetics of Space*. Trans. Maria Jolas. Boston, MA: Beacon Press.

Berry, Thomas. 1999. *The Great Work: Our Way into the Future*. New York: Bell Tower.

Cullinan, Cormac. 2011. *Wild Law: A Manifesto for Earth Justice*, 2nd edn. Totnes, Devon: Green Books.

Deleuze, Gilles. 1994. *Difference and Repetition*. Trans. Paul Patton. New York: Columbia University Press.

Deleuze, Gilles and Félix Guattari. 1987. *A Thousand Plateaus: Capitalism and Schizophrenia*. Trans. Brian Massumi. Minneapolis: University of Minnesota Press.

——. 1994. *What is Philosophy?* Trans. Hugh Tomlinson and Graham Burchell. New York: Columbia University Press.

Eiseley, Loren. 1957. *The Immense Journey: An Imaginative Naturalist Explores the Mysteries of Man and Nature*. New York: Random House.

Emerging Earth Community. 2014. "About." http://EmergingEarthCommunity.org/about (accessed December 2, 2014).

Gassendi, Pierre. 2002. *The Life of Copernicus (1473–1543)*. Fairfax, VA: Xulon Press.

Grim, John and Mary Evelyn Tucker. 2014. *Ecology and Religion*. Washington, DC: Island Press.

Guattari, Félix. 2000. *The Three Ecologies*. Trans. Ian Pindar and Paul Sutton. London: Athlone Press.

Harding, Stephan. 2006. *Animate Earth: Science, Intuition, and Gaia*. White River Junction: Chelsea Green Publishing.

Hardt, Michael and Antonio Negri. 2009. *Commonwealth*. Cambridge, MA: Harvard University Press.

Kaza, Stephanie. 2008. *Mindfully Green: A Personal and Spiritual Guide to Whole Earth Thinking*. Boston, MA: Shambhala Publications.

Kolbert, Elizabeth. 2014. *The Sixth Extinction: An Unnatural History*. New York: Henry Holt.

Morin, Edgar. 1999. *Homeland Earth: A Manifesto for the New Millennium*. Trans. Sean M. Kelly and Roger LaPointe. Cresskill: Hampton Press.

Prigogine, Ilya and Isabelle Stengers. 1984. *Order Out of Chaos: Man's New Dialogue with Nature*. New York: Bantam Books.

Rolston, Holmes. 2012. *A New Environmental Ethics: The Next Millennium of Life on Earth*. New York: Routledge.

Schneider, Stephen H., James R. Miller, Eileen Crist, and Penelope J. Boston (eds). 2004. *Scientists Debate Gaia: The Next Century*. Cambridge, MA: MIT Press.

Snyder, Gary. 1990. *The Practice of the Wild*. Berkeley, CA: Counterpoint.

Swimme, Brian and Thomas Berry. 1992. *The Universe Story: From the Primordial Flaring Forth to the Ecozoic Era – A Celebration of the Unfolding of the Cosmos*. San Francisco, CA: HarperCollins.

Swimme, Brian and Mary Evelyn Tucker. 2011. *Journey of the Universe*. New Haven, CT: Yale University Press.

Westra, Laura and Mirian Vilela (eds). 2014. *The Earth Charter, Ecological Integrity and Social Movements*. New York: Routledge.

8   Cosmic connections

Whole Earth thinking is about seeking ecological wisdom, reinventing the human, and nurturing the emergence of a vibrant Earth community. There are many ways to do those things, as is indicated by the different approaches of the geologian Thomas Berry and the geophilosophers Gilles Deleuze and Félix Guattari (see Chapter 2). Depending on your personal dispositions and the context in which you are thinking, some ways may be more useful to you than others. To practice whole Earth thinking, you start where you are at, with your mindset and your ecological and social setting. You start in your place, from your own unique and intimate connection with the whole. "You start with the part you are whole in" (Snyder, 1990: 41). Insofar as Earth has its wholeness as part of the evolving universe, to find your place in the whole Earth community also means to find your place in the whole cosmos. Committed to cultivating mutually enhancing human–Earth relations, whole Earth thinking draws deeply from ecological perspectives, and because Earth is itself enmeshed in the dynamics of cosmic evolution, whole Earth thinking also draws from cosmology.

Scientific cosmology is defined as the study of the origin and development of the universe. However, there are innumerable ways of thinking and speaking about the universe, cosmos, or world. Even if one has no knowledge of science, ideas about the world are nonetheless implicit in one's experience of things. Everyone has some sense of the world. It could be inaccurate, but everyone has one nonetheless. For instance, one has some sense of the extent to which the world displays a fixed and determined progression, like fate or destiny, and the extent to which it is undetermined and spontaneous, exhibiting freedom, chance, and luck. Is the world basically benign and benevolent, or is it threatening and cruel? Is it created by a deity, or populated by spirits? Does it feel like home, or does home seem elsewhere? Even if you do not think about those kinds of questions, the actions you take and the stories you tell indicate what your response might be. The things you say and do reflect whether you trust the world or find it threatening, whether you feel at home or alienated, whether you feel free or fated, and so on. The cosmological perspectives implicit in one's everyday experiences may be referred to as "folk cosmology" (El-Aswad, 2002).

Art, activism, cooking, politics, business, parenting, gardening, playing, education, and all human endeavors are situated in some sense of the world. When that sense of the world is explicitly expressed, it transitions from folk to formal cosmology, which can take many forms, including philosophical, scientific, and religious. When cosmologies are formally expressed with symbols, myths, and ritual actions, they may be described as religious cosmologies. Religious interpretations of the cosmos provide the context within which religious practitioners understand human–Earth relations. The concept of religious cosmology is articulated by John Grim and Mary Evelyn Tucker (2014: 63):

> Religious cosmologies in world religions describe the origin and unfolding of the universe, Earth, and life. Religious ecologies are functional cosmologies that express an awareness of kinship with and dependence on nature for the continuity of life. . . . They assume cosmological stories and embedded cultural practices that weave humans into the life systems of the cosmos, of the Earth and of bioregions.

While religions use myths to understand the cosmos, philosophy and science focus on logic. The opposition between stories (*muthos*) and rational discourse (*logos*) has been part of philosophy and science since their ancient Greek beginnings.

When one's interpretation of the universe is primarily oriented around reason, it can be called philosophical cosmology, which began in ancient Greece with thinkers like Plato, Aristotle, and Democritus, who, respectively, conceived of the real substance of the cosmos as an immaterial idea or form, as activity or energy (*energeia*), and as a collection of atoms. Philosophical cosmology generally includes scientific methods of observation while also speculating on questions beyond the scope of observation but within the scope of rational thought (e.g., questions about the soul, beauty, and justice). When a sense of the world is articulated based on empirical observations and measurements, it can be called scientific cosmology. Moreover, although philosophy, religion, and science are distinct, especially in modern academic contexts, they each overlap with one another in various ways throughout history. Philosophers, scientists, and religious practitioners all have tendencies to wander into the territories of the other.

It was not until the modern world that scientific cosmology clearly and distinctly marked itself off from philosophical and religious ways of interpreting the universe. Proponents of the modern scientific method saw little to no use in philosophical speculation or religious stories. Empirical observation and measurement would be the only guides for knowledge. The invention of the telescope in the early seventeenth century provided the means for obtaining more detailed observations of celestial phenomena, including observations whereby people like Galileo supported the Copernican theory that Earth revolves around the sun (King, 2003). Cosmological observations are still becoming more detailed today, and the scientific picture of the universe is coming into sharper focus. Whereas early modern science generally represented the universe mechanistically, reducing everything to passive objects obeying mechanical laws, the increasingly detailed knowledge of scientific cosmology has radically changed that picture.

In the twentieth century, cosmologists came to the consensus that the universe is evolving. What was thought to be static is actually dynamic, and what were thought to be independent, passive objects are actually interrelated beings with self-organizing dynamics. In contemporary scientific cosmology, the universe appears less like a collection of objects and more like a communion of subjects (Berry, 1999: 82; Swimme and Berry, 1992: 243). The cosmos is not a rigid system of inert objects that move according to fixed formulas. It is more like a dragon than a machine (Swimme, 1984). It is an open-ended, complex network full of spontaneity and creative agency. The cosmos is an unfolding process, always moving and changing, always crossing over into chaos. It is a process of "chaosmosis" (Guattari, 1995). As Deleuze (1994: 57) says, the cosmos is "a complicated, properly chaotic world," a "*chaosmos.*"

Whereas early modern science opposed itself to religious cosmologies, the former finding the universe to be a passive machine, and the latter often finding the universe to be a sacred and even divine reality, contemporary scientific cosmology is developing a picture of the universe that is much more open to religious cosmologies. Practitioners of scientific and religious ways of knowing have more opportunities to cross paths and enter into dialogue about the meaning, mystery, and creativity pervading the universe. Through such dialogue, religious and scientific cosmologies are beginning to develop a shared vision of a sacred universe, a vision that provides a context for humans to understand their place in the Earth community (Kauffman, 2008; Berry, 2009). For whole Earth thinking to support comprehensive and inclusive responses to the challenges facing planetary coexistence, scientific knowledge of our evolutionary context is necessary. To address values, cultural diversity, and multiple ways of knowing, religious cosmologies are also a necessary component of whole Earth thinking. Following an outline of cosmic evolution as understood in contemporary science, the remainder of this chapter considers how religious and ethical perspectives can enter into dialogue with scientific cosmology in collaborative efforts to transition out of the current period of planetary destruction and into a period of mutually enhancing human–Earth relations.

The evolving universe

Since Copernicus, Galileo, and others demonstrated that Earth revolves around the sun, humans have been gradually realizing that they live on a moving body – a planet orbiting the sun. However, the movement does not stop there. The sun is itself moving, orbiting the center of our galaxy: the Milky Way (Swimme and Tucker, 2011: 21). That fact was discovered by Harlow Shapley in 1918, under a century ago. At the time, the only galaxy that scientists knew about was the Milky Way (p. 17). It was debated whether other galaxies existed. Indeed, throughout the history of philosophical and scientific cosmologies, the existence of multiple planets, worlds, and universes (the multiverse) has been an ongoing debate, one which always touches on religious themes as well by raising questions about cosmic creativity, infinity, and the beginning of all things (Rubenstein, 2014).

Having realized that the planet is spinning around the sun, which is itself spinning around the center of our galaxy, the spinning movement intensified even further with the discovery that, in fact, other galaxies do exist. The Milky Way is not alone. Moreover, there are not just three or four galaxies, and not just hundreds or even thousands. There are billions. It is a startling fact. Furthermore, they are all moving. Our planet orbits the sun, which orbits the center of our galaxy, and our galaxy is one among "several dozen galaxies revolving around each other. This system as a whole is moving around the Virgo Cluster of galaxies," which is among "other groups revolving about the Virgo Cluster, and this entire system is called the Virgo Supercluster" (Swimme and Tucker, 2011: 21).

We inhabit a planet in one solar system of the Milky Way, which is in the Virgo Cluster of galaxies, moving with other clusters in the Virgo Supercluster. It is dizzying, but not simply decentering. It decenters the anthropocentric human, and it provides a context for a reinvention that recenters the human species in a complex, dynamic universe. "We now realize that we dwell in one center in a universe that is composed of millions of such centers" (p. 22). In other words, the discovery that the universe is constantly moving and swirling does not take away one's own center. It shows that the center is everywhere. "We live in a multicentered universe and are only now awakening to this great discovery" (p. 21). We inhabit "an omnicentric evolutionary universe, a developing reality which from the beginning is centered upon itself at each place of its existence. In this universe of ours to be in existence is to be at the cosmic center of the complexifying whole" (Swimme, 1996: 85–86).

There are two cosmological observations which contribute to an understanding of the universe as an omnicentric or multicentric evolutionary process. Consider the more recent observation first. In the 1960s, Arno Penzias and Robert Wilson detected the thermal radiation left over from the Big Bang. It is "the dim glow left over from the eruption of the universe" (p, 78). The space between stars looks dark to the naked eye and even through an optical telescope. Using a sensitive radio telescope, Penzias and Wilson detected a dim glow in the background between stars, a faint radiation that showed up in the radio spectrum, particularly in the microwave region of the spectrum, hence its name: Cosmic Microwave Background. Evidence which proves that a crime has taken place is often called a "smoking gun." The empirical observation of the Cosmic Microwave Background is the smoking gun of the Big Bang, providing evidence for the theory that our universe evolved from an explosive event. It is the smoldering remainder of the initial explosion, the glowing cinders of "the great Flaring Forth" (Swimme and Berry, 1992: 20).

The observation of the Cosmic Microwave Background came a few decades after Edwin Hubble made an observation which demonstrated that the universe is expanding. In the 1920s, through the use of a high-powered telescope, Hubble observed that distant galaxies appear to be receding, moving further away, which indicates that the universe is expanding (Swimme and Tucker, 2011: 6). More specifically, Hubble noticed a slight color change in the appearance of distant galaxies, a redshift. When light from distant cosmological objects moves away, it shifts into the red area of the color spectrum, whereas light from objects that are moving closer shifts toward the blue (blueshift), similar to the doppler effect, when sounds become higher pitched as they approach and lower pitched as they depart (Duncan and Tyler, 2009: 136). Wherever one is at in the universe, if you look out with a telescope and observe distant phenomena, your location will appear to be a stable center away from which everything else is moving.

Observations of cosmic expansion and the Cosmic Microwave Background provide evidence that the cosmos is not stable, static, and unchanging. It is evolving, constantly swirling and changing. It is a chaosmos, a term which Deleuze and Guattari adapt from the experimental prose of James Joyce's (1982: 118) *Finnegans Wake*: "every person, place and thing in the chaosmos of Alle anyway connected with the gobblydumped turkery was moving and changing every part of the time." Everything is changing, becoming different, yet all differences are implicitly connected, as all things emerge from the same complex evolutionary process, the same flaring forth. The chaosmos is a "world of differences implicated in one another," where every "difference passes through all the others" – "a complicated, properly chaotic world" (Deleuze, 1994: 57).

This is not to say that the world is merely chaos or that order (*kosmos*) is reduced to disorder (*chaos*). The point is that the order of the cosmos is intimately intertwined with disorder – the chaotic dynamics of change, transforming, becoming different. The universe exists at the edge where cosmos and chaos meet. This is evident in the characteristics of the Big Bang and the early universe. The force of expansion in the Big Bang struck a creative balance at the edge of chaos. "If the rate of expansion had been slower, even slightly slower, even one millionth of a percent slower, the universe would have recollapsed," and, on the other hand, "if the universe had expanded a little more quickly, even one millionth of one percent more quickly, the universe would have expanded too quickly for structures to form," diffusing and disintegrating (Swimme and Tucker, 2011: 10–11). The balance between expansion and attraction (gravity) allowed stable structures to form and endure, providing conditions for the emergence of elementary particles, galaxies, stars, and eventually life and human beings.

The ordered systems and stable strata of the universe are all a hair's breadth away from complete destruction. In the chaosmos, to be is to be on the edge of chaos. "The universe thrives on the edge of a knife. . . . Every being that thrives does so in a balance of creative tension" (Swimme and Berry, 1992: 54). Too much or too little water will kill a plant. Too high or too low a temperature will kill a human being. Too much or too little carbon dioxide in the atmosphere and the greenhouse effect necessary for life degenerates into chaos. Too much or too little gravity and our galaxy will collapse or fly apart. Existing in an evolving universe means that, in order to thrive, one must inhabit the creative edge where chaos meets order.

The observations of cosmic expansion and light from the Big Bang show that the universe is evolving, and furthermore, those observations indicate that the universe is omnicentric or multicentric. On the one hand, the observation of light from the origin of the universe indicates that we are at the edge of the universe.

The light of the central point from which the universe first flared forth appears at the greatest distance we can observe. On the other hand, the redshift of distant phenomena indicates that our perspective is a stable center away from which everything else is expanding. The central point of the cosmic beginning has expanded and complexified to become the vast universe and everything in it, such that everything occupies the center of the universe. In other words, "the cosmos is centered on its own expansion" (Swimme, 1996: 83). The universe is a complex world of different centers implicated in one another, where every center interrelates with all the others. "*The center of the cosmos is each event in the cosmos*" (p. 112).

The idea of a universe in which everything is a center is not new. Variations of the idea may be found many centuries earlier than the empirical observations that support it. For instance, it may be found in the Renaissance philosophies of Nicholas of Cusa (1401–1464) and Giordano Bruno (1548–1600). Cusa famously expressed a formula stating that the universe is a sphere that has its "center everywhere" (*centrum ubique*) and its "circumference nowhere" (*circumferentia nullibi*). This formula has precursors, appearing as early as the twelfth century, but Cusa and Bruno present their concepts more explicitly than previous formulations (Casey, 1997: 116). Cusa understands the universe as a process that unfolds into different beings while folding together with the creative source of beings: God. To say that the center of the universe is everywhere is to say that every unfolded being implicitly contains the complex whole of the universe folded together with the divine.

Bruno takes up Cusa's sense of the unfolding (*explicatio*) and enfolding (*complicatio*) of the universe, but he goes further to add that, if everything is the center, one could just as well say that the universe is a sphere in which everything is the edge or circumference with a center nowhere (p. 123). Everything is the center, but each center is itself an edge of all other centers. Bruno's cosmology suggests that to be is to be on the edge of other beings and on the edge of the whole world. If everything is the center of the world, it does not mean that anything has total freedom. It does not mean that anything has a special privilege that justifies access or power over others. If everything is the center of the world, each center is bound and limited by other centers. A key difference between Cusa's and Bruno's visions and their contemporary counterpart is that Cusa and Bruno are theological, saying something about the presence of the creative agency of the divine folded into every center. In contrast, contemporary scientific cosmology bases its understanding of the multicentric universe on empirical observation with no explicit talk about God. Does this mean that scientific cosmology has nothing to say about creative agency in the universe? No.

While scientific cosmology does not speak directly of God, it does speak about a kind of creative agency in the universe: self-organizing dynamics. Self-organization (autopoiesis) may be found at all scales of cosmic activity, including matter, life, and human culture (Kauffman, 1995). Atoms, galaxies, and all structures in the universe emerge out of self-organizing dynamics. Consider the emergence of a star (Swimme and Tucker, 2011: 29). A cloud of hydrogen and helium atoms accumulates, and as their mass increases so does their gravity. At some point, the cloud gets so big that its own gravitational attraction pulls its atoms together. Vibrating, colliding, and imploding, the atoms thus heat up gradually until the particles get so hot – millions of degrees – that they undergo nuclear fusion, fusing into new relationships and producing new elements while exploding into starlight. As the fusion process explodes, gravity pulls the explosion together, preventing it from simply dissipating. The star exists on a knife's edge, a "seething disequilibrium" that strikes a creative balance between fusion and gravity, a balance that emerges out of the self-organizing dynamics of the star (p. 30).

The star organizes itself, pulling itself together through the gravity of its own mass, exploding into starlight through the fusion of its own particles. In short, the star is self-generating, self-creating. The star has agency. It is a subject. This does not mean a star is conscious. It means that it generates and maintains itself. It has itself as a value. Every center of the multicentric and evolutionary universe exhibits some form of subjectivity or self-organizing dynamics, a hurricane, an eagle, a galaxy, a star, a person, an anthill, and the whole Earth. Every center is implicated in the others, each unfolding from the same flaring forth, the same complex and chaotic process of the cosmos: chaosmosis.

The spirit of the chaosmos

Through the articulation of a multicentric and evolutionary universe, contemporary scientific cosmology sees the world as a communion of subjects, not a collection of objects. This poses an immense challenge to ethical perspectives oriented around the idea that only humans have subjectivity and thus only humans have value in themselves. If everything admits of some degree of subjectivity or self-organization, then everything has itself or its system as a value. Scientific cosmology depicts a world where creative agency and value is everywhere. However, scientific perspectives do not say what humans should do about that value. How should we act if the cosmos is a communion of subjects, a chaosmosis of singularities? Ethics must somehow account for the subjectivity or intrinsic value of all beings. This is a task to which philosophical and religious perspectives can contribute.

As the environmental philosopher Anthony Weston (2009: 89–90) puts it, this is the task of transitioning from anthropocentrism to "multicentrism," which is oriented around "*diverse centers*, shifting and overlapping but still each with its own irreducible and distinctive starting-point," each existing as its own "world with separate though mutually implicated centers." No particular centrism should hold all value, not anthropocentrism, biocentrism, or ecocentrism. For multicentrism, the center is everywhere. The task of transitioning to a multicentric outlook is a task of caring for multiple centers enmeshed in shifting and overlapping relationships distributed across the chaosmos. The transdisciplinary theologian Catherine Keller provides an example of how philosophical and religious perspectives can enter into dialogue with scientific cosmology to facilitate a transition to ethical care in an evolving, multicentric universe. This may be seen in her recovery of the Christian symbol of the trinity, which she situates in a contemporary cosmological context by reconstructing the trinity in terms of Deleuze's complex chaosmos.

The Christian trinity expresses the unity of the three persons of God: God the Father, God the Son (Jesus Christ), and spirit (*ruach*, Hebrew; *pneuma*, Greek). Keller reconstructs the notion of God the Father by retrieving a profound feminine element in God, which is also indicative of the chaos in the cosmos which God creates. That feminine element is *tehom* ("deep"), which is mentioned in the Hebrew Bible like a feminine name (a feminine gendered noun without an article like "the" or "a") in the opening of the first book of the Bible, Genesis: "In the beginning when God created the heavens and the earth, the earth was a formless void and darkness covered the face of the deep, while a wind [*ruach*] from God swept over the face of the waters" (Gen. 1:1–2). Keller (2003: 12) shows how this passage indicates that the Hebrew vision of the creation is not a vision of a statically ordered cosmos but a chaosmos, where order emerges from the hovering, vibrating movement of spirit sweeping over the chaos of the deep.

Against what theologians have traditionally said, God does not create "out of nothing" (*ex nihilo*). God creates "out of the deep" (*ex profundis*). The image of God as a Father creating out of nothing, suppressing the chaos of dynamic relationships, is not unlike the pattern of domination whereby humans exploit the natural world. A related pattern of domination is at work in sexism and hetero-sexism whereby male-dominated (patriarchal) social systems suppress feminine wisdom as well as women and members of the LGBTQ community (lesbian, gay, bisexual, transgender, and queer). Keller makes a poignant pun when she notes that there is "an incipient *tehomophobia*" in biblical religions, a phobia that "prepares the way for the *creatio ex nihilo*," sexism, homophobia, and other forms of domination (p. 26). Creating out of the deep, God does not impose order and suppress chaotic conditions whereby beings organize themselves. Less dominating and more loving, God creates by unfolding the uncertain and complex capacities of chaos.

The image of God the Father may thus be reconstructed such that God names the complexity of the chaosmos – the *complicatio* from which order unfolds and in which everything folds together. Adapting Deleuze's (1994: 123) secular trinity, which is derived from Cusa and Bruno, Keller (2007: 143) reconstructs God the Father, Son, and Spirit as *complicatio*, *explicatio*, and *implicatio*. As *complicatio*, God is less of a dominant father and more like an infinite matrix or womb, the complex chaosmosis that creates out of the deep. If God is *complicatio*, then the Son is *explicatio* (p. 144). Represented as Christ – the Word (*logos*) or wisdom (*sophia*) of God – *explicatio* refers to the unfolding (explicating) of the different structures of the universe. The Word of God resonates in the evolutionary emergence of different centers, different self-organizing systems. The third capacity – *implicatio* – names the mutuality that relates the infinite depths of the chaosmos (*complicatio*) to the different structures unfolding from it (*explicatio*) (p. 145). This mutuality or relationality is traditionally represented as "the *spirit of God*," the spirit vibrating over the face of the deep, intensifying differences by bringing beings (explications) into contact with their divine ground (chaotic complexity) (Keller, 2003: 232).

With support from Deleuze's philosophical cosmology, Keller reconstructs the trinity in a way that resituates it within the multicentrism of an evolutionary chaosmos. God does not impose a static order but unfolds a dynamic order out of chaos. Christ is not the only center of divinity in the universe but represents the unfolding of multiplicities of different centers, and spirit is not just a personal connection with God but is the relationality and mutuality whereby all centers relate to one another and to the creative depths of the chaosmos. Furthermore, Keller also points toward possibilities for bringing multiple religious cosmologies into dialogue. For instance, she suggests a possible connection between the chaotic matrix of *tehom* and the flowing "Way" (*dao*) expressed in the Chinese traditions of Daoism and Confucianism (p. 14).

Elaborating on this connection, Hyo-Dong Lee (2014) considers philosophical and theological conceptions of spirit in comparison with the Daoist and Confucian principle of *qi* (sometimes spelled *ch'i*). Lee translates *qi* as "psychophysical energy," but there are many alternative translations, including "material force," "vital energy," or "psychophysical stuff," and like the Greek and Hebrew words for spirit, it derives linguistically from words like "steam," "breath," and "wind" (p. 42). *Qi* is not unlike spirit hovering over the chaotic waters of the deep. It is complex, constantly moving and changing as it intimately intertwines material with ideal, physical with psychological, and energetic with mental; it is the generative source that unfolds all things; and it is the intensifying energy that connects beings to one another in their creative matrix.

The complex, unfolding, and intensifying characteristics of *qi* parallel Deleuze's and Keller's trinities. Lee compares those trinities with a trinity expressed in Neo-Confucianism, which emerged out of Confucianism approximately 1000 years ago with efforts to present a more philosophically robust Confucianism. *Qi*, like the spirit of God, may be understood in terms of three capacities, although not three persons. As with Deleuze, there is no personal God in Daoism or Confucianism, but there is still a concept of ultimate reality, which is described in more impersonal, cosmological terminology. The Neo-Confucian trinity views the psychophysical energy of *qi* in terms of *yi* (Change), *dao* (Way), and *shen* (Spirit), which corresponds with Deleuze's *complicatio, explicatio, implicatio* (p. 199).

Yi is the process of chaosmosis, the constantly fluctuating movement that makes possible the structure of the world and myriad things. It is the creative matrix of the universe. *Dao* is the way in which structure or pattern (*li*) unfolds from *yi* and becomes different self-organizing things, each of which explicates a configuration of passive (*yin*) and active (*yang*) aspects of *qi* (e.g., a mountain is considered *yang*, whereas a valley is *yin*; sunlight and fire are *yang*, and shade and ice are *yin*). *Shen* is the relationality and affective mutuality whereby things fold into a communion of subjects. The terminology here can be confusing.

Shen represents spirit as the third capacity of the trinity, whereas *qi* refers to spirit in the sense of the psychophysical energy that has three capacities (*yi, dao, shen*). The overall point is that the trinity grounds humans in a cosmic community, wherein the dynamic process (*yi*) of the universe unfolds myriad beings along a path (*dao*) of yin–yang configurations that are always in communication and communion (*shen*). In short, the religious cosmology and ecology of Neo-Confucianism is anthropocosmic (Grim and Tucker, 2014: 113).

Lee does not claim that the Neo-Confucian trinity is the same as Keller's reconstruction of the Christian trinity or Deleuze's trinity of the chaosmos. It is important to recognize the differences between those trinities (e.g., the Christian trinity is theistic, the others are not; the Confucian trinity relates to traditions of Chinese medicine and internal martial arts; Deleuze's trinity is aligned more with science than with religion). Nonetheless, those trinities resonate with one another. They implicate one another, pointing different ways toward shared concerns for engaging cosmology not only as a scientific endeavor but also as an ethical and existential commitment.

For Deleuze, Keller, and Lee, cosmology provides a context within which one can scientifically understand that we live in an evolutionary universe, and, more than that, it also provides a context within which philosophical concepts and religious symbols can reorient the human species and rejuvenate the Earth community. Philosophical and religious cosmologies can reorient humans toward an existential affirmation of our place in the chaosmos, and they can renew human participation in the world, empowering the cultivation of mutually intensifying human–Earth relations. The trinities expressed in Keller's vision of Christianity, Deleuze's philosophy, and Lee's Neo-Confucianism can do great work together, forming a powerful trinity in their own right. They can empower the multitude of humans to resist the domination and destruction currently colonizing the planet and replace it with vibrant planetary coexistence. They can support efforts to resituate the multitude "within a planetary web of life characterized by the interdependent flourishing of all, that is, the democracy of creation" (Lee, 2014: 41).

The point of integrating scientific, philosophical, and religious cosmologies is not just to interpret the universe. The point is to facilitate intimate participation in the unfolding epic of evolution, engaging in its chaotic process (*complicatio*), attending to the way in which self-organizing centers unfold (*explicatio*), and caring for the mutuality that connects all beings together in the same process (*implicatio*). The point is to reinvent the human, to resituate the human amidst a communion of subjects, which is to say, amidst the innumerable interdependent centers of the unfolding chaosmos. That would provide a context within which the human species could orient itself toward a multicentric concern for the cultivation of mutually enhancing human–Earth relations. By entering into dialogue with the contemporary scientific understanding of the evolutionary and multicentric universe, philosophical and religious cosmologies articulate a context for empowering and enhancing the interdependent flourishing of the emerging Earth community.

References

Berry, Thomas. 1999. *The Great Work: Our Way into the Future*. New York: Bell Tower.

———. 2009. *The Sacred Universe: Earth, Spirituality, and Religion in the Twenty-first Century*. Ed. Mary Evelyn Tucker. New York: Columbia University Press.

Casey, Edward S. 1997. *The Fate of Place: A Philosophical History*. Berkeley: University of California Press.

Deleuze, Gilles. 1994. *Difference and Repetition*. Trans. Paul Patton. New York: Columbia University Press.

Duncan, Todd and Craig Tyler. 2009. *Your Cosmic Context: An Introduction to Modern Cosmology*. San Francisco, CA: Pearson.

El-Aswad, El-Sayed. 2002. *Religion and Folk Cosmology: Scenarios of the Visible and Invisible in Rural Egypt*. Westport, CT: Praeger.

Grim, John and Mary Evelyn Tucker. 2014. *Ecology and Religion*. Washington, DC: Island Press.

Guattari, Félix. 1995. *Chaosmosis: An Ethico–Aesthetic Paradigm*. Trans. Paul Bains and Julian Pefanis. Bloomington: Indiana University Press.

Joyce, James. 1982. *Finnegans Wake*. New York: Penguin Books.

Kauffman, Stuart. 1995. *At Home in the Universe: The Search for Laws of Self-organization and Complexity*. Oxford: Oxford University Press.

———. 2008. *Reinventing the Sacred: A New View of Science, Reason, and Religion*. New York: Basic Books.

Keller, Catherine. 2003. *Face of the Deep: A Theology of Becoming*. New York: Routledge.

———. 2007. "Rumors of Transcendence: The Movement, State, and Sex of 'Beyond.'" In *Transcendence and Beyond: A Postmodern Inquiry*, ed. John D. Caputo and Michael J. Scanlon, 129–150. Bloomington: Indiana University Press.

King, Henry G. 2003. *The History of the Telescope*. Mineola, NY: Dover Publications.

Lee, Hyo-Dong. 2014. *Spirit, Qi, and the Multitude: A Comparative Theology for the Democracy of Creation*. New York: Fordham University Press.

Rubenstein, Mary-Jane. 2014. *Worlds without End: The Many Lives of the Multiverse*. New York: Columbia University Press.

Snyder, Gary. 1990. *The Practice of the Wild*. Berkeley, CA: Counterpoint.

Swimme, Brian. 1984. *The Universe is a Green Dragon*. Santa Fe, CA: Bear and Company.

———. 1996. *The Hidden Heart of the Cosmos: Humanity and the New Story*. Maryknoll: Orbis Books.

Swimme, Brian and Thomas Berry. 1992. *The Universe Story: From the Primordial Flaring Forth to the Ecozoic Era – A Celebration of the Unfolding of the Cosmos*. San Francisco, CA: HarperCollins.

Swimme, Brian and Mary Evelyn Tucker. 2011. *Journey of the Universe*. New Haven, CT: Yale University Press.

Weston, Anthony. 2009. *The Incompleat Eco-Philosopher: Essays from the Edges of Environmental Ethics*. Albany: State University of New York Press.

9 Narrative imagination, dangerous dreams

Whole Earth thinking envisions humans as participants in an emerging Earth community situated within the dynamics of the evolving universe. Thomas Berry describes this vision in terms of the reinvention of the human, which he considers to be the crucial challenge of our era of planetary interconnectedness. As previous chapters discuss, the reinvention of the human takes place at the species level and with critical reflection (Chapter 6), and it reorients humans to their place within the complexity, community, and subjectivity of the Earth community (Chapter 7) and the unfolding cosmos (Chapter 8). This chapter focuses on the final part of Berry's call to reinvent the human. The reinvention of the human takes place "by means of story and shared dream experience" (Berry, 1999: 159).

Scientific perspectives make important contributions to the ecological wisdom that a reinvention of the human requires. However, they are not sufficient. For instance, you can explain climate change to someone by saying that there is too much carbon dioxide in the atmosphere for our climate to remain stable, but that is rarely sufficient to motivate a response. If the facts alone were sufficient, international institutional action in response to climate change would have begun years ago. However, such action has yet to really begin, although an international grassroots climate movement is growing. What empowers responses and motivates change? It is not just the facts. To inspire concerned action, there has to be something like a vision, a song, a dream, or an image. In short, narrative imagination is a crucial component of whole Earth thinking. Without a story that communicates a shared dream of a vibrant Earth community, how can people make sense of the facts of the ecological crisis and orient their action? "The dream drives the action" (p. 201).

Gilles Deleuze and Félix Guattari make a related point. Whereas the geologian calls for the reorientation of the human species to a vibrant Earth community, Deleuze and Guattari propose a geophilosophy that creates concepts for planetary renewal and a reinvention of humanity. "The creation of concepts in itself calls for a future form, for a new earth and people that do not yet exist" (Deleuze and Guattari, 1994: 108). Furthermore, the task of developing geophilosophical concepts must be grounded in the real world. The concepts must be immanent, expressed here and now in a way that is relevant to the relations and contexts of real beings. This contextuality and relationality is a commitment that geophilosophy shares with the sources of wisdom in indigenous traditions and feminist perspectives (see Chapter 5). It means that geophilosophy must experiment with non-philosophical or non-conceptual ways of knowing, relying on measures that are not included within the purview of scientific or rational knowledge.

> These measures belong to the order of dreams, of pathological processes, esoteric experiences, drunkenness, and excess. We head for the horizon, on the plane of immanence, and we return with bloodshot eyes, yet they are the eyes of the mind. . . . To think is always to follow the witch's flight.
>
> (Deleuze and Guattari, 1994: 41)

For thinking to facilitate real transformation and to empower humans to become different, to become planetary, thinking must become visionary.

To practice whole Earth thinking, one must undertake flights of imagination, not unlike the flights of some witches, shamans, and yogis, and not unlike the flights that inspire artists, scientists, and philosophers. One must find an entrancing vision that can be communicated to others. One must perform a song that others can hear and understand as well as participate in for themselves. Ultimately, for a song to orient people to the planet and the universe, it must be rooted in the universe, and not only in the sense of a song that sings about the universe. Such a song must come from the resonating cosmos itself. It must come from "the song of the universe" (p. 189). Berry (2014: 18–19) makes a similar point:

> We need to see the sequence of earthly transformations as so many movements in a musical composition. In music, the earlier notes are gone when the later notes are played, but the musical phrase, indeed the entire symphony, needs to be heard simultaneously. We do not fully understand the opening notes until the later notes are heard. Each new theme alters the meaning of the earlier themes and the entire composition. The opening theme resonates through all the later parts of the piece.

The dream that motivates concerned action for the Earth community is a dream of Earth (Berry, 1990). It is a dream of the Earth community, by the Earth community, and for the Earth community. The entrancing story that can orient humans to the universe as a communion of subjects is the story of the universe.

Integrating perspectives from the humanities and sciences, Berry presents his "new story" with the cosmologist Brian Swimme in *The Universe Story*, "the first comprehensive narrative of universe, Earth, and human emergence" (Grim and Tucker, 2014: 59). The book concludes with the point that the myriad stories that are told about the universe are part of one unfolding journey, one evolutionary epic, "one story, the story of the universe" (Swimme and Berry, 1992: 268). The universe itself is storied. It is epic. In other words, "the universe is unfolding and has a story – a beginning, a middle (where we are now), and, perhaps in some unimaginable future, an end" (Swimme and Tucker, 2011: 6). For some anthropocentric perspectives, nothing in the universe can imagine or communicate except for humans, in which case it seems impossible for the universe to be a story or a dream. Before considering how narrative imagination can facilitate a reinvention of the human, it is important to clarify how capacities for stories, images, dreams, and songs are distributed across the universe and are not confined in human beings.

Stories, dreams, refrains

In a communion of subjects, all beings have agency in interdependent and interconnected relations with other beings, which is to say, all beings are enmeshed in networks of communication. To be is to be communicative, capable of producing messages. Each message starts at some point and, sooner or later, stops. Each message has a beginning and an end, and thus displays something like a narrative structure. Accordingly, storytelling should not be considered an exclusively human endeavor. The anthropologist Gregory Bateson (1979: 12) provides some clarification of this point:

> Now I want to show you that whatever the word "story" means . . . thinking in terms of stories does not isolate human beings as something separate from the starfish and the sea anemones, the coconut palms and the primroses. Rather, if the world be connected, if I am at all fundamentally right in what I am saying, then thinking in terms of stories must be shared by all minds, whether ours or those of redwood forests and sea anemones . . . the evolutionary process through millions of generations whereby the sea anemone, like you and me, came to be – that process, too, must be of the stuff of stories.

Gary Snyder (1990: 71) makes an analogous point about how nature may be understood as a text:

> A text is information stored through time. The stratigraphy of rocks, layers of pollen in a swamp, the outward expanding circles in the trunk of a tree, can be seen as texts. The calligraphy of rivers winding back and forth over the land leaving layer upon layer of traces of previous riverbeds is text.

The idea that everything is made of the stuff of stories or meaningful messages is not new. It may be found in indigenous traditions, classical religions, and throughout the history of philosophy.

In indigenous traditions, an example of a world made of stories may be found in the Aboriginal people of Australia, particularly in the notion of a Dream Time or Dreaming. The time of Dreaming is an ancestral time, a time of creation when humans and nonhumans shifted shapes, transforming and blending into one another. It is the time of the emergence of the intimate relationships and lineages that make some beings kin, and kin are never just other members of the same species. Kin are always entangled in multispecies relationships. The human in this context exists within a multispecies kinship group, intimately related to certain animals, plants, and places. For instance, the dingo – a wild dog – is considered a close relative to the human (Rose, 2000).

The Dreaming is an ancestral time, a time of creation, a time of the emergence of kinship groups. However, it is not simply a time in the past. It is ongoing.

> "Dreaming" or "dreamtime" refers to a time of fluidity, shape-shifting, inter-species conversation and intersexuality, radically creative moves, whole landscapes being altered. It is often taken to be a "mythical past," but it is not really in *any* time. We might as well say it is *right now*.
>
> (Snyder, 1990: 91)

Dreaming is here right now. The tracks of its creativity are distributed across the landscape. Deborah Bird Rose, an anthropologist and leading figure of environmental humanities, describes her encounter with the tracks of Dreaming while visiting sacred sites as part of her research in Aboriginal country. "We learned that the desert is crisscrossed with Dreaming tracks, and that people's lives are part of these tracks because people are born into the stories and places of Dreaming sites and songlines" (Rose, 2011: 13).

The tracks of Dreaming are the stories of the places, stories of the emergence and transformation of the landscape, its inhabitants, and their kinship groups. They are not just stories people tell about those places. They are stories embedded in the places. Dreaming sites are storied places. The tracks of Dreaming may be read like stories. Dreaming tracks are like lines of a song. Aboriginal people follow those tracks, renewing their connections to their places and their multi-species kinship groups by telling the stories distributed across the terrain, singing the "songlines" of the land (Chatwin, 1987). Telling the stories of the land is a way of connecting one's body to the land and folding the past into the present. Singing the stories of Dreaming tracks can open up future possibilities for renewing human–Earth relations and for recovering and reconstructing past traditions and lineages. Sometimes the stories of Dreaming tracks fail to open up future possibilities, indicating instead the foreclosure of those possibilities as Aboriginal traditions are suppressed or backgrounded in the wake of colonialism, modernism, and industrialization. For instance, Snyder recounts an experience of traveling by truck in the desert of central Australia, when an elder member of the Pintubi people began speaking very quickly to him.

> He was talking about a mountain over there, telling me a story about some wallabies that came to that mountain in the dreamtime and got into some kind of mischief with some lizard girls. He had hardly finished that and he started in on another story about another hill over here and another story over there. I couldn't keep up.
>
> (Snyder 1990: 88)

Snyder realized shortly thereafter that those stories were supposed to be told not in a moving truck but while moving at a much slower pace: walking.

When trucks and other products of industrial technology mediate human–Earth relations, it is difficult for people to maintain intimate contact with their surroundings, their traditions, and their kin. Losing place-based stories means losing everything, losing cultural diversity, losing traditional ecological knowledge that preserves biodiversity, and losing one's "*title* to the land" (p. 7). The disruption of native stories has gone hand in hand with the colonization and exploitation of native lands in Australia and worldwide.

Recuperating a sense of the storied landscape is crucial for recuperating the cultural and biological diversity of the whole Earth community. Along with indigenous perspectives on the dreams, songs, and stories inscribed on the world, classical philosophical and religious traditions can also contribute to a sense of intimate participation in a storied universe or a communicative cosmos. Although classical traditions of philosophy and religion often focus on human–human or human–divine relations to the exclusion of human–Earth relations, the anthropocosmic strands of those traditions that do not restrict the meaning-making forces of narrative imagination to humans but recognize that meaning-making forces are at work in all life and the whole universe. Meaning-making activities may be found in the wild, self-organizing dynamics of the universe, whereby each being tells its own story and finds itself implicated in the stories of others. In his proposal for a contemplative ecology, Douglas Christie (2013: 189) suggests that the song of the wild world can be heard in multiple religious traditions.

It can be heard in Hindu, Buddhist, and Jain accounts of *dharma*, which refers variously to a cosmic order or law as well as a phenomenon or true teaching. To do your duty, attend to the world, and walk a path of wisdom is to follow the *dharma* inscribed on the world. Along those lines, Christie also considers the ancient Chinese understanding of *dao*, which suggests that meaning is not located exclusively in the human but emerges along the unfolding way (*dao*) of the universe (p. 188). A sense of a meaning-making universe may also be found in biblical understandings of wisdom (*hokmah*/*sophia*) emerging in the contexts and relations of places (see Chapter 5). It may also be found in the Christian concept of Jesus Christ as the *logos* ("word") of God, which is not just the person of Jesus but is a capacity of the trinity (God, Christ, Spirit). The *logos* of God is the creative expression through which the universe unfolds self-organizing structures (see Chapter 8).

> *Dao, Dharma, Hokmah/Sophia, Logos*: here is language that invites us to consider again the cosmological sensibilities of our great religious traditions, and the informing spiritual principles that arise from paying close attention to the wild. The wild world has its own voice, its own language. Learning how to listen – whether in a field by the ocean or in a chapel in the Redwood forest, or anywhere – is part of our common task.
>
> (Christie, 2013: 189)

Furthermore, philosophy can contribute to this common task. The Christian *logos* intersects with the concept of *logos* inherited in philosophical studies of logic and the "-ologies" of the sciences (e.g., biology, ecology, cosmology, sociology, anthropology, psychology).

Christie notes that the cosmically creative *logos* of Christianity resonates with the understanding of *logos* in the ancient philosophical tradition of Stoicism (p. 193). For the Stoics, the words (*logoi*) that becomes expressed in human speech are only the explicit manifestation of a cosmic *logos* that permeates everything. That cosmic *logos* is a seed (*logos spermatikos*), a rational meaning folded into the universe. This is not quite the same as saying that the universe is a creative dream, a story, or a sacred meaning (i.e., Christ). Typical of philosophy, the Stoics privilege a rational (logical) to a storied (mythical) universe. This distinct separation of logical from mythical thinking is important for the intricate and specific work done in scientific ways of knowing (-ologies). However, in the dynamic, creative context of an evolving universe, the story of the universe is clearly more than rational. Its rational, calculable, measurable side also has a wild side. Its order (*kosmos*) is entangled with the spontaneous change of disorder (*chaos*).

The voice of the chaosmos is not simply rational. From a geophilosophical perspective, the voice of the chaosmos is uproarious, loud, noisy, obstreperous, and wild. "A single voice raises the clamour of being" (Deleuze, 1994: 35). That clamor does not always make sense to reason. It communicates the voice of "the whole thousand-voiced multiple," like a confused nonsense that fuses together every sense of every being (p. 304). The clamor of being is chaotic yet communicative, multiple yet singular. To be is to participate in a "unique event in which all events communicate with one another," "the nonsense of all senses in one," "a single voice for every hum of voices and every drop of water in the sea" (Deleuze, 1990: 180). What is this clamoring voice if it is not simply reason? What is this voice that can also be heard telling stories, singing songs, sharing dreams, teaching *dharma*, speaking the creative *logos* and *sophia* of God?

Perhaps it may be understood as a little ditty, what musicians call in Italian a *ritornello* ("little return"). It is something like a pattern that comes back and repeats itself in innumerably different stories, songs, dreams, words, patterns, teachings, and more. This is what Deleuze and Guattari (1987) call a "refrain." In music, a refrain is any line that repeats. The chorus of a song is often called a refrain or contains a refrain. Deleuze and Guattari expand upon the musical definition of refrains, and they develop it into a geophilosophical concept for which the whole universe is a song made up of different repetitions of refrains. The clamor of being is the song of the wild world, the story of the chaosmos. As with other concepts of geophilosophy, refrains involve a dynamic tension between order (territorialization) and chaos (deterritorialization). This may be understood in terms of three components of refrains.

First, the territorializing component begins to draw some degree of order out of chaos, like a lost child whistling in the dark to find some comfort in a terrifying situation. In this way, a refrain territorializes chaos. It opens up a "center in the heart of chaos," which is to say, it creates "a circle around that uncertain and fragile center" (Deleuze and Guattari, 1987: 311). Second, the emerging order goes from organizing to organized, from territorializing to territorialized. Whistling in the dark barely makes one feel at home, whereas this component exists when one's sense of home is secured and its boundaries firmly stabilized, so that walls, fences, and roofs have been put up, a mailing address has been obtained, a garden has been planted, and you have a favorite room in the house where you like reading or listening to music. Third, the refrain deterritorializes boundaries and structures. It opens up possibilities to let things in or out of the territory. This does not mean breaking down into chaos. It chaotically breaks through territories in order to build connections with the universe; that is, "in order to join with the forces of the future, cosmic forces. One launches forth . . . to join with the World, or meld with it" (p. 311). One can use one's habitual structures as a hub from which to launch into many creative endeavors to build mutually intensifying relationships with people, places, and the universe. In sum, refrains find and stabilize ordered structures and they creatively disorder those structures.

Everything in the universe is a refrain, a narrative imagining itself, a pattern organizing itself at the edge where order and chaos meet. Sometimes refrains become highly organized (like geological strata), and sometimes they undergo periods of radical disorganization (like earthquakes). Too much order chokes out creativity, and too much disorder makes things collapse. On the edge of chaos, every particular being unfolds itself, singing its refrain, telling its story. Ultimately, the relative refrains of all beings open out onto the single clamoring refrain of the universe – "the songs of the Molecules," the refrain of the chaosmos, "an immense deterritorialized refrain" (p. 327). To be is to be a refrain sharing in the single clamor of the universe, the immense refrain of "rhythm-chaos or the chaosmos" (p. 313). "Everything begins with refrains," and the refrains of all beings – material, living, and human – are implicated in one another in "the great Refrain," "the song of the universe" (Deleuze and Guattari, 1994: 189).

Dreaming dangerously

The clamoring song of the universe is chaotic, but its chaos harbors patterns, structures, self-organizing dynamics. In the current era of planetary interconnectedness, it is by means of shared participation in the song of the universe that humans can reinvent themselves and support the emergence of vibrant modes of planetary coexistence, becoming a renewed people, inhabiting a renewed Earth community. The universe story reorients humans to their ecological and evolutionary contexts, not just by communicating facts and reasons, but by communicating a vision – a sense of the whole Earth community unfolding in a cosmic journey. The universe story communicates a dream. It provides a context for participating in the dream of an Earth community of interdependent flourishing.

The dream of a flourishing Earth community is a dream of peace, justice, and mutuality. It is not unlike the dream expressed by Martin Luther King, Jr., whose famous "I have a dream" speech delivered on April 28, 1963 put into words the dream driving the civil rights movement, a dream for a more just and peaceful world, a dream for mutuality instead of domination. King's dream was not just wishful thinking or wide-eyed optimism. He was well aware of the nightmare of racism and injustice, but he did not dwell in negativity, cynicism, and criticism. He envisioned a way to become different. "Let us not wallow in the valley of despair. . . . so even though we face the difficulties of today and tomorrow, I still have a dream" (King, 2001, p. 85). The same may be said of the current difficulties facing planetary coexistence. Even though we face those difficulties, some of us nonetheless have a vision of emancipation, a vision of freedom from the domination and exploitation running rampant through the environments, societies, and subjects of Earth.

Dreams of planetary emancipation resist the destructive dreams of anthropocentrism – dreams of consumerism, infinite economic growth, and technological progress. The tension between dreams of mutually enhancing relationships and dreams of domination is increasing around the planet. More people are participating in the dream of mutuality, but at the same time destruction and exploitation continues to spread. This tension is evident in some of the worldwide revolutionary political actions of 2011. As the philosopher Slavoj Žižek (2012: 127) describes it, "2011 was the year of dreaming dangerously, of the revival of radical emancipatory politics all around the world." The democratic clamor of the multitude could be heard in riots in the United Kingdom, the Occupy Wall Street movement, and the Egyptian Revolution and other protests and riots associated with the Arab Spring. The year 2014 too was one of dangerous dreams flaring forth in numerous protests, demonstrations, and riots around the world (Hampson, 2014). Alongside the clamor of emancipation one finds the monotonous refrains of domination. Alongside "emancipatory dreams" there are "destructive dreams," the former aiming to mobilize the multitude, the latter seeking to maintain power over people and territories (Žižek, 2012: 1).

Both kinds of dreams are dangerous. Destructive dreams are dangerous to all life on Earth. Dreams of control and domination are propagating poverty and inequality among humans, destroying biological and cultural diversity, destabilizing the climate, and polluting the land, water, and air. Dreams of control and domination are destructive even for those who are in positions of power. By controlling and dominating others, those people become dissociated from their own humanity and their place in the unfolding universe. They become confined to prisons of individualism, where any happiness and meaning attained in life are but brief flashes of light in a vast darkness of loneliness and meaninglessness. Dreams of emancipation not only aim to emancipate the oppressed. They also seek the emancipation of oppressors, so that those in power can reinvent themselves and renew their participation in the Earth community.

Dreaming of emancipation is dangerous because it threatens the status quo and refuses to accept business as usual. Emancipatory dreams are dangerous to the government and corporate elites that currently hold power. They are dangerous to complacent and apathetic attitudes that pretend nothing needs to change. They are dangerous to all those who seek to control and possess the Earth community. They are also dangerous because those who dream of emancipation risk retaliation from those with opposing dreams, which envision domination instead of emancipation.

Dreaming of freedom is risky. Protestors risk their bodies, risking exposure to violence, risking imprisonment, risking their lives. The assassination of Martin Luther King is a poignant reminder that dreaming of peace, justice, and mutuality is dangerous.

Singing the song of Earth is a way of joining in the emancipatory dream of the multitude, reconnecting humans to the Earth community and to the indomitable creativity of the cosmos in and through which all things unfold. Telling the story of the universe is a radical political act. It is a political act insofar as it provides a context for demanding institutional support for the freedom and flourishing of subjects. It is a radical political act insofar as it recognizes that subjects are not exclusively human but include all material and living beings in the cosmos. In a communion of subjects, "every being has rights to be recognized and revered," which entails that humans "have no rights to disturb the basic functioning of the biosystems of the planet" (Berry, 1999: 5). No being can be the absolute owner of another, and to the limited extent that institutions of ownership or property can exist, they must be situated in relationships of concern for the values intrinsic to the property. If you own land, you have to care for that land and not treat it as a mere resource or object to be used for human benefit.

The radical democratic politics implicit in Earth-based storytelling may be described as participatory ecological democracy, facilitating the participation of humans and nonhumans in the decision-making processes that affect them and their places. For the Indian environmentalist and ecofeminist Vandana Shiva (2005), this may be described as "Earth democracy," which respects the rights of all beings to sustenance, values the intrinsic worth of all species, people, and cultures, promotes cultural and biological diversity, and advocates peaceful, caring, and compassionate relationships. Earth democracy reflects the Hindu values embedded in Shiva's culture, for which all of the human and nonhuman beings of Earth are envisioned as a whole Earth family (*vasudhaiva kutumbakam*) (p. 1). This also resonates with the vision of shared values presented in the Earth Charter (see Chapter 7). Participatory ecological democracy is not just left or right politics, not simply liberal or conservative, democratic or republican. This emancipatory dream challenges all the current divisions between political parties. It is a dream that envisions a new context for politics, the ecological context of the emerging Earth community. This dream envisions a new division, and not into a new left and new right. It is not a division into social classes, ethnic groups, or religious sects. "It is a division based on the human as one of the components within the larger community of the planet Earth" (Berry, 1999: 107). It is a division between the emancipatory dream of participation in mutually enhancing human–Earth relations and the destructive dream of human superiority and control.

While the clamor of democracy has risen up many times since the beginnings of democracy in ancient Greece, from the American and French revolutions to the Arab Spring and the Occupy movement, the emancipatory dream of the Earth community has been dormant and even suppressed, supplanted by dreams of human superiority. In the development of classical and modern societies, humans have lost contact with the storied landscape. So many humans have forgotten how to read the texts of the wild world, forgotten how to participate in the dream of the Earth community. Berry (1999: 165) observes that most people "probably have not had such participation in the dream of the Earth since earlier shamanic times," and since then humans have gradually transitioned into an "exaggerated and destructive" dream of human superiority and an "entrancement with industrial civilization."

The task of renewing human participation in the songs of Earth and the cosmos calls for humans to break free of the entrancing dreams of human superiority and of ongoing technological and economic progress. It calls for humans to become sensitive and open to "a new revelatory experience"; that is, "an experience wherein human consciousness awakens to the grandeur and sacred quality of the Earth process" (p. 165). Participating in a dream of planetary renewal is not just a radical political act. It is a visionary act, a sacred experience. A new revelatory experience would be similar to the visionary experiences of shamans or other healers in indigenous communities, who undergo trances and extraordinary states of consciousness that provide visions with which healers can empower and heal. A new revelatory experience need not be derived from indigenous traditions or any particular religious tradition. It can come from many sources. The flights of imagination and "dream awareness" that artists experience also provide a model for humans to receive "a vision of the future sufficiently entrancing that it will sustain us in the transformation of the human project that is now in process" (p. x).

Along with religious visions and artistic flights of imagination, geophilosophical thinking makes room for a vast multiplicity of methods for rejuvenating human participation in the song of the universe. As Deleuze and Guattari point out, participation in the Great Refrain can be motivated by many non-conceptual or non-rational methods, including art, dreams, sickness, intoxication, and secret or suppressed spiritual practices, like those of sorcerers or witches. Almost anything can empower a new dream. You have to experiment. The point of those methods is thus not to build a system of ideas or express a final answer or solution to the challenges of planetary coexistence. The point of those methods is to facilitate experimentation with different ways of participating in the Great Refrain, which means opening up the refrains of the human species so that they connect to the creative forces of the cosmos, becoming "hypersensitive to the cosmos" (Guattari, 2011: 11). "Produce a deterritorialized refrain . . . release it in the Cosmos – that is more important than building a new system. Opening the assemblage onto a cosmic force" (Deleuze and Guattari, 1987: 350).

Deleuze and Guattari are not particularly concerned with where a refrain comes from – science, painting, philosophy, sickness, drunkenness, poetry, ecstatic visions, sex, dreams, etc. They are concerned with connecting the refrain to the creative forces of the cosmos. Those connections are uncertain and unpredictable. Accordingly, Deleuze and Guattari (1994: 41) caution that the kind of thinking demanded by geophilosophy is "a dangerous exercise." A renewal of people and the planet is far from a guaranteed success. New structures emerge from the seething disequilibrium of the chaosmos. Too much order (territorialization) chokes out creativity, and too much disorder (deterritorialization) causes things to collapse. Along these lines, there is another sense in which dreams of planetary emancipation are dangerous. As was said above, they are dangerous to those who want to maintain their dreams of human superiority and domination, and they are dangerous because the people who participate in those dreams risk their lives by invoking alternative ways of being in the world that challenge the status quo. Participating in the dream of mutually intensifying human–Earth relations is also dangerous because such a dream opens up to the source of all danger and risk, the churning chaos of the evolving universe.

We do not yet know the outcome of the dream of vibrant planetary coexistence. It is possible that new attitudes, habits, and institutions will emerge that build mutually enhancing relationships between humans and the other members of the emerging Earth community. However, it is also possible that emerging relationships of mutuality will fail to grow. They could fall off of either side of the knife's edge upon which cosmic creativity unfolds. On one side, they are in danger of becoming suffocated by excessive order and domination, letting cruelty and cynicism take the place of mutuality and intimate interconnectedness. On the other side, they are in danger of becoming too chaotic, too dreamy, too open-minded with no discerning vision. Experiments in transforming refrains and narratives must observe "extreme caution" (Deleuze and Guattari, 1987: 502).

There is no system that can tell us in advance whether a dream will work, whether it will mobilize the multitude, whether it will facilitate the emergence of more peaceful, just, and sustainable ways of being in the world. Perhaps the dream of domination is too entrenched to change, too resistant to transformation. Perhaps the emancipatory dreamers are not sufficiently grounded in paths of ecological wisdom. Perhaps those who dream of planetary flourishing are not strong enough to commit to the dream, to live the dream. Deleuze and Guattari (1987: 350) provide a poignant reminder that "we can never be sure we will be strong enough, for we have no system, only lines and movements." So we must experiment. Dream big, whether that means dreaming like a poet, a shaman, or Martin Luther King. Dream intensely, whether that means dreaming like a geologian or geophilosophers. With care and caution, dream of the whole Earth, open up to the unfolding epic of evolution, learning to listen and respond to the songs emanating from the planet's habitats and inhabitants. Starting where you are at, from your place in the emerging Earth community, experiment with different ways of telling the story of the evolving universe and sharing in the dream of interdependent flourishing for all.

References

Bateson, Gregory. 1979. *Mind and Nature: A Necessary Unity*. New York: Dutton.
Berry, Thomas. 1990. *The Dream of the Earth*. San Francisco, CA: Sierra Club Books.
——. 1999. *The Great Work: Our Way into the Future*. New York: Bell Tower.
——. 2014. *Selected Writings on the Earth Community*. Ed. Mary Evelyn Tucker and John Grim. Maryknoll: Orbis.

Chatwin, Bruce. 1987. *The Songlines*. New York: Viking Press.

Christie, Douglas E. 2013. *The Blue Sapphire of the Mind: Notes for a Contemplative Ecology*. New York: Oxford University Press.

Deleuze, Gilles. 1990. *The Logic of Sense*. Trans. Constantin V. Boundas. New York: Columbia University Press

——. 1994. *Difference and Repetition*. Trans. Paul Patton. New York: Columbia University Press.

Deleuze, Gilles and Félix Guattari. 1987. *A Thousand Plateaus: Capitalism and Schizophrenia*. Trans. Brian Massumi. Minneapolis: University of Minnesota Press.

——. 1994. *What is Philosophy?* Trans. Hugh Tomlinson and Graham Burchell. New York: Columbia University Press.

Grim, John and Mary Evelyn Tucker. 2014. *Ecology and Religion*. Washington, DC: Island Press.

Guattari, Félix. 2011. *The Machinic Unconscious: Essays in Schizoanalysis*. Trans. Taylor Adkins. Los Angeles, CA: Semiotext(e).

Hampson, Rick. 2014. "2014 Protests: From Ferguson to Hong Kong, Impact Unclear." *USA Today*, December 25. http://www.usatoday.com/story/news/nation/2014/12/25/ferguson-staten-island-protest-2014/20435471 (accessed December 26, 2014).

King, Martin Luther, Jr. 2001. *A Call to Conscience: The Landmark Speeches of Dr. Martin Luther King, Jr.* Ed. C. Carson and Kris Shepard. New York: Warner Books.

Rose, Deborah Bird. 2000. *Dingo Makes Us Human: Life and Land in an Australian Aboriginal Culture*. New York: Cambridge University Press.

——. 2011. *Wild Dog Dreaming: Love and Extinction*. Charlottesville: University of Virginia Press.

Shiva, Vandana. 2005. *Earth Democracy: Justice, Sustainability, and Peace*. Cambridge: South End Press.

Snyder, Gary. 1990. *The Practice of the Wild*. Berkeley, CA: Counterpoint.

Swimme, Brian and Thomas Berry. 1992. *The Universe Story: From the Primordial Flaring Forth to the Ecozoic Era – A Celebration of the Unfolding of the Cosmos*. San Francisco, CA: HarperCollins.

Swimme, Brian and Mary Evelyn Tucker. 2011. *Journey of the Universe*. New Haven, CT: Yale University Press.

Žižek, Slavoj. 2012. *The Year of Dreaming Dangerously*. London: Verso.

10 Energy

Planetary coexistence requires energy. It takes energy to build and maintain a civilization. Houses, hospitals, schools, transportation, and businesses all need sources of energy to exist. You have to eat to live. All life uses energy. Indeed, there has to be energy for anything whatsoever to happen. Without energy, there would be no Earth, no sun, no stars, no Big Bang, no universe. Everything in the universe is a transformation of the same energy. This is the first law of thermodynamics: energy cannot be created or destroyed, only transformed. The energy in the world now is the same energy from the Big Bang, the same energy that "erupted as a single quantum" (Swimme and Berry, 1992: 17). From the perspective of contemporary scientific cosmology, "our universe is a single immense energy event that began as a tiny speck that has unfolded over time to become galaxies and stars, palms and pelicans, the music of Bach, and each of us alive today" (Swimme and Tucker, 2011: 2).

In recent centuries, with developments in science and industrial technology, humans have become capable of harnessing tremendous amounts of energy, using far more energy than ever before throughout their entire history. Humans accomplished this amazing feat through the increasing use of fossil fuels (oil, coal, and natural gas) beginning with the Industrial Revolution in the eighteenth century. This increase in energy usage has allowed the human population to grow at an incredible rate, exploding from less than one billion people in the eighteenth century to over seven billion people today.

> It took from the beginning of time until 1800 for the world's population to reach its first billion. It then took only 130 years (1930) to add the second billion. Just 30 years later (1960), the world population hit three billion. The time it took to reach the fourth billion was cut in half, to only fifteen years (1975). Then just twelve years later (in 1987), the total reached five billion, in another twelve years it hit six billion (in 1999), and in yet another twelve years it hit seven billion (in 2011).
>
> (Henslin *et al.*, 2014: 503)

There are indications that the population will level off around the middle of the twenty-first century, but in the meantime, the trend toward population growth is continuing. Along with population growth, economic growth is another crucial feature of human energy consumption. "At current rates of growth, the world economy will double in size in less than two decades" (Speth, 2011: 6). While growth benefits a limited number of people, a problem with this remarkable growth in the human presence on Earth is that the increasing use of energy has been accompanied by an increasing amount of waste. This is the second law of thermodynamics: systems of energy tend toward entropy.

When energy is used, it dissipates. For instance, when fire burns wood, it eventually burns out. The wood is now burnt, and you cannot un-burn it. The organization of the wood has become disorganized. It can no longer turn outward in the form of fire, so it turns inward on itself. That turning inward is called "entropy" (the prefix "en-" means "in" and "-tropy" comes from the Greek *tropos*, "turning"). While attempting to build a wondrous world full of conveniences like personal automobiles, airplanes, plastics, computers, fast food, and phones, industrial civilization has produced an unprecedented amount of waste. "Our quest for wonder-world," as Thomas Berry (1999: 68) says, "is making wasteworld. Our quest for energy is creating entropy on a scale never before witnessed in the historical process." Moreover, all uses of energy create entropy. Even renewable energies produce some kind of waste. For example, in the construction of solar panels and wind farms, resources have to be extracted and transported, and those processes of extraction and transportation use up materials. Nonrenewable energies (e.g., coal, oil, and the materials used in nuclear power plants) pose a unique problem because they do not replenish themselves once they are completely consumed, at least not at a time-scale that is relevant to human life.

Using renewable energies, a civilization has a chance of sustaining itself indefinitely into the future. A civilization built on nonrenewable energies like oil, coal, and natural gas cannot be sustained. Today's global civilization is undergoing an energy crisis due to the increasing difficulty of obtaining the non-renewable energy of fossil fuels, especially oil. However, the energy crisis is not just a problem of peak oil or the looming scarcity of other fossil fuels. It is also a problem of the waste that is produced when they are consumed. Greenhouse gases are an entropic by-product of fossil fuels, including the greenhouse gas that is most responsible for global warming: carbon dioxide (CO_2). The energy crisis is intimately intertwined with the climate crisis. "Peak oil and global warming are two interrelated expressions of one fundamental problem" (Crockett and Robbins, 2012: 89). In the mid-eighteen century, prior to the worldwide use of fossil fuels, the concentration of CO_2 in the air amounted to around 250 parts per million (ppm). That amount has increased to over 400 ppm, far exceeding what climate scientists have determined is the upper limit of a safe amount of CO_2, namely 350 ppm, hence the title of one of the leading climate activist organizations: 350.org.

If the planet's climate is to remain relatively stable and inhabitable, it requires that humans replace fossil fuel energy sources and implement a worldwide transition to alternative energies. People have been calling for such a transition for decades, and in some places that transition is well underway. For instance, throughout the first half of 2014, Germany – a worldwide leader in the transition to alternative energies – produced approximately one-third of its energy through renewable energies, such as solar, wind, biomass, and hydroelectric, which is more than twice the percentage produced by the United States, where renewable sources made up only 13 percent of its total energy production as of the end of 2013 (Kroh, 2014). However, in many places, the transition toward sustainable energy is still moving at a dangerously slow pace.

Climate change threatens many organisms, ecosystems, and even humans as seasons shift, temperatures and sea-levels rise, and droughts, floods, heatwaves, and other extreme weather events become the norm. Why would people, governments, and corporations move so slowly? To some extent, it is a lack of another kind of energy. Many people lack the personal motivation to change their habits, and many governments and corporations lack the political will to transition away from a global economy based on fossil fuels. In other words, the challenges of climate change do not just call for the development of alternative energies. They call for an understanding of the ways in which the personal and political energy of human beings relates to the sun, wind, life, chemical reactions, and other nonhuman energies of the cosmos. They call for a new understanding of what energy is and how it is distributed across environments, societies, and subjects.

A new understanding of energy must include perspectives from contemporary sciences. More specifically, no conception of energy is adequate if it does not account for thermodynamics and the problem of entropy. Without the scientific perspective of thermodynamics, it is impossible to understand the current energy crisis. However, sciences in themselves are not sufficiently capable of responding to the ethical and existential challenges posed by the energy crisis. While sciences have a lot of power in society, particularly because of their practical and technological applications, they are insufficient to address questions about the value or meaning of energy or questions about personal and political energy. Those are the kinds of questions addressed in the humanities, but the humanities in themselves lack the factual knowledge necessary for understanding the physical characteristics of energy.

> We could say that the sciences, at their limit, cannot think insofar as they are cut off from the most acute and important philosophical questions, whereas the humanities, including philosophy and religious studies, are rendered largely impotent because they are disconnected from real forces and powers in the world today.
>
> (Crockett, 2014: 272)

An integrative concept of energy must cross the boundaries of sciences and humanities. Separated from one another, sciences and humanities both lose their ability to make any significant impact upon contemporary problems.

The geophilosophy of Gilles Deleuze plays an important role here, both because his work does not suffer from a separation between sciences and humanities, and because he presents a concept of energy which rethinks entropy in a way that is relevant to personal and political responses to global climate change. Deleuze's concept of energy encourages a shift away from the superficial pleasures of consumerism toward a more joyous affirmation of life, away from a civilization oriented toward growth for the benefit of the few toward a planetary civilization oriented to participatory ecological democracy. The following sections of this chapter cross fields of science, philosophy, and religious studies to articulate an integrative concept of energy and consider possibilities for summoning the personal and political energy to cultivate mutually enhancing human–Earth relations. In this context, responding to the energy crisis calls for a realization that energy is something to cultivate and nurture, and not merely something to be controlled and consumed. Energy is not just physical or objective stuff to be used up. It is the unfolding complexity of chaosmosis. It is the unfolding communion of subjects, a mystery that calls for human participation, not domination. "We live immersed in a sea of energy beyond all comprehension. But this energy, in an ultimate sense, is ours not by domination but by invocation" (Berry, 1999: 175).

Ancient sunlight

The sun converts "four million tons of its mass into energy every second" (Swimme and Tucker, 2011: 43–44). Relative to human existence, that is a tremendous flaring forth of energy, like a herd of four million bison exploding into light every second. That energy has been radiating onto Earth since the planet formed. Life on Earth developed a way of using energy from the sun within millions of years after the first living cells emerged around four billion years ago: photosynthesis. Bacteria first developed the capacity of photosynthesis, which uses sunlight as well as carbon dioxide and water to produce carbohydrates for energy and expel oxygen as a waste by-product. Plants inherited photosynthesis from those bacteria. Photosynthesis plays a crucial role in life on Earth. Thinking of the climate crisis, many people think of photosynthesis in terms of its function in taking carbon dioxide out of the air. Planting trees is a way to reduce the greenhouse effect causing global warming. However, photosynthesis is not just important for regulating the balance of oxygen and carbon dioxide in the atmosphere. Photosynthesis is the primary source of energy for life on Earth, harnessing the energy of sunlight to support the existence of photosynthetic organisms, and those organisms in turn are an energy source for animals, and those animals become a source of energy for other animals. Sunlight helps tomatoes grow, then a deer eats a tomato plant, and a wolf eats the deer. The waste and decomposing remains that are left over from that feast become fertile soil for plant life to continue the cycle.

The evolution of plant life provided energy for the evolution of fish, reptiles, birds, and mammals. Approximately 200 million years ago, flowering plants (angiosperms) emerged, providing an abundant energy source for the evolution of mammals through the reproductive strategy of encasing seeds in transportable packages (e.g., the fruit of an orange or the spore of a dandelion) (see Chapter 7).

The "fierce energy" of mammals was "maintained on a high, effective level, through hot days and frosty nights, by the concentrated energy of the angiosperms" (Eiseley, 1957: 74). Flowering plants provided the energetic conditions required for the emergence of the primate ancestors of humans. Along with plants, another source of energy that facilitated the emergence of the human species is fire, which itself is dependent upon the sunlight stored in plants. The control of fire is a way of "shaping the Sun's energy that had been stored in sticks" (Swimme and Berry, 1992: 11).

The control of fire made possible the invention of cooking, and the extra nutrition and energy made available through cooking provided the conditions required for the development of the complex brain that marks the emergence of the human species approximately 200,000 years ago (Wrangham, 2009). Throughout its evolution, the human species has continued to revolutionize its energy use. Approximately 10,000 years ago, humans found a supplement to the energy made available through the use of fire and the use of resources accumulated by gathering and hunting. That supplement arose with domestication and agriculture, which provided new means for obtaining the energy stored in plants and animals. Growing crops and domesticating animals provided so much energy that food began to be produced in surplus amounts. This allowed for the human population to expand. It also led to the development of cities, which were hubs for the production and consumption of the energy provided by domestication and agriculture.

Following the Agricultural Revolution, the Industrial Revolution marks the next revolution in the way humans relate to energy. During early human evolution through the development of agriculture, humans were always using energy that had been converted from sunlight into plants and animals. If you were eating grains, the sunlight that helped those grains grow would have touched Earth's surface within recent seasons or years. During the Industrial Revolution, humans began the widespread use of fossil fuels for energy. Berry (1999: 150) calls this period "the Petroleum Interval." Unlike the energy sources used throughout the prior history of humanity, the energy sources used in this period are fossils. When we use that energy, we are not using sunlight that was stored in plants or animals within recent seasons or years. We are using the remains of "ancient sunlight" (Hartmann, 2004).

Oil deposits are the fossilized remains of microscopic plants that existed over 300 million years ago. The energy generated by burning oil and other fossil fuels is derived from solar energy that was stored, buried, and fossilized in the remains of those plants. That energy source is being used up quickly, and it will not come back in any foreseeable future. Even if it did come back, it would not necessarily be worth digging up. As Berry notes, the industrial period of human history has been dominated by anthropocentric values which orient the concerns of humans around themselves, with little or no concern given to the rest of the Earth community. From the perspective of whole Earth thinking, it would be important to consider the value of fossil fuels for planetary systems and not only for humans. What function is provided by the burial of fossil fuels in the first place? It stabilizes planetary chemistry, maintaining the self-organizing dynamics of the interdependent systems of life, land, water, and air. Planetary systems organize themselves in such a way as "to bury the vast amounts of carbon in the coal and petroleum in the depths of the Earth and in the forests so that the chemistry of the atmosphere, the water, and the soil could be worked out with the proper precision" (Berry, 1999: 158). Through the extraction and burning of fossil fuels, massive amounts of carbon have been unleashed into the atmosphere, disturbing the stability of the climate and thus endangering the integrity of Earth systems that have been evolving together for billions of years. "Because of our need to fuel the industrial world, we have created a technosphere incompatible with the biosphere" (p. 167).

Global civilization is running out of the energy sources from which it was built and upon which it has become dependent, and as it is burning through that energy, carbon dioxide and other entropic by-products of fossil fuel use are destroying planetary systems. One could argue that the energy crisis is mainly a problem of too much consumption, in which case a reduction in energy use would be the best solution. One could also argue that the energy crisis is mainly a problem of too much waste, in which case the best solution to the energy crisis is the development of more efficient, presumably renewable, energy sources. Doubtless both points are partially right. Overconsumption is a problem, and a reduction in energy use would alleviate that problem. Likewise, waste is a problem, and a transition to renewable energy sources would alleviate that problem. However, there is another problem. Energy is thought of primarily in terms of a physical property that dissipates and cools off. What if dissipating heat is just the surface? What if energy means more than that? That could change everything.

Integrating energies

There are scientific, philosophical, and religious resources for moving beyond the definition of energy in terms of disorganization and heat loss. Regarding the science of thermodynamics, Eric Schneider and Dorion Sagan (2005) present a radical rephrasing of the second law of thermodynamics. Whereas entropy is normally phrased in terms of the dissipation or disorganization of energy, Schneider and Sagan note that such a definition only applies in closed systems, like a cup of hot tea becoming cold as it dissipates into its environment. However, throughout material, living, and human strata of the universe, nothing is a completely simple, closed system. At the very least, every being has gravity pulling on it, complicating it, and opening it up to dynamics outside of itself. Everything in the cosmos is open to some chaotic changes. Everything harbors dynamics of seething disequilibrium. The standard scientific model of thermodynamics cannot account for such rampant disequilibrium. It is thus transitioning to a model of non-equilibrium thermodynamics (NET). The NET version of entropy sees energy as more than just the dissipation of heat. "The NET version of the second law" is that "nature abhors a gradient" (p. 51).

Energy tends toward equilibrium, getting rid of the differences that make gradients (like temperature, density, or pressure gradients). For instance, in a relatively simple, closed system like a cup of hot tea, this means that the tea becomes the same temperature as the surrounding room, finding equilibrium with the room. However, a cloud of atoms is an open system, changing and transforming in the churning dynamics of the unfolding universe. For example, for a cloud of hydrogen and helium atoms, there is no stable equilibrium. Rather, equilibrium is in the making, unfolding along the knife's edge of self-organizing dynamics, the edge where order emerges out of chaos. Gravity activates the self-organizing dynamics whereby the cloud of atoms contracts, condensing its atoms into intensifying vibrations, eventually generating enough energy to ignite the birth of a star (see Chapter 8). The energy of nuclear fusion synthesizes new, complex atoms within the stars (Swimme and Tucker, 2011: 33). Through that process (nucleosynthesis), hydrogen and helium atoms become carbon, oxygen, silicon, and heavier elements. When the star eventually spends all of its fuel it becomes a supernova, exploding and scattering its diverse elements across the universe. However, the death of the star does not mean that the star simply dissipates. Those elements then pass into other open systems and enter into other self-organizing dynamics, including the self-organizing dynamics of living systems.

The atoms that make up living organisms were all forged in stars. "The essence of the universe story is this: the stars are our ancestors" (p. 29). Humans, life, and the material universe interconnect with one another in the self-organizing dynamics of the same energy event. The dissipation of energy is only one aspect of it. The dissipation of stars provided the conditions for the emergence of life. Similarly, living beings do not simply cool off and dissipate into their environment. They build ecological connections to energy sources in their environment to form increasingly complex systems, growing, reproducing, and communicating. Living beings die, but their energy never simply dissipates or disorganizes. It does not simply degenerate into chaos. A decomposing organism unfolds new physicochemical structures at the edge where chaos and order meet. Even in death, nature abhors a gradient, seeking equilibrium in a universe far from equilibrium, seeking structure in the chaosmos. From the Big Bang to the present day, the single energy event of the universe has been abhorring gradients, reducing the differences between things, always reaching for order at the edge of chaos.

The philosophical concept of energy developed by Deleuze fits with the scientific definition of entropy in non-equilibrium thermodynamics (Crockett, 2014). The dissipation of heat is only the extensive dimension of energy, the unfolded or explicated aspect of the energy. There is also an "intensive factor" involved in the dissipation of energy (Deleuze, 1994: 229). Energy is the way that intensity "is deployed and nullified in an extensive state of affairs" (Deleuze and Guattari, 1994: 21). To say that nature abhors a gradient is to say that it cancels or nullifies extensive differences. The intensive aspect of energy is not cancelled out in dissipation. Intensity preserves and repeats differences, implicating differences in one another and thus deploying complex structures. For example, the extensive aspect of a supernova is found in the dissipation of heat and the scattering of elements. It is the death of a star. The intensity of a supernova is found in the way in which the supernova preserves the different atomic structures produced in the star, which are then repeated in the complex structures of living organisms and human beings. The extensive aspect of a star dies during a supernova. The intensity of supernovas undergoes complex repetitions in the body of every fish, bird, mammal, and human. The intensity does not die.

In its extensive aspect, entropy sounds like bad news. Everything dissipates. Hot soup gets cold. Fuel runs out. Ideas and traditions get old and boring. All living things die. Creativity becomes stagnant over time. However, the extensive differences that are cancelled out in dissipation, aging, death, and stagnation are only the surface. Underneath the surface, intensity is churning with the seething disequilibrium of the chaosmos, preserving and repeating those differences in the unfolding complexity of the chaosmos. In its intensive aspect, entropy is affirmative. "It makes difference itself an object of affirmation," it "makes the lowest an object of affirmation" (Deleuze and Guattari, 1994: 234). The energy event of the universe is not simply cooling off or running down, cancelling out the differences that make up the texture of the universe. Its intensity is affirming differences, implicating differences in one another, unfolding the self-organizing complexity of the chaosmos. Energy is not just a physical property that is transferred as heat. It is not merely stuff that dissipates. The energy event of the cosmos is unfolding the communion of subjects, explicating the chaosmosis of singularities.

If energy is not just unfolding heat, but is unfolding the complexity, community, and subjectivity of the universe, then it is possible to articulate an integrative concept of energy, such that energy may be understood without reducing it to objective, physical, or material stuff as opposed to subjective, psychological, or spiritual dimensions. Energy is chaosmosis – the chaotic creativity of the cosmos – which unfolds self-organizing dynamics (subjectivity) that are implicated with one another in the same energy event (community). Transformations of energy are thus less about heat and more about the kind of "psychophysical energy" expressed in Daoist and Confucian senses of *qi*, which resonate with biblical senses of spirit (Lee, 2014).

Qi describes the whole of reality. It harbors the churning intensity of difference or change (*yi*). It is the way (*dao*) in which self-organizing patterns unfold. It is also the mutuality (*shen*) that implicates patterns in one another. This trinity of *yi*, *dao*, and *shen* may be read parallel to the Christian trinity of God's three persons: the Father, the Son, and the Holy Spirit (see Chapter 8). Spirit can refer to the entire trinity: the intense depths of creativity (God), the unfolding of self-organizing structures (Christ; the word or wisdom of God), and the relationality that implicates beings in community (spirit). In this context, it would be a severe misunderstanding to think that energy is merely physical stuff transferred as heat. If energy is like *qi* or spirit, then it harbors capacities of creativity, self-organization, and interconnectedness. Attending to those capacities of energy could change everything.

Pleasure and joy

If energy is not just a property of objects but is more like *qi*, spirit, chaosmosis, or a communion of subjects, then a comprehensive response to the energy crisis must do more than find ways to reduce energy consumption and develop alternative energy sources. As important as those options are, they are not sufficient to reinvent the human and facilitate the interdependent flourishing of the whole Earth community. Those options still treat energy like a property of objects that dissipates with use. In other words, those options still view entropy as bad news, as a dissipation that generates waste. That view of entropy treats life and the whole universe as a problem that we must react against if we are to survive: we must not use too much energy, and what we use we must use efficiently. Other people have the opposing attitude that we might as well make the best out of a bad situation, which entails burning up as much energy as we want, without worrying about restraint or efficiency. Those people also view life as a bad situation, a problem that we must react against, except instead of reacting with restraint and efficiency they react with desires for unlimited energy to support unlimited growth, including territorial growth in war and militarism and economic growth in money (Crockett and Robbins, 2012: 73).

Advocates for unending economic growth and militarism join in the same refrain as environmentalists advocating for restrained and efficient energy use. They are telling the same story, wherein humans find themselves in a universe in which everything dies and becomes undone. In that story, to find happiness humans must react against the universe, either by implementing restraint and efficiency so as to extend life for as long as possible, or by using excessive amounts of energy to provide enough money and territory to suppress the fact that everything eventually dies. That story is not true, or at least it is not the whole story. Everything dies and becomes undone, but intensity is preserved and repeats itself in the emergence of complex, self-organizing, interdependent systems.

Finding a fulfilling or flourishing way of being in the world does not require that one react against the unfolding of the universe. Quite the opposite: by reacting against the dynamics of evolution, humans have brought about unprecedented crises that generate tremendous suffering for the human and nonhuman members of the Earth community. Finding a fulfilling or flourishing way of being in the world requires intimate participation in the energy event connecting humans with Earth and the universe. This provides a comprehensive context for responding to the energy crisis, which is also a crisis of climate change, a crisis of industrial technology and consumer culture, and a crisis of the stories and values that orient human existence. Drawing upon Deleuze, Clayton Crockett and Jeffrey Robbins (2012: 110) make the point that the "answer to our current energy crisis, which is also a crisis of belief, is the Earth." Similarly for Berry (1999: 67), a response to our current situation begins with a reorientation toward the evolutionary energy of Earth.

In our question for understanding, we might begin with the observation that the Earth is the manifestation of a vast amount of energy caught up in a diversity of designs for which there is no accounting in terms of human understanding or imagination.

(Berry, 1999: 167)

The task of renewing our participation in the energy of the Earth community calls for a complete reinvention of the human. It means doing something entirely new to facilitate mutually enhancing human–Earth relations. At the same time, the entirely new is not entirely different. It means participating in the intensity of what we already do. It means that the main thing we need to do is "what we've been doing – evolve . . . again" (Crockett and Robbins, 2012: 96). This is the same point that Naomi Klein (2014) makes in her insightful and provocative analysis of the social and environmental challenges of climate change. For Klein, climate change calls for a radical reinvention of human civilization, particularly our economic and political models, and a renewal of our evolutionary intensity. Climate change is thus a "civilizational wake-up call. A powerful message – spoken in the language of fires, floods, droughts, and extinctions – telling us that we need an entirely new economic model and a new way of sharing this planet. Telling us that we need to evolve" (p. 25).

Evolving means opening up to the creative, self-organizing, interdependent capacities inherent in the energy of the universe. In other words, it means joining in the unfolding story of the universe, which is not a story of physical energy as opposed to psychological or spiritual energy. It is a story of *qi*, spirit, or chaosmosis. It is a story of psychophysical energy. It is a story of solar energy, fossil fuels, and hydroelectric dams, but it is also a story that speaks about what practitioners of yoga consider the energy centers (*chakras*) of the body, a story about the *qi* cultivated in internal martial arts (e.g., taiji and qigong), a story about the energy lines (meridians) that map the body for practitioners of acupuncture and Traditional Chinese Medicine (Kaza, 2008: 102). Recovering the psychic dimension of the universe's psychophysical energy is a crucial part of our evolutionary challenge. "As physical resources become less available, psychic energy must support the human project in a special manner," providing a sense of intimate communion that overcomes the alienation of humans from the cosmos, and providing new energies "to support the human venture. These new energies find expression and support in celebration" (Berry, 1999: 170).

Instead of thinking that the dynamics of energy are something against which humans must react, whole Earth thinking affirms energy. Whole Earth thinking celebrates the wondrous display of the single energy event of the universe. In Deleuze's terminology, this could be called an ethics of affirmation, which is an approach to ethics that actively participates in the universe instead of reacting against it (Crockett and Robbins, 2012: 83). It is an ethics of joy or love, which is to say, "an active ethics of participation, an ethics of attraction" which cultivates interconnectedness and mutuality between humans and all other beings, whether human, living, or inorganic (p. 85). This approach to ethics celebrates energy.

Instead of reacting against heat death either by wallowing in despair or by pursuing personal pleasure (hedonism), this approach to ethics joins the theologian

Catherine Keller (2012: 15) in affirming the vision of energy expressed by the English poet and painter William Blake, "Energy is eternal delight":

> The energy of eternal delight is the alternative to a hedonistic indulgence in bursts of pleasure. Pepsi peppiness and consumer glee are draining, not energizing, the planet. The manic excitations produce depressive effects in a vicious circle that, if undiagnosed, blocks the circulation of our spontaneous interactivity. For our souls live indissociably from these bodies that are folds of the living planet. Its life would be the pulse of its energy. As the Blakean delight it is akin to musical or poetic rhythm, to oceanic ebb and flow, to the pulse of blood and the breath of meditation. So this energy, far from a homogeneous linear flow, signifies the creative throb of life itself, beyond the distinction of human and nonhuman.

The celebration of the creative intensity of the single energy event of the universe energizes our participation in the story of the universe and the emerging Earth community. It energizes personal and political action to respond to the challenges of climate change and the growing scarcity of fossil fuels. It energizes our capacity to restrain our energy consumption, and it energizes our resolve to develop sustainable alternatives to fossil fuels. Yet it does much more as well.

Ethical approaches to energetic affirmation and celebration facilitate a transformation of values. They change the story. They change the dream driving global civilization, shifting values away from the destructive dreams of individualism and human superiority toward the egalitarian and emancipatory dreams of mutuality, which are much more supportive of concern for the challenges of climate change (Klein, 2014: 36). Indeed, joyous participation in the energy event of the universe changes everything. A participatory celebration of energy intensifies our entanglement in the whole Earth community. It intensifies the mutuality and interdependent flourishing of planetary coexistence.

References

Berry, Thomas. 1999. *The Great Work: Our Way into the Future*. New York: Bell Tower.

Crockett, Clayton. 2014. "Entropy." In *The Future of Continental Philosophy of Religion*, ed. Clayton Crockett, B. Keith Putt, and Jeffrey W. Robbins, 272–281. Bloomington: Indiana University Press.

Crockett, Clayton and Jeffrey W. Robbins. 2012. *Religion, Politics, and the Earth: The New Materialism*. New York: Palgrave Macmillan.

Deleuze, Gilles. 1994. *Difference and Repetition*. Trans. Paul Patton. New York: Columbia University Press.

Deleuze, Gilles and Félix Guattari. 1994. *What is Philosophy?* Trans. Hugh Tomlinson and Graham Burchell. New York: Columbia University Press.

Eiseley, Loren. 1957. *The Immense Journey: An Imaginative Naturalist Explores the Mysteries of Man and Nature*. New York: Random House.

Hartmann, Thom. 2004. *The Last Hours of Ancient Sunlight: The Fate of the World and What We Can Do About It Before It's Too Late*. New York: Three Rivers Press.

Henslin, James, Adam Possamai, and Alphia L. Possamai-Inesedy. 2014. *Sociology: A Down-to-Earth Approach*, 2nd edn. Frenchs Forest: Pearson Australia.

Kaza, Stephanie. 2008. *Mindfully Green: A Personal and Spiritual Guide to Whole Earth Thinking*. Boston, MA: Shambhala Publications.

Keller, Catherine. 2012. "The Energy We Are: A Meditation in Seven Pulses." In *Cosmology, Ecology, and the Energy of God*, ed. Donna Bowman and Clayton Crockett, 11–25. New York: Fordham University Press.

Klein, Naomi. 2014. *This Changes Everything: Capitalism vs. the Climate*. New York: Simon & Schuster.

Kroh, Kiley. 2014. "Bye-bye Brown Coal: Germany's New Renewables Mark." *Business Spectator*, July 10. https://www.businessspectator.com.au/article/2014/7/10/renewable-energy/bye-bye-brown-coal-germanys-new-renewables-mark (accessed November 6, 2014).

Lee, Hyo-Dong. 2014. *Spirit, Qi, and the Multitude: A Comparative Theology for the Democracy of Creation*. New York: Fordham University Press.

Schneider, Eric D. and Dorion Sagan. 2005. *Into the Cool: Energy Flow, Thermodynamics, and Life*. Chicago, IL: University of Chicago Press.

Speth, James Gustave. 2011. "The Limits of Growth." In *Moral Ground: Ethical Action for a Planet in Peril*, ed. Kathleen Dean Moore and Michael P. Nelson, 3–8. San Antonio, TX: Trinity University Press.

Swimme, Brian and Thomas Berry. 1992. *The Universe Story: From the Primordial Flaring Forth to the Ecozoic Era – A Celebration of the Unfolding of the Cosmos*. San Francisco, CA: HarperCollins.

Swimme, Brian and Mary Evelyn Tucker. 2011. *Journey of the Universe*. New Haven, CT: Yale University Press.

Wrangham, Richard. 2009. *Catching Fire: How Cooking Made Us Human*. New York: Basic Books.

11 Conclusion

Whole Earth thinking is about coming to terms with the startling realization that humans inhabit an increasingly interconnected planet situated within an evolving universe. Humans are connecting with one another in unprecedented ways through computers, social media, telecommunications, tourism, trade, and multicultural dialogue. Along with the connections humans have with one another, humans are also becoming increasingly connected with the nonhuman inhabitants and habitats that make up the whole Earth. Indeed, humans are becoming increasingly interconnected with planetary systems, which are so massive that it is difficult to imagine that humans could have an impact at that scale.

Since industrial technology and dreams of human domination spread around the globe in the modern period, there is now no place on Earth that does not bear the impact of some human presence. Humans are not only affecting a species here and a landscape there. Problems like ocean acidification, soil erosion, desertification, pollution, and deforestation are happening around the planet. Humans are affecting the chemical composition of Earth's atmosphere (climate change), altering the genetic makeup of species (genetically modified organisms), and precipitating a loss of biological diversity the likes of which has not been seen since the dinosaurs went extinct sixty-five million years ago (mass extinction).

The challenges of our era of planetary interconnectedness are immense. They call for new ways of thinking that can guide our understanding of and responses to the planetary scale of coexistence. Insofar as the challenges of the planetary era arise from increasing connections, relations, and interdependencies, they may be described as ecological challenges. In other words, they are challenges that must be addressed at the level of complex networks of relationships between organisms and environmental conditions, and such networks are precisely the purview of ecological inquiry. However, scientific perspectives on ecology are not sufficient to address the challenges of our planetary era. Organisms and environments never relate to one another in a vacuum. Their relationships intersect with human beings. They intersect with our ideas, practices, values, feelings, cultures, technologies, economic institutions, and religious traditions. Along these lines, scientific perspectives on ecology must be in dialogue with religious ecologies (see Chapter 2). More generally, ecology must overcome the separation of academic disciplines, integrating perspectives from the sciences and the humanities and opening up to multiple ways of knowing.

Becoming more integrative, ecological inquiry can develop more comprehensive and inclusive articulations of ecological relationships, accounting for complex systems and environmental problems as well as social relationships, cultural values, and subjective dynamics of thinking, feeling, and acting. Integrative approaches to ecology cultivate an ecological wisdom (ecosophy) that brings together environmental (complexity), social (community), and mental (subjectivity) registers of ecological phenomena (see Chapter 4). Along with the integration of multiple ways of knowing to investigate the environments, societies, and subjects of ecology, whole Earth thinking aims to understand how those environments, societies, and subjects are distributed across the planet. In other words, whole Earth thinking brings ecological wisdom into the context of planetary coexistence.

The idea of developing more integrative and planetary approaches to contemporary ecological problems is not something I came up with myself. Living enmeshed in ecological relationships, it seems impossible for me or for anyone to come up with any idea that is completely independent of assistance or inspiration. The approach to whole Earth thinking expressed in this book serves as an open-ended introduction to a variety of ecologically oriented thinkers who provide integrative and planetary perspectives for navigating the complexity, community, and subjectivity of planetary coexistence, thinkers coming from diverse backgrounds, including religious studies, literature, environmental studies, cosmology, philosophy, psychology, physics, Earth systems science, and more. There is not just one way to engage in whole Earth thinking.

The phrase "whole Earth thinking" comes from the environmental scholar Stephanie Kaza (2008), whose work integrates perspectives from Buddhism and complex systems theory to address the interlocking environmental, social, and psychological crises facing the Earth community. Kaza's work envisions "how to reduce harm and how to be with harm as a witness and compassionate advocate for the earth" (p. 33). This follows from her adherence to the Four Noble Truths of Buddhism, which state that (1) all life is suffering, (2) there are causes of suffering, (3) and suffering can be reduced by addressing its causes, which one can do by (4) following the path of complete or right ways of beings in the world (p. 28). In that sense, whole Earth thinking is about reducing suffering and promoting mutual flourishing for all members of the Earth community. However, whole Earth thinking involves more than that. It involves intimate participation in something like a sacred or spiritual intensity of Earth, participation in the mysterious, wondrous, creative splendor of the planet. It involves "a sense of awe for the earth as a miraculous whole" (p. 26).

Kaza considers the work of Gary Snyder to exemplify whole Earth thinking (p. 9). A Beat poet and essayist, Zen Buddhist practitioner, wilderness advocate, and bioregionalist, Snyder's ecological thinking wanders across the boundaries of the humanities and the sciences to find practices for resituating humans in the wild world. He considers humans to be an indicator species, which is a term used by biologists to refer to a species whose condition indicates the condition of the entire system or region of which they are a part. Just as the spotted owl is an indicator for some conifer forests, and buffalo (bison) were considered an indicator for the condition of the Great Plains of the North American continent, the human species is an indicator species. The story of the owl is the story of the forest, the story of the bison is the story of the plains, so what is the story of humans? The forest says "owl," and the plains say "bison." Snyder (1990: 117) asks, "what says 'humans'? What sucks our lineage into form? It is surely . . . the whole of this earth on which we find ourselves more or less competently at home." The story of Earth is the story of humans, which means that the condition of the human species is an indicator of the condition of the whole Earth community.

While Kaza and Snyder offer many contributions to the development of integrative approaches to ecology that facilitate the participation of humans in our planetary context, they are not alone. Their Buddhist perspectives may be understood in the context of the field of religion and ecology, which explores religious ecologies from multiple traditions and puts them into dialogue between ecological perspectives from science and other intersecting disciplines (economics, policy, and philosophy). Along those lines, the approach to whole Earth thinking introduced in this book situates Kaza and Snyder in a creative contrast between two groups of thinkers. The first group is represented by the American geologian Thomas Berry, whose work has been highly influential in the development of the field of religion and ecology (Grim and Tucker, 2014) and in the articulation of narrative accounts of cosmic, Earth, and human evolution (Swimme and Berry, 1992; Swimme and Tucker, 2011). The second group is represented by the French geophilosophers Gilles Deleuze and Félix Guattari, who are highly influential in diverse fields of inquiry, including areas of philosophy, psychology, critical theory, cultural studies, and postmodernism. Despite their relatively atheistic orientation, their influence is even felt in theology and religious studies (Bryden, 2001; Justaert, 2012; Ramey, 2012).

Considered separately, the former group opens up possibilities for religious engagements in whole Earth thinking, while the latter group opens up possibilities for whole Earth thinking to draw from sources outside of religious traditions and institutions. However, when put together in dialogue, the two groups become different. They become energized by their creative contrast (see Chapter 3). The geologian draws out the spiritual side of geophilosophy, and the geophilosophers draw out a side of the geologian that is critical of the anthropocentrism and authoritarianism of religions. They converge in challenging traditional (religious) and modern (secular) approaches to religion, affirming a postsecular integration of religious and secular perspectives. The geophilosophers join the geologian in criticizing the individualist and consumerist values of modernism, and they also join together in criticizing the cynicism and apathy that characterize much of what is called postmodernism. They share an orientation to theories and methods that cross the disciplinary boundaries of the humanities and sciences, and they share a common aim of facilitating participation in the work of reinventing the human species and cultivating mutually enhancing modes of planetary coexistence.

Together, these two groups point toward multiple, overlapping roots of eco-logical wisdom, including the traditional ecological knowledge of indigenous traditions, the wisdom embedded in feminist perspectives and women's experi-ences, the classical traditions of philosophy and religion, and contemporary scientific perspectives (see Chapter 5). One can draw from these roots to pursue wisdom that is grounded in contexts and relationships, wisdom that supports values of care and mutuality. Such wisdom facilitates a reinvention of the human, carrying out a transition from humanist to posthumanist ways of beings in the world, which is a transition from anthropocentric dreams of human superiority to anthropocosmic dreams of the intimate intertwining of humans with the cosmos (see Chapter 6).

The reinvention of the human resituates the human species in the environ-mental, social, and subjective dynamics of the whole Earth. In this context, humans are not dominators or owners of Earth. We do not live on Earth. We inhabit Earth. We are creative participants living within the emerging Earth community (see Chapter 7). Whole Earth thinking does not stop at the edges where Earth opens out into the rest of the cosmos. The reinvention of the human resituates the human in the community of life on Earth and in the evolutionary development of the cosmos. Whole Earth thinking considers the evolutionary dynamics of order and chaos that gave rise to Earth, cosmological dynamics of creativity, self-organization, and mutuality (see Chapter 8). Furthermore, whole Earth thinking is whole Earth dreaming, singing, imagining, and storytelling.

The task of resituating the human species in intimate contact with Earth and the wild world – the chaosmos – cannot be achieved through critical reflection alone. The action of reinventing the human must be driven by story and dream (see Chapter 9). Whole Earth thinking calls for dangerous dreams of emancipation, dreams of freedom from the destructive refrains of domination and oppression. It calls for a vision of a more peaceful, just, and sustainable Earth community, a vision of participatory ecological democracy. Moreover, an entrancing vision of flourishing planetary coexistence cannot come out of humans alone. It cannot be another anthropocentric vision. It can only arise through participation in the dreaming landscapes and storied places of Earth. In other words, songs of planetary liberation emerge through participation in the song of the universe, the Great Refrain repeated throughout cosmic, Earth, and human evolution.

Whole Earth thinking provides ways of listening to and communicating the story of cosmic, Earth, and human evolution. The point is not just to tell an interesting story, but to energize personal and political action for the work of rein-venting humanity and cultivating mutually enhancing human–Earth relations. Along these lines, whole Earth thinking provides an integrative concept of energy, where energy is not merely a property of physical objects that dissipates and dis-organizes over time. Energy is less like a physical property of objects and more like a communion of subjects. It does not just give off heat and cool over time. It intensifies relationships and enhances mutuality, like spirit in Christianity or *qi* in Confucian and Daoist traditions. Such an integrative concept of energy indi-cates how the current crisis of fossil fuel use (an energy crisis, climate crisis, and economic crisis) may be addressed not only through restrained and efficient energy use but more primarily through intimate and celebratory participation in the intense energies of Earth and the cosmos (see Chapter 10).

To some people, the idea of whole Earth thinking may sound countercultural, particularly because of the *Whole Earth Catalog* and other works by Stewart Brand (2009), whose vision of the whole Earth was inspired by some converging trends in the 1960s, including the growing environmental movement, the growing number of photographs of Earth taken from space, and growing disillusionment with the confining norms and traditions of mainstream culture. Along those lines, whole Earth thinking resonates with countercultural movements that emerged around the 1960s, including the Beat movement, of which Gary Snyder is a member, as well as environmentalism, civil rights, free speech, feminism, anti-war, anti-nuclear, and gay rights movements. Whole Earth thinking can embrace this countercultural legacy while also maintaining critical reflection and accounting for the limitations of countercultural thinking. There are three limitations to bear in mind.

First, an important limitation to keep in mind is that the 1960s counterculture in general and Brand's *Whole Earth* network in particular did not yield an ecological culture or a planetary civilization. Instead of countering dreams of progress and technological control, they actually played crucial roles in facilitating the development of computer and information technologies, and the emergence of a consumer society of decreasing regulations and restrictions on economic development (Turner, 2010). Whole Earth thinking is not opposed to technological innovation and economic growth, but it does call for ecological wisdom with which to situate technological and economic development within the dynamics of the emerging Earth community, nurturing the development of something like a whole Earth economy (Brown and Garver, 2009).

Second, countercultural efforts converged with postmodern trends in criticizing the oppressive aspects of cultural norms and values while often failing to account for the beneficial contributions that those norms and values have made or could make to the flourishing of the whole Earth community. Not all aspects of our cultural traditions need to be countered. They can also be retrieved, re-examined, and reconstructed (Grim and Tucker, 2014: 86). Whole Earth thinking attempts to criticize the problems and limitations of different traditions and different ways of knowing while also engaging constructively in their promises and beneficial contributions.

Third, Brand's account of the whole Earth describes Earth as a primarily natural or material basis on which humans exist, but in the twenty-first century there is no part of Earth that is free of human influence (Boes, 2014). It is now more appropriate to understand Earth as a complex system which includes the human sphere along with spheres of air, water, land, and life. In contrast to Brand's countercultural account of Earth, whole Earth thinking has entered the Anthropocene (Whitehead, 2014). In other words, Earth is no longer thinkable as a primarily material and biological ground, as that ground is inextricably intertwined with the human species.

Whole Earth thinking is countercultural and more. If you engage in whole Earth thinking as a geologian, a geophilosopher, or some combination thereof, you make countercultural commitments more complex. Whole Earth thinking appreciates technological innovation and economic freedom while also transitioning from dreams of human superiority and progress to dreams of vibrant planetary coexistence. It criticizes traditions and conventional norms for their limitations while also recognizing their benefits and promises. It does not view Earth as a simply natural system but as a complex system of energy that cannot be reduced to binary oppositions between natural and culture, physical and psychological, or material and spiritual.

Whole Earth thinking may be summarized as a way of thinking of, by, and for the Earth community. It is of the Earth community in the sense that is about Earth, contemplating the entangled environments, societies, and subjects of Earth through perspectives of religion, ecology, and philosophy. It is by the Earth community in the sense that thinking and wisdom is not something isolated in the human brain or distributed across networks of computers, libraries, and universities. "Wisdom sits in places" (Basso, 1996: 121). Thinking emerges through participation in the creative, self-organizing, and interdependent dynamics of Earth's energies. Finally, whole Earth thinking is for the Earth community in the sense that its contemplative participation in planetary coexistence is achieved with the aim of cultivating mutually intensifying human–Earth relations, facilitating the interdependent flourishing of the whole Earth community. Of, by, and for the Earth community, whole Earth thinking unfolds along many paths. You can find a path to ecological wisdom anywhere. You start from where you are at, with your subjective mindset and your environmental and social setting. You start in your place, from your own unique and intimate connection with the whole.

References

Basso, Keith. 1996. *Wisdom Sits in Places: Landscape and Language among the Western Apache*. Albuquerque: The University of New Mexico Press.

Boes, Tobias. 2014. "Beyond Whole Earth: Planetary Mediation and the Anthropocene." *Environmental Humanities* 5: 155–170.

Brand, Stewart. 2009. *Whole Earth Discipline: An Ecopragmatist Manifesto*. New York: Viking Press.

Brown, Peter G. and Geoffrey Garver. 2009. *Right Relationship: Building a Whole Earth Economy*. San Francisco, CA: Berrett-Koehler.

Bryden, Mary (ed.). 2001. *Deleuze and Religion*. New York: Routledge.

Grim, John and Mary Evelyn Tucker. 2014. *Ecology and Religion*. Washington, DC: Island Press.

Justaert, Kristien. 2012. *Theology after Deleuze*. New York: Continuum.

Kaza, Stephanie. 2008. *Mindfully Green: A Personal and Spiritual Guide to Whole Earth Thinking*. Boston, MA: Shambhala Publications.

Ramey, Joshua. 2012. *The Hermetic Deleuze: Philosophy and Spiritual Ordeal*. Durham, NC: Duke University Press.

Snyder, Gary. 1990. *The Practice of the Wild*. Berkeley, CA: Counterpoint.

Swimme, Brian and Thomas Berry. 1992. *The Universe Story: From the Primordial Flaring Forth to the Ecozoic Era – A Celebration of the Unfolding of the Cosmos.* San Francisco, CA: HarperCollins.

Swimme, Brian and Mary Evelyn Tucker. 2011. *Journey of the Universe.* New Haven, CT: Yale University Press.

Turner, Fred. 2010. *From Counterculture to Cyberculture: Stewart Brand, the Whole Earth Network, and the Rise of Digital Utopianism.* Chicago, IL: University of Chicago Press.

Whitehead, Mark. 2014. *Environmental Transformations: A Geography of the Anthropocene.* New York: Routledge.

Index

Aboriginal 122–3
actors 3, 61–2, 72, 80, 106; *see also* subjectivity
Africa 85–6, 103
agriculture 19, 21–2, 86–7, 103, 136
animism 71, 75–6
Anthropocene 6, 14, 87–8, 103, 148
anthropocentric 20–3, 26, 52–3, 73, 89–94, 107, 146–7
anthropocosmic 23, 90–5, 106, 118, 124, 147
Aristarchus 4, 97–8
Aristotle 19, 25–6, 110
art 12, 20, 69, 109, 129
autopoiesis 56, 61, 94, 100, 114; *see also* self-organization

Bachelard, Gaston 92, 106
Bateson, Gregory 47, 62, 122
Beat Generation 7, 145, 148; *see also* counter-culture
Berry, Thomas 32–5, 37–42, 45–7, 56, 70, 84–5, 120–1, 146
the Bible 75–6, 116, 124
Big Bang 56, 80, 94, 112–13, 132, 138
biocide 5, 83
biology 17, 24, 50,
bioregionalism 7–8, 72, 75, 145
Bodhisattva 23, 76, 103, 107
Brand, Stewart 5, 148
Bruno, Giordano 114, 116
Buddha 47, 75–6, 89
Buddhism 22–3, 41, 50, 53–4, 65, 145; anthropocentric 89; Tibetan 52; Zen 46–7, 68; *see also* Bodhisattva; Buddha; *prajña*

CAFO 17, 87
capitalism 42–3, 54, 59–60, 83, 88

care 23, 47, 66, 74–5, 84, 103–5; *see also* ethics; mutuality
Cenozoic Era 104
chaos 27, 58, 79, 100–1, 113, 125–6, 138; *see also* chaosmos
chaosmos 111, 113, 115–18, 139–141, 147
Christianity 11, 22, 34–6, 52, 68–9, 76; *see also* God; Jesus; spirit; trinity
Christie, Douglas 66, 124; *see also* contemplative ecology
climate change 3, 6, 83, 120, 134–5, 140–2; *see also* global warming
communion 38, 59–6, 62, 80, 117–18, 139–41; *see also* mutuality
complexity 14, 50, 56–8, 80, 102, 116–17
consumerism 7, 60, 72, 104, 127, 135; *see also* capitalism
Confucianism 9, 37, 41, 76, 93, 117–18; *see also* Confucius; *qi*; *yi*
Confucius 75, 89
Copernicus 2–4, 97, 110
Cosmic Microwave Background 112–13
Cosmogenetic principle 14, 56
Cosmology 41, 94, 109–111, 114–15, 132
Counterculture 5, 148–9
Crisis 1, 6, 52, 73, 102, 133–7, 140
Cusa, Nicholas of 114, 116

Dao 67, 93, 117–18, 124, 139
Daoism 22, 35, 46, 68, 147; *see also* Dao
Darwin, Charles 18, 27, 68, 85
Deleuze, Gilles 11–13, 32–39, 42–45, 57, 99, 111, 116–118, 138–141; *see also* geophilosophy; postmodernism; poststructuralism
democracy 34, 105, 118, 127–8, 135, 147; *see also* the multitude
Descartes, René 61

deterritorialization 43, 69, 100–1, 125–6, 129–30
dharma 124–5
domination 74, 104, 116, 126–7, 130
dream 41–2, 44, 85, 120–130, 142, 147–9

Earth 1–3, 10, 43, 53–8, 109–11, 135–7, 140; community 40, 70, 84, 98–9, 104–6; democracy 128; photographs 4; *see also* Anthropocene; Gaia; geophilosophy; planet; *Whole Earth Catalog*
Earth Charter 99, 105, 128
ecology 3, 17–20, 78, 144–6; contemplative 66, 76, 124–5; deep 8, 12, 21, 90–1; social 58–62, 103; religious 20–4; scientific 24–8, 94; integral 29, 51–3, 55; religion and, 9–10
ecofeminism *see* feminism
Ecozoic Era *see* Cenozoic Era
Eiseley, Loren 101
empire 22, 60, 87, 103–5
energy 27–8, 83, 87, 101–3, 110, 117–18, 132–42
ethics 29, 44–47, 58, 73–5, 90, 141
evolution 26–9, 41, 94, 111, 118, 135–6; Darwin and 18, 85; of plants 101, 135
existentialism 12, 89

feminism 5, 12, 61, 70, 73–6, 90–1, 147–8
food 7–8, 19, 26, 86–7, 136
Forum on Religion and Ecology 9, 46, 99, 105
fossil fuel 15–83, 87, 137–137, 147

Gaia 2, 5, 102
Galileo 97, 110
geophilosophy 12–13, 43–4, 55, 78, 121
global warming 30, 56, 98, 133
globalization 54, 72, 104, 137
God 18, 23, 35–6, 45, 52, 116–17
gravity 100, 113–15, 137–8
Grim, John 9, 99, 105, 110
Guattari, Félix 12–14, 32–5, 42, 55–63

Haeckel, Ernst 18–20, 27
Hinduism 9, 22, 39, 50, 76
hokmah 65, 76, 124
humanities 28–30, 39, 50–3, 99, 134

imagination 14, 25, 62, 92, 120–1, 129; *see also* dream
indigenous 7, 21–2, 70–3, 76, 122–4
industrialization 7, 39, 54, 104, 123

integral 10, 29, 39–41, 51–3, 102
Islam 9, 23, 46, 65, 94

Jainism 9, 46, 50, 55, 124
Jesus 75, 103, 116, 124
joy 135, 140–2
Judaism 9, 22, 35, 65, 94
Justice 25, 54–5, 60, 98, 110, 126–8

Kant, Immanuel 42, 89
Kaza, Stephanie 6–8, 10, 46–7, 53, 145
Keller, Catherine 115–18, 142
King, Martin Luther 126–8, 130
Klein, Naomi 83, 141–2

Laruelle, François 44
Latour, Bruno 53, 61; *see also* actors
Leopold, Aldo 3, 28–9
logos 17, 24, 77, 110, 116, 124–5

Maimonides 45–6
Marx, Karl 54–88
mass extinction 6, 87, 98, 101, 104
meaning 11, 35–6, 45, 52, 58–62, 124–5
Mesozoic Era 101, 104
modernism 11, 38, 72, 88, 123
Morin, Edgar 53–5, 58, 103
Morton, Timothy 30
the multitude 104–5, 118, 127–8
mutuality 59, 116–18, 126–8, 139, 142, 147
myth 22, 24–5, 77, 110, 125

narrative 24, 36–8, 75, 80, 93, 122; *see also* imagination; refrain; story
Native American 8, 21
Nietzsche, Friedrich 42, 77
nomadology 43, 55, 69

oil 87, 132–3, 136; *see also* fossil fuel

philosophy 10, 25–6, 43–4, 65, 69, 77; *see also* geophilosophy; humanities; *logos*
photosynthesis 101–2, 135
place 7–8, 21–2, 71–3, 75–7, 123–4, 149
planet 1–6, 8, 38–9, 83–5, 97–9, 112; *see also* planetary era
planetary era 14, 54–5, 103–5, 144; *see also* globalization
plants 19, 25–6, 68–70, 78, 101, 103; *see also* photosynthesis
Plato 10, 25, 77, 110

politics 23, 36, 42, 53, 128;
  see also democracy
postcolonialism 88
posthumanism 88–90, 147
postmodernism 11–12, 35–9, 79, 88
postsecularism 44–7, 54, 88, 146
poststructuralism 11–12; *see also*
  postmodernism

qi 117–18, 139–41, 147

rationality 14, 24–5, 35–7, 45, 88; see also
  logos
refrain 43, 125–6, 129–30
relationality 74–5, 117, 120, 139
religion 8–10, 23–5, 34–5, 44–6, 54, 146
revolution 33–5, 69, 79, 86–7, 127, 136
rights 6, 29, 73, 106, 128

salvation 22, 54
science 18, 24–8, 50–6, 68–70, 78–80, 134
self-organization 79–80, 94–5, 100–2,
  106–7, 114–18, 137–141; *see also*
  subjectivity
shaman 71, 121, 129–30
Shinto 9, 46, 68
Shiva, Vandana 128
Sloterdijk, Peter 66
Snyder, Gary 6–8, 90, 106–7, 123; *see also*
  Beat Generation; bioregionalism
Socrates 10, 25, 75, 77, 89
sophia 14, 24, 77, 116; *see also hokmah*

spirit 7, 106, 115–18, 124, 139–41
stars 37, 93, 97, 107, 138
stewardship 23
Stoicism 125
Story 7, 37, 75, 80, 121, 146
strata 86, 100–2, 113, 126, 137
subjectivity 19, 27–8, 42–3, 55, 60–3,
  104–7
Swimme, Brian 10, 37, 56, 80, 99, 105

technology 22, 62, 79, 87, 104; *see also*
  industrialization
Technozoic Era *see* Cenozoic Era
Teilhard de Chardin, Pierre 41
territorialization *see* deterritorialization
traditional ecological knowledge (TEK)
  14, 21–4, 70, 78, 124, 147
trinity 55, 116–18, 139
Tucker, Mary Evelyn 9, 39, 46, 80, 99, 105

virtue 66, 77

water 4–6, 8, 17, 103, 116–17, 135
Whole Earth Catalog 5, 148
wisdom 2, 40, 55, 65–70, 103, 107; *see*
  also sophia
wonder 40–1, 80, 86, 94, 133

yi 117–18, 139,
yin and *yang* 93, 117–18

Žižek, Slavoj 65, 70, 127

Made in the USA
Las Vegas, NV
06 September 2023